D1551326

SigHT:

Unveiling Black Student

Achievement

and the Meaning of Hope

Amanishakete Ani

Foreword by Molefi Kete Asante

Chicago, Illinois

Front cover illustration by Damon Stanford

Copyright © 2012 by Amanishakete Ani

First Edition, First Printing

Printed in the United States of America

ISBN #: 1-934155-80-2
ISBN #: 978-1-934155-80-6

Dedication

To African American youth, playing hopscotch and double-dutch in the neighborhood, riding your bikes, hoopin at the community court, or dancing to music probably too loud for your eardrums, this is for you. To African children everywhere, your intelligence, creativity, and possibilities energize me to keep working and never settle in comfort or defeat. Keep on believing, and keep going. We're working on it for you.

Contents

Acknowledgments v
Foreword by Molefi Kete Asante vii
Preface: Where I Stand x
Introduction: On Understanding the Terms and Conditions
of Black Student Life xv

Part 1: Laying the Foundation

Chapter 1: Hope Theory Reviewed 1
Chapter 2: Toward an Afrocentric Hope Theory 7
Chapter 3: Context, Participants and Methodology of the
SigHT Study 25

Part 2: Black Student Achievers Speak

Chapter 4: Ture 43
Chapter 5: Talib. 57
Chapter 6: Kwame. 67
Chapter 7: Assata. 75
Chapter 8: Kenya. 97
Chapter 9: Aisha. 107
Chapter 10: Follow-Up Questions 117

Part 3: Putting SigHT to Work

Chapter 11: Messages to the Grown-Ups:
What the Student Narratives Mean 127
Chapter 12: A Hope Epidemic: How Your Black
Students Can Do It Too 143
Chapter 13: Conclusion: Hoping for the Best in Black
Students 159

Appendix A: Basic Template for Identifying Beliefs and
Values 163
Appendix B: Basic Template for Tapping into
Strengths and Interests 164
Appendix C: Basic Template for Goal-Setting 165
Appendix D: Basic Template for Goal Achievement 166

References 168

Index 189

Acknowledgements

I have been privileged to receive both life education as an African American girl born and raised in inner city Los Angeles, California, and formal education at Spelman College, a prestigious historically Black college. Following these, I received training at the University of Wisconsin at Madison, an impressive predominately White institution. For further exception, Drs. Marian Fukuda and Molefi Kete Asante and their families, accepted me as a niece, daughter, and sister in spirit at important stages of my development. Now still, as my journey on the path toward enlightenment and restoration continues I am honored to know and grow close to the honorable Heru Ankh Ra Semahj Se Ptah, Abu Tepi (Elder Guide) of the Shrine of Ptah.

Baba Asante, brother of Harriet Tubman and Cheikh Anta Diop, you are like the modern day Ramses II, Moses, and Du Bois all rolled into one. Where would so many of us be today without your conceptualization of Afrocentricity and without your spirit of grace, always giving to whomever needs your wisdom and time? Ashe, ashe, ashe. Asante sana, sana to you and your family for teaching me through your actions what it means to be proudly African and nobly human. The world is far better because of you all. I walk in your glow. May the conditions of our people and the knowledge of all people be improved because our love and agency.

Nswt (King) Semahj as I lovingly call you, your contributions to the knowledge, health, both spiritual and physical, and immortality of so many brothers and sisters are immeasurable. As you have lived fully for the legacy of the world's greatest civilization your very existence offers us today the experience of Maat during the first time, where others know only books and concepts. You have surely gone above the call of duty and done your father very proud. You wear the names of the mighty Heru, Ra and Ptah in the fashion of the Neteru, of which you have earned entrance. Tua-em-k Ntr for your presence and gifts as living demonstration of the masculine principle and compliment in all things. There is more to come from us, Tu? Ankh.

Auntie Marian, I love you! Long before I knew of Dr. Asante and Nswt Semahj you were there— Japanese, European American, and from the better part of LA as far as I knew. Thank you for being so beautifully human and for seeing human beauty and possibilities in everyone. Thank you for always seeing the greatness in me. You represent the possibility of reciprocity in America. How many times have we debated over issues of race and world evolution, you always simply wanting the best for me and me wanting you to just say that I am right to fight? Still our laughter and positive memories are many, and counting. I am eternally grateful for the intersection of our paths wonderful one.

To my maternal grandmother, Lorean Davis (Mom), I carry your spirit with me everywhere I go, and I hope that you are watching over me with protection and pride. To all of my family, beautiful and full of love, talent, and justice—here is to our legacies, children, and posterity: My mother and sister, Frantzetta and Ramona Chandler, Pop Marcus and Mama Tammy Jackson, Mama Majisa and Poppa Kenny Boyd (loving parents in spirit), Mama Portia Hunt (my teacher and mastermind guardian angel!), Baba Ogun Kemi (peace please!), Mama Asante, and Dr. Santipriya Khonsu, Cousin Negretta, Sisters Venus, Danielle, Tanisha, Markeda, Nikki, Nedra, and Rachel, Brothers Charles, Rocky (loml), Miciah (thank you for your light Sun), Philip (Philly! We are coming of age in your likeness), Chad (Rasta bredrin of St. Kitts and Nevis), JJ, Ausar Henry Tabe (my Cameroonian Sen, loving "editor", and wonderful kindred African spirit), Jonathan, Brandon, Damon, Prentiss, Remi, Scott, Sean "the Real" Mckoy (one love!), and last but not least, Little Bros Marcus Jr. and Terrell. Thank you all.

Finally, my life has been one of contrasting racial, cultural, and psychological juxtapositions. It took a lot of struggle, but I understand now that while my social and economic conditions growing up said that I would conclude my life with the inner city blues of Black American "ghettoes," my historical and cultural position foretold an existence of peace, dignity, stability, and prosperity. All of my experiences and achievements were meant to culminate into this work so that I could help usher more Black girls and boys through the struggle and back to our legacy. For their contributions to my victory over the spiritual, racial, and cultural battles that continue to plague so many African people, I offer up endless gratitude and respect to Divinity, my Ancestors, family, friends, and the would-be hope-killers, too, that I have encountered along the way. You have encouraged me through to know the full power of standing always in the light of the sun.

Senet (Sister) Amani

Foreword

SigHT: Unveiling Black Student Achievement and the Meaning of Hope by Dr. Amanishakete Ani is in the same tradition as the works of Jawanza Kunjufu and Asa Hilliard. This is a book of immense importance to educators. Ani's book is necessary because the conditions that we find, especially in the large urban areas of the industrialized American cities, North and South, are the same that we have experienced since the dawn of the 20th century. The persistent cultural sabotage and self-destruction in the African American community demands an immediate, skillful, and loving response from trained intellectuals. Dr. Ani (Daphne Chandler) brings a brilliant analysis and an equally enlightening, or endarkening, quest for solutions based on her strong love for the African American community. This book is a plea for action and results, Ani is not content to simply give us an analysis of what is wrong with our youth. Too many analysts have tried to identify the problems in the lives of young people, but we have not had enough who truly appreciate the role of culture and identity in the rise of victorious consciousness. Now we have a champion on this front who walks in the same path as Na'im Akbar, Wade Nobles, Jawanza Kunjufu, Asa Hilliard, and other deeply rooted psychiatrists, scholars, and behaviorists. Amanishakete Ani is not afraid to tackle the thorniest issues in the discourse on success. This is the value of her reflections.

The key to her analysis and interpretations is the fact that she based her research on solid empirical data gathered in Cleveland, Ohio, a city that has been predominately black for more than a generation. Ani followed six junior high school students who consistently exceeded state exam standards despite the fact that they were in schools that were considered poor in academic and economic terms. By asking them a series of questions about family and identity, culture and spirituality, she discovered that there were certain values that might support success.

As an Afrocentrist I am encouraged by this type of research because it goes to the African American students to discover in their lived student experiences the possible mechanisms for success. Furthermore, she has demonstrated how educational thinkers such as Kunjufu, Hilliard, Beverly Daniel Tatum, and others have often been marginalized in thinking about student success from the standpoint of the students' own agency. After all, these scholars have understood for a long time, a much longer time than is recognized, that black students are capable of succeeding in academic situations. Yet we know that too many black students are in special education, directed toward non-college preparation, and simply dismissed as inferior students. *SigHT* seeks to provide us with an in-depth appreciation of the role of cultural identity in the making of successful students. Who is black? What does it mean to be a black student in a hegemonic society? How do we intervene in the academic lives of black children in such a way that it produces positive results? But this book is not simply about a few black students who do well because they are centered, the author seeks to offer all black students and their families in public and private schools the kind of hope that produces results. This is why the HBCUs must be a part of the formula for our complete success in education.

Ani provides us with a strong portrayal of achievement based on self-knowledge, cultural identity, and character. The students in the study who have been most successful know more than the average student about identity and culture. They tend to have a good sense of their power and possibility, and they utilize the long-term memory, that is, historical memory of their people's struggles. They seem to understand that knowledge not only gives them truth but a sense of place, that is, a sense of power. Students who operate on the bases of cultural esteem and even a sliver of optimism appear to have an intense commitment to achieving their goals. Ani suggests in this book that we have always known what our children need, the problem is that the hindrances of the society have been overwhelming and we have not been given the freedom to teach our children or to intervene in the way that we know will be beneficial.

The Yoruba people teach that character, *iwa,* is the highest value. In this regard I have come to believe that this is precisely what is essential to our young people, the teaching of character. When the Yoruba used the word "iwa," it almost always went with the word "pele," meaning "good character." The concept is substantial and has the meaning of strength, the ability to absorb blows and to rebound on the basis of a strong cultural foundation. It creates confidence, cultural esteem, and prepares students to challenge all obstacles. I am not disappointed in the research base and work of Amanishakete Ani because she has produced a volume that speaks to the same enduring values as her ancestors.

What is it that disinherits our youth if not the lack of a connection to the agency that created the resilience that they exhibit? *SigHT: Unveiling Black Student Achievement and the Meaning of Hope* tells us that we may not be what we ought to be but we know the way to the truth. Ours is a fight for the salvation of our children's minds. Rescuing them from the abominable damage that has been done is one of our sacred tasks. Alongside their protection and security we probably have no other real task but the recovery of our mental sanity. I am so inspired when I read this book because it lets me know that there are young scholars, the brightest among us, who have not forgotten the wisdom of their elders. Ani walks in the way of Anna Julia Cooper, Harriet Tubman, and Fannie Lou Hamer, and she has honored the nurturing mothers of our intellectual tradition like Joyce King, Nah Dove, Ama Mazama, Delores Aldridge, Marimba Ani, and Tiamoyo Karenga. She tells the truth in the same manner as the giants who have written their names forever in the hearts of their people because she knows, as they knew, that the only ultimate value in life is to be able to have those who follow you say that you had integrity, walked with character, and sought to improve the conditions of the oppressed. The added glory of this sister is that she has wrapped her intellectual brilliance in the same mantle as the educational theorists and psychological thinkers who laid the foundation.

SigHT: Unveiling Black Student Achievement and the Meaning of Hope shows me that Amanishakete Ani is familiar with Wade Nobles's *Sakhu* and Carter G. Woodson. They have both given profound judgments on the cause of our children's misorientation. I am not going to repeat their words here because Ani has gone on to tell us precisely how we can recover our orientation. Woodson, allow me to say, predicted Wade Nobles, Joyce King, Susan Goodwin, Chris Wiggins, and so many more Afrocentric educators when he said something to the effect that the conditions we see today have been determined by what happened in the past. Amanishakete Ani spends considerable energy in her book reminding us of the condition but also of the prospect for victory. Here she walks in the path of Maulana Karenga, the great harbinger of transformation and cultural ethics. If we are to be who we know that we can be and if our children are to stand on the human stage, then we must always listen to the language of culture as taught by Karenga in his magisterial *Introduction to Black Studies*. I see in Ani's book an author who knows that all education is political and that we are either educated to love and honor the traditions of our ancestors or the traditions of someone else's ancestors. For the African child, in America and in Africa, I will say, the single hardest change is to free oneself from the enslavement of Eurocentric thinking in education, religion, beauty, excellence, ideas, and culture. In *SigHT: Unveiling Black Student Achievement and the Meaning of Hope,* Dr. Amanishakete Ani has stepped into the pit, ready to win the victory for black children. I give a hearty Afrocentric salute to this young scholar who refused to allow either Spelman or Wisconsin, especially Wisconsin, to make her chattel.

Molefi Kete Asante, Ph.D.
Philadelphia

Preface: Where I Stand

Question: What does a successful life look like? Answer: "Uh, not many worries. Success is to be able to have all the things in life that you always wanted and not really have to turn them back in after a month or something because you didn't pay your bills. It's like where you can do everything and anything that you like...as long as it's in the law, that you could really do, that you felt like you wanted to do for a long time."

—Ture, 7th grade

When I speak of hope I am referring to the specific set of thoughts, behaviors, and beliefs that drive people toward achieving their goals. Even more specific, in the case of *SigHT, strength-based hope theory,* hope refers to the cognitive, behavioral and principle ingredients that come together to form experiences of achievement for Black youth in school. This is an important concept for a couple of reasons. The first is that very little work in the social sciences and education have ventured into the task of asking Black children directly about their strivings and experiences with school *achievement,* not failure, in "neocolonial" earth—that is, in world life after colonization of Africa. The second is more central to my heart: Black children have been given a bad wrap (or rep) and nearly impossible opportunities to be happy.

Two of my educational and professional experiences have enlightened me to some of the most effective curriculum and instruction strategies for Black children. The first is that I was fortunate to attend Spelman College beginning in my sophomore year. The second, ironically, is that I also attended predominately White institutions (PWIs)—the University of Oklahoma during my freshman year as an undergraduate and the University of Wisconsin at Madison, where I received my master's and doctorate.

I enjoyed being taught at Spelman, with its ethnic-enriched curriculum and Maat-centered culture that emphasized spirit, reciprocity, and harmony within the various relationships on campus. While there, my consciousness was profoundly awakened. In stark contrast to Spelman were the University of Oklahoma and the University of Wisconsin-Madison, two of the largest PWIs in North America. No school experience was more frustrating than my years of training at the latter two schools. The education and support that I received at Spelman was extraordinary in its effectiveness for me. Never was I more enthused, inquisitive, or reflective as a student than during my first two years at Spelman. I began to see with new vision during this time. Here is where I learned that Egypt is a part of Africa, Africa is a huge part of me and that Black people are a "minority" in a numerical sense only in some locales of the African Diaspora.

It was at Spelman College that I was encouraged intellectually, professionally, personally, and spiritually. For the first time in my school career I felt supported by my instructors, mentors, *and peers*, even when I erred in judgment, wore African American urban dress, or performed below my academic potential. By virtue of the care at the school, below potential performance was a rare occasion. I was not judged because of my family background, which was low-income and uneducated in the academic sense. My college family was genuinely concerned about me. My self-esteem and cultural-esteem grew by leaps and bounds. Not only did I begin to feel better about myself, my grades began to improve. Cultural-esteem led to impenetrable self-esteem, which led to extraordinary achievement in my life.

I have incorporated belief in Black children's capabilities and desire for Black history and dignity in my curriculum and intervention strategies with countless students in community centers, schools, and detention facilities to the delight of their teachers, parents, and judicial authorities who are often stunned at the positive changes in their attitude and behavior. Best of all, I have been tearfully thanked by Black youth and young adults alike for helping them realize their natural strengths, values, and goals through therapy and mentorship. As a practicing psychologist I have learned that often all it takes to adjust Black youth's behavioral difficulties or lack of motivation is a couple of sessions infused with Black history and cultural principles, brief ones at that, and the transformation begins. Colleagues have recognized that I tend to have a higher "show" rate (versus "no shows") than most. All too often, Black clients drop out of therapy early or come too inconsistently to make any significant change in their thoughts and behaviors. I am often asked to share my "secrets" in getting clients to come to sessions.

You may wonder how I am able to reach these young people. Do I have a gift for building rapport? Is it my college and university training? Or is it something more insightful regarding the nature and concerns of Black people? When it comes to helping any people, formal educational training can only take you so far. Cultural consideration is the key to understanding and service. For this matter, no exception to the rule of ethnicity and culture is given here to persons of multi-ethnic or mixed race heritage with African ancestry. Unless you (or the person you are reading for) are someone of mixed heritage in a state of self-avoidance, then I am confident that you will take as much positive information away from this book as any other Black person.

In my practice working predominately with people of African descent, I am guided by Afrocentric principles and activities such as those outlined by W.E.B. Du Bois, Carter G. Woodson, Molefi Kete Asante, and Na'im Akbar. Interestingly, the youth and families that I have aided may not themselves know the term Afrocentric in an intellectual sense, but they know the feeling of Afrocentricity as African people. Of course my approach is different when I work with youth and families from other ethnic groups, but I switch with ease because I understand the brilliance of diversity and importance of culture.

I draw from five main sources as I share principles and strategies that are successful with motivating and connecting to Black children in this book:

- My direct experiences of working with Black youth and their families
- The paradigm of Afrocentricity as described by Dr. Molefi Kete Asante
- My study of African American junior high school students, which lays the foundation for this book with its support for a theory of hope from the African descended person's worldview
- A literature review of African history related to contemporary African American, and for that matter other African Diasporic experiences
- Congruence between the study results and my own awakening as a conscious and *hopeful* African American woman

I have taken care to present information that is historically and anthropologically accurate, as well as psychologically and behaviorally meaningful. I write as an academic, consultant, sister, aunt, daughter, therapist, and ally in the struggle to liberate the minds of all people, and especially Black children. I am passionate about Black youth reaching their full potential for life success with far greater frequency than we have seen so far in the 20th and early 21st centuries.

While it is true that I am an African American woman, I am first African given that my cultural upbringing was always markedly "Black" in culture. My experiences in America and abroad have been largely segregated, divided between an unspoken physical and philosophical color line of Black on one side and White on the other (Ani, 2012; Chandler 2010). The fact is "Black" as many Americans have taken a liking to using to identify people of African descent is just that—African. I am an African American woman whose rhythm, values, and energy come from Africa by way of ancestry, intergenerational transference of culture, and consciousness. I am comfortable with my Blackness. As a result, I am neither ashamed of nor confused about my African-ness. My daily experience is of being referred to and accepted as a "sistah" far more often than an American, and I am quite conscious of my reality. This is true for most all Black people in America, whether they admit it or not. We are in actuality Africans in America.

African belief systems and cultural factors have directly impacted Black people for more than 10,000 years. Black people have been in

Preface

America and other parts of the Diaspora in mass numbers for only the past 500 years. What a time difference! The intergenerational effects of cultural values, traditions, languages, and communication styles are far-reaching and long lasting. Black people are not the same as White people and White people are not the same as Black people, neither phenotypically nor philosophically. It is imperative that we all accept this reality if our children are to perceive themselves as right and laudable creations of God (whomever yours is) and act as future leaders for universal order.

I-em-hotep (I welcome you in peace!),
Amanishakete Ani, Ph.D.

One senses that hope is celebrated to hold back the forces of despair...What if our authors could discover a few silver clouds, a few sunlit places where people have taken hold of hope, and where the human spirit has won out against the negatives?

(Mazama, 2007)

Introduction: On Understanding the Terms and Conditions of Black Student Life

Q: What are some things that might stand in your way?
A: No.
Q: No. Nothing?
A: Nothing. –Talib, 7ᵗʰ grade

In the African American community, "the truth" is a colloquialism used to describe a laudable invention, person or thing that resonates in the spirit as righteous and affirming. For example, in a poetry or hip hop forum, a young African American person might say, "Yeah, he's *the truth!*" In this book, my goal is to illuminate that which successful Black youth in the 21ˢᵗ century find as righteous, affirming or laudable in their strivings during the achievement process. Further, if we can persuade low performing students, their parents and teachers, to adopt these truths, we will launch a revolution that will stun the world.

While Black youth have their truths, as we all do, they have had to confront the unfortunate reality of a great many lies and misconceptions in the one place, *school*, where the truth should be in abundance but appears to be missing in action. Black children are often told that they represent an "at-risk" group. That they are less intelligent and likely to succeed based on biased "intelligence tests." They are also expected to believe that race is a nonissue today, and that their ethnic culture exists only within European, White "mainstream" culture. Why, the U.S. has experienced its first African American President, and "mixed race" children are on the rise. Meanwhile, history and culture are far more enduring than occurrences of elected officials and conditions of social orientation.

The effects of these lies have led to academic failure, high suspension, expulsion, and dropout rates, disproportionate placement in special education, and a deep mistrust of the system and the authority figures that work therein. Black children can see nothing good or laudable through this one-sided, unjust scenario and so, many of them, mixed or not, resonate hopelessness rather than hopefulness. Their fortitude is imperative for basic survival let alone grand feats like completion of graduate school today, and thus the criticalness of ensuring that they have the "SigHT" to see beyond fallacies and undesirable conditions, the sight to really see themselves.

I believe that hope is a verb, denoting goal-driven action grounded in intra- and intercultural understanding and informed by conscientious thinking and feeling about society. In easier terms, real hope involves self-awareness and social attention that work together to help us meet our goals. Consider this, a student's desire to be a doctor or lawyer in adulthood is but wishful thinking, or pointless dreaming unless that student is consciously thinking and acting on that goal in their daily striving. Goal-pursuit must be completed in ways that are harmonious to the students' family and cultural values and customs, and alert to both social resources and toxins if the goal is to be achieved. Especially in situations of mired opportunities, children must know their strengths, friends and foes to excel. This is the truest meaning of a "strength-based" theory or model of practice. A strength-based model is needed for Black youth everywhere to prevent more dreams deferred, or worse lives stolen.

In a just, free, and humane world, this book would be unnecessary. Where the playing fields of school and society were in fact level, and cultural diversity were truly celebrated over categorization and assimilation, Black students would be achieving much more frequently because intelligence and innovation comes natural to them. Many psychological theories have been developed to explain human behavior and specifically that of (European/Caucasian) children and adolescents, however, rarely do these theories explain *how* thought-patterns are formed or behaviors are manifested, which is what we must understand—the process by which African children succeed. For example, Abraham Maslow's widely accepted hierarchy of needs theory, and applied behavior analysts' notions of behavior functioning and conditioning have some utility in assessing behavioral *configurations*, but they do little by way of informing us of behavioral *processes* (Hockenbury & Hockenbury, 2000; O'Donohue & Fryling, 2007). That is to say that we must understand what those we intend to educate and develop optimally are made of, what informs their thinking and behaviors the most.

It is unsurprising then that even the most "enlightened" or "liberal" policymakers and educators still do not understand what inspires and frustrates African descended children. From Africa to Europe, India, the United States, Canada, Brazil, Asia and the Caribbean, pictures of powerlessness and hopelessness are painted regarding Black youth. Often-cited statistics of underachievement, delinquency, and depression about Black youth defy natural laws of human thought and ambition to pursue fulfillment under ideal conditions of freedom and opportunity. The underlying premise of this book is that we should begin to listen to the true experts of Black student achievement—high performing Black students themselves, rather than looking to adults for answers—who may never even interact with Black students, much less understand them.

Where the vast majority of American teachers are White, lack of recognition and appreciation of value systems and behavioral norms distinct from the White community runs high. Consider that 90% of the U.S. teaching force, for example, is of European descent (Boser, 2011; National Collaborative on Diversity in the Teaching Force, 2004). It is unsurprising then that many Black children, especially Black boys, begin to taper off in spirit, effort, and
cooperative behavior in U.S. schools during the third and fourth grades (Kunjufu, 1995; 2005). It is now common knowledge that Black children are disproportionately labeled in schools and placed in special education. The same is true of mis-diagnosis and over-medication in psychiatry

and psychology, wherein Black children are over diagnosed with mental and behavioral dysfunctions and subsequently treated with spirit, mind and behavior supressing chemicals (e.g., Children's Defense Fund, 2007). These are cycles of practice that suggest imminent doom for Black children and families indeed, rather than hope and achievement.

Yet, in spite of this dismal picture, there are some Black students who are overcoming tremendous obstacles and beating the odds. Some youth of African descent successfully matriculate through school with high grades and their spirits relatively intact, despite the disaffection they often feel from those charged with educating them. Given the negative school environments within which many Black students must learn and make good grades, their success is nothing short of a miracle (Kozol, 2005; Loewen, 2007)—and an underreported one at that.

SigHT outlines the results of a study[1] designed to define the components of hope among African American junior high school achievers raised and educated in Cleveland, OH, a spiritually and materially impoverished, predominately African city in North America. Herein I extrapolate information from this study that should prove to be important to teachers, school administrators, school psychologists, legislators, and parents of African and African Diasporic children. The purpose is to inform each group of the components which appear to be essential to developing high-achieving, self-determined Black children. In stating the purpose of this book, it is evident that people in roles outside of the core family and school personnel readership, such as policymakers, social workers, and professors of education, psychology and Africana/Black Studies programs who will also find this book important in their work with or for Black children.

Key Terms Defined
Schooling vs. Educating. The words "schooling" and "schooled" are not interchangeable with "educating" and "educated." I have narrowly defined these terms for the purposes of this analysis, which deals not only with the thoughts and processes of African people, but also with the reorientation of these people following centuries of miseducation. Education involves the bestowing of knowledge that is important to an individual's experience. Education leads to wisdom, which syncretizes spiritual, psychological, and intellectual development and serves as a guide in daily living (Asante, 2011b).

On the other hand, schooling involves the training of one's mind and containment of spirit. The schooled individual is trained to serve those leading the prevailing social and political order. Understanding the difference between the two terms is critical as we seek meaning in the narratives of the study participants and general contents of this book. Where Black children and families value education, they may hold little appreciation for schooling. To increase school achievement among Black youth then, schooling must be somehow connected to education, meaning life-adding or improving.

Reform vs. Restore. "Reform" or "reformation" in the educational context usually refers to modifying curricula, pedagogy, or school culture to make them relevant and effective for diverse student achievement. These terms are also used, disturbingly, in reference to "modifying" Black students themselves to fit into foreign school cultures and bring about modicums of achievement. I use the accurate terms of "restore" and "restoration" instead in recognition of the virtues and intellectual capacities inherent within Black students. The former set of terms implies that the American school structure was once fit for connecting with Black children, or that Black children are deficient in some way and require fixing or restructuring themselves. Neither one of these is the case.

The reality is that most Black children are primed to exercise their intellectual and cultural talents, but their teachers, administrators, and even some parents are unaware of their brilliance. When we speak of restoring Black consciousness and educational and cultural practices that work rather than "reforming" Black children or modifying strategies that were designed for other cultures, we are closer to recognizing what we once enjoyed culturally and academically. We come closer to fixing post-colonial and neo-colonial issues rather than creating and recreating false notions and pathologies. We begin to lift the veil. I believe that this is what Molefi Kete Asante meant when he wrote in 1980,

> Europe claims that you are universal if you do not write about black people while all the time they are writing about white people. If you write about white people, then it should be within the context of your historical experiences. Isolate, define, and promote those values, symbols, and experiences [that] affirm you. Only through this type of affirmation can we really and truly find our renewal, this is why I speak of it as a reconstruction instead of a redefinition. Actually what we have to do is not difficult because the guidelines are clearly established in our past. (p. 54)

Race vs. Ethnicity. Much confusion now exists with regard to the definitions of and differences between race and ethnicity. The conflation of these terms has brought about confusion on the meaning and pervasiveness of culture. In brief, it should be understood that race was for a long time treated as a hard scientific fact of biological determinism. Africans were decidedly African based on their physical features, and Europeans, Asians, Latinos, etc. the same, and from this intelligence and ability were supposedly concluded. Now, however, scholars and scientists agree more than not that race is primarily a social construct that was constructed and pushed throughout the past three centuries to maintain a caste system of better and lesser humans, intellectual and imbecile, and rich and poor along a continuum of "White" to "Black" and all shades in between (Bauval & Brophy, 2011; Gould, 1996). To the contrary, ethnicity or ethnic groups refers to ancestral lineage in relation to land and culture. Most enlightened people understand, for instance, that African Americans are more than a racial group. We have ethnic ties to Africa and cultural heritage related to Africans on the continent and across the African Diaspora.

Yet, understanding that many people across ethnic lines and education levels still speak in terms of race rather than ethnicity, I have opted to employ the terminology of race-ethnicity in this particular work. I hope that this strategy will help to ease the reading and increase the knowledge of those who might otherwise not connect African Americans to ethnicity. Quintana (2007) explains well that, heretofore,

> ...the proposed solution of reclassifying racial groups as ethnic groups has been criticized because it appears to exclude the racial basis of the social distance among sociocultural groups. An obvious third alternative, proposed by Cross and Cross (in press), to these two classification strategies is to use a hybrid approach: classifying groups as racial-ethnic. This approach would acknowledge that the social distance and treatment of Latinos or Hispanics is based on racial as well as ethnic features. Similarly, there are important ethnic features to African Americans' racial identity, and there is a growing number of calls to theorize and investigate the ethnic foundation to African Americans' identity. (p. 260)

I certainly recognize that African Americans are an ethnic group. I also recognize that the African American experience has been in many ways a volatile one where upon the primary political agenda by European American sociopolitical powers has been to erase any memory of and pride in our ethnic history and continued culture of origin. Sadly, the 17th to 21st century agenda has been largely effective, resulting in many African Americans themselves identifying and thinking as racial beings without ethnic awareness (Goffe, 2012; Woodson, 1933/2000). My intention in this work is to be sensitive to this conditioning while simultaneously urging African American parents, students and their teachers beyond racial training. Inasmuch, you will notice that I capitalize Black and White as "racial-ethnic" identifiers in the same way that I do geographically and culturally substantiated terms of African, European, etc. Hopefully in time, racial color devices will no longer be of concern as we re-enter our proper ethnic domains in full.

Afrocentricity vs. Africanity. At the outset readers must understand the meaning of Afrocentricity in its intellectual and political form. Afrocentricity refers to cultural awareness and political consciousness among Black peoples everywhere, and often employs "African" as the natural ethnic identifier for people of African descent since the dawn of civilization in Kush, and most illuminated through the Nubian and Kemetic dynasties of Kemet. It is a Pan African idea embraced to support unity and development within the continent and across the African Diaspora. Three terms are critical to understanding what Afrocentricity means in thought and practice: (1) subject, which refers to the humanity and ability of African people to think, speak and act for ourselves from our own sources of history and contemporary innovation, (2) agency, referring to action performed by Africans from their subject place for the development of the community, and (3) object, as in objectification, which helps to identify when African people are treated not as human beings but as objects such as during chattel slavery in the Arabic, European, and Spanish subject histories (Asante, 1980/2003; 1998). The professional sports and entertainment corporations at large are contemporary examples of the object term.

When we say that a research study is completed through an "Afrocentric analysis," we mean that the very development and analysis of the research was done through the lenses of African people in terms of history, culture and experience. It means that we have done our best to remove any and all notions of Black people being intellectually or culturally dependent on others to direct or speak for them. Only in this way can we claim to be "Afrocentric" or "African-centered" in our approach toward understanding and supporting African people.

On the other hand, Africanity "broadcasts identity" and refers to customs, traditions, and traits of Africans continental and Diasporan (Asante, 1998, p. 19). Africanity is observed when African women wear their hair naturally and when African men wear dashikis, for example. It is the expression or symbols of culture, conscious or subconscious, whereas Afrocentric is the conscious exercising of cultural legacy and dignity as a person of African descent. While both terms are important, Afrocentricity encompasses Africanity. Ironically, for example, while some African Americans are comfortable at times with expressing their Africanity, the same men and women might reject being referred to as African or members of the cultural legacy and political situations of other Africans. They look the part and have all of the necessary tools to play the part but fail to do so. They are the lions without teeth. Again, it is the reality of this situation that leads me to employ the term "Black" even though I understand that it is a dated term of mental and political colonization and African is far more accurate historically, culturally and even politically.

> We are not [simply] African Americans without Africanity; we are an African people, a new ethnic group to be sure, a composite of many ancient people, Asante, Efik, Serere, Touculur, Mande, Wolof Angola, Hausa, Ibo, Yoruba, Dahomean, etc. And quite frankly our politics, like the expressiveness [of] our religion, is more often similar in sentiment to that of Africa than of white America. (Asante, 1980/2003, p. 87)

Introduction

As we Africans share common biological, cultural and political bonds I am encouraged to use the term *African* as a global referent when discussing those of greater melanin on the continent and abroad, so I often do. Rather than prove the point of Africanity running deeper than hair texture, clothing, or skin complexion in African people everywhere, I intend instead to reach the hearts and minds of readers by illuminating truth about the achievement needs of our children, thus Black is used as well as African. Africa and Afrocentricity find homes in the words and activities of the youth presented in Chapters four through 10 no matter the technical terms used to relay their messages. Africa lives where they do.

The Context of Struggle

Much of psychological and educational programming lack the information critical to effectively serving Black and other non-White young people simply because the bulk of the literature used to create the various theories, behavioral interventions, and school curricula are based on information gleaned from the culture, heritage, historiography and resulting assumptions of White people only. Whiteness is a matter of fact around the world today so much so that a contemporary term has been created in its honor, *mainstream* (e.g., Caracciolo, 2008; Rios, Stewart, & Winter, 2010). Mainstream is often used within the education and psychology fields to describe championed teaching strategies, curricula, behavioral interventions and the like. One can be sure that any time the term "mainstream" appears it is meant to reference that which is considered to be "normal" or "right" in curriculum, instruction, and psychological service, context ignored. Any practice or content that does not reflect the assumptions and model of the mainstream is considered to be "alternative" and "unconventional"—wrong. Just as the saying went in the 1960s, "White is right" remains the banner of status quo supporters today.

Mainstream thoughts and behaviors are rightly codified as an *ism* because they denote devotion to a singular doctrine. In American schools and other parts of the world where the interests of Europeans dominate, *Eurocentrism* has acted as the mainstream. When Eurocentrism pervades in school culture and pedagogy, multicultural intolerance and intellectual silencing pervade. Eurocentrism prevails at the expense of the development and achievement of non-Europeans. This is wrong and would also be the case if Afrocentrism, Asiocentrism, or Indiocentrism were the dominant *isms*, however, none of these exist on a global, imperialist scale (Penang Conference, 2011). Centricity on the other hand, seeks to center people on their own ground without imposing on others.

Intellectuals and activists, including Yosef Ben Jochannan, John Henrik Clarke, Molefi Kete Asante, Asa Hilliard, Na'im Akbar, Amos Wilson, Wade Nobles, Ivan Van Sertima, and others have documented the problems that Eurocentrism with its ethnocentric prejudices and imperialist actions has created for all Black people who dare to hope and succeed. The authors also address decolonization of the mind and the achievement of Black people before European imperialism. Much attention is given to the disease of Eurocentrism also in the pages of this book, by virtue of necessity really, rather than desire. So says *Njia*, the wisdom of African people; "Never allow evil to burn in your hearts. Go to the one who offends you and lay the matter on the line" (Asante, 1980/2003, p. 140).

In every way Eurocentrism in our school curricula and overall school culture is an offense to the dignity and abilities of those of us who live outside of the European existential reality. We who care for children cannot allow it to persist. Instead we must choose to struggle in protest against it as necessary. The African principle of *Sankofa*, and the many proverbs stemming from it, teach that we must know our past in order to move intelligently into our future, lest we repeat errors or make futile attempts toward progression.

What becomes of children who are taught that they have no history? What becomes of children who are taught that their own history is limited to imitating or reacting to others'? These are the lessons Black children are learning today in schools around the world at times overtly and at others covertly. Not only are Black children taught that they come from a people devoid of remarkable history through the exclusion of their history in most school curricula, but they are taught that they have always had to rely on the people who are glorified in the curriculum and are therefore are incapable of contributing to society in any meaningful way today. To add insult to injury as the North American idiom goes, the curriculum inflicted upon Black children surreptitiously honors the fact that the same people glorified in schools raped, enslaved, and murdered their grandmothers and grandfathers. What must Black children think of themselves and their Ancestors in light of their exclusion from school curricula and culture other than to be insulted? What must so many Black children think about their abilities to set and reach important goals? What right do they have to hope?

Certainly not all teachers, administrators or policymakers hold ill intentions toward educating Black children meaningfully. The hard reality, however, is that unless you are a part of the solution, meaning actively *de*moting schooling and *pro*moting education for Black children, then you are in fact a part of the problem. Silent, "color-blind" educators speak just as loud in their silence and omissions than do overt racists. When you ignore or belittle important factors in service you say in your inaction that you support the current system (while simultaneously citing it as broken and failing). While many call for simple solutions to the nation's educational problems in nicely wrapped packages, the truth is that the current state of education was created by a complexity of events from an often ignored, and very ugly history.

Many lies and misunderstandings about Black people and history have been propagated, all of them ending in failure for African, European, Asian, Latin, and Indigenous American children alike, although mostly for Black children. Given the state of emergency facing Black children, there can be no expectation of convenience, only hope, which requires centric input and action from everyone. Let it be understood that White issues are in many ways Black issues, and Black issues White ones, if for no other reason that we must coexist.

Understanding African Youth Today

African American youth in schools today are the children of parents or grandparents who lived through J. Edgar Hoover's COINTELPRO, which targeted the destruction of Black political and religious organizations like the Black Panther Party and the Nation of Islam. They are the grandchildren of elders who survived Jim Crow and the economic improprieties of the sharecropping system (Churchill & Wall, 2002; Reuf & Fletcher, 2003). Continental African and Caribbean youth of today are the children of those who participated in or lived through 20th century Independence wars and protests (e.g., Swan, 2011).

While much of Africa was fighting to regain political Independence, at least on paper, during the 1950s to the 1990s, African Americans were winning the fight for respectable treatment and public facilities, and celebrating the first Black governor elected in 1990 (i.e., Carl Stokes of Ohio) (Collins & Smith, 2007; Ture & Thelwell, 2003). As South Africans were celebrating Nelson Mandela's prison release in 1990 and the dismantling of the vile Apartheid system in 1994, African Americans were celebrating unprecedented literary and political honors with Toni Morrison's Nobel Prize in 1993, Charles Fuller before her for his politically charged *A Soldier's Play* in 1982, and the Million Man March in 1995 (A&E Television Network, 2009; Asante, 2011a). Black youth today speak in and act through the language and views of their elders first as matters of both culture and protest (Asante, 1998).

Despite the distinct differences and difficult history between the two races, most Blacks and Whites agree on the value of education. In the 21st century, many African American parents find themselves vying for choice vouchers that will enable them to send their children to more academically rigorous schools (The Heritage Foundation, 2009; Sackler, 2010). In 2011, an African American woman from Akron, Ohio, risked imprisonment for attempting district placement falsification in order to send her children to better schools in a nearby suburban area (Johnson, 2011). Yet, many teachers and administrators still believe the misnomer that African American parents do not care about their children's education.

The truth is, Black parents interact with systems in ways that make sense for their cultural and social experiences. Prior to desegregation in 1954, many African American parents were content with separate but equal education for African children due to the American traditions of racism and ethnocentrism (e.g., see Ture & Thelwell, 2003; Weiner, 2009). In the 21st century, many African Americans continue to question the merit of Black children being educated, or rather mis-educated as Woodson (1936/1968) aptly pointed out, in environments that virtually ignore their experiences and question their cognitive, emotional, and behavioral normality (Clark, 2009; Merry & New, 2008, Orfield, 2001). And African Americans are right to question.

Research shows that Black youth are conscious of the existence and social implications of racism beginning in childhood (Clay, 2006; Quintana, 2007). The middle school period is especially shaped by racial-ethnic identity and public perception (e.g., see Hughes, Hagelskamp, Way, & Foust, 2009; Rivas-Drake, Hughes, & Way, 2009). In the general society, Black children witness police brutality and judiciary discrimination, such as with the nationally televised murder of Oscar Grant III on January 1, 2009, in California, the unchecked brutality of Black people until 2010 by Massachusetts police officer Jeffrey Asher, the beating of teenage Chad Holley of Texas in 2011, and the murder of Trayvon Martin by a would-be police officer on February 26, 2012. Stories like these are played and replayed on the nightly news and YouTube.com across the world, and even more are witnessed in local neighborhoods.

It has been theorized that Black youth, especially African American, express their dissonance and discontent in school through oppositional identities and cool poses. Ogbu (1993) recognized oppositional identities among Black students as attitudes and behaviors that oppose any belief or behavior embraced by members of the White community, whose cultural habits have been largely oppressive. According to Ogbu (1989, 1993), oppositionality may be observed when Black students use Ebonics in the classroom, even when they know that Standard English is the institutional rule. Further, he found that school achievement itself was opposed by many of the youth, both for themselves and their peers.

Majors and Billson (1992) defined the cool pose as the construction of a symbolic universe of unique patterns of speech, walk, and demeanor designed to maintain poise under pressure. Referring mostly to African American males, the conceptualization of the cool pose was based on assessment of the "tense encounters" with psychological and social impositions inflicted by racism against Black masculinity, such as in police brutality and racial profiling (p. 2). Cool poses give African American youth the sense of having a voice and right to feel dignified in spite of the incessant messages of degradation they receive from the wider society (Majors & Billson, 1992). Majors & Billson's theory of the cool pose extended Thompson's (1974) theory of "cool" in Africa as a product of creativity and intellect. Both Ogbu and Majors & Billson's works continue to be referenced in social science discourses today.

Oppositional identity, the cool pose, and hip hop are all contemporary symbols and sounds energized by the African mythoform of resistance to cultural confusion and racism. Like other cultural microcosms, hip hop includes dialect, dress style, a code of ethics, disposition, social interests, and music, and it pervades all life domains for those connected to it of which African American youth are the arbiters and primary innovators (Kubrin, 2005). Erykah Badu (2008) said that hip hop is bigger than even religion and money. On a recent album entitled

Introduction

New Amerykah, Part 1, she called hip hop *The Healer* that transcends geographical and social boundaries. To many Africans Americans, hip hop is more than beats, fast speech, and entertainment. Like reggae and gospel music, hip hop is a source of affirmation, therapy, joy, and freedom (e.g., Banfield, 2004; Clay, 2006; Rosenthal, 2006). We cannot presume to know and understand the carriage of African youth today, and especially in America, without paying attention to hip hop.

M.K. Asante, Jr. (2008) understands that hip hop is a socio-political artistic expression borne out of the creative genius of African American youth and young adults from the inner cities of North America. So integral is the cool in the African American hip hop community that songs have focused solely on what the cool is, such as in Lupe Fiasco's "The Coolest" on his 2007 album titled *The Cool,* and The Roots' *Stay Cool* (2004). Lupe Fiasco warns in his "tales of The Cool," that getting lost in materialism and youthful excitement gained from living life carelessly is "guaranteed to go and make you fail from your school, and seek unholy grails like a fool." Yet, to many educators and policymakers, and even to some Black parents, hip hop music and attitudes are viewed as antithetical to scholarship, creativity, propriety, or motivation for school achievement.

Understanding why African youth speak, think, and act the way they do is critical to educating, counseling, and mentoring them. More importantly, understanding the dynamics of African youth culture(s) is necessary to nurturing their strengths—it's cool to be cool, and even cooler to be cool *and* successful in school. It has always been cool to be smart and demonstrate excellence in Africa, and Black youth today should know that.

Educating African American Youth Today

African youth are seldom understood culturally and therefore rarely nurtured in schools or clinical practice. Issues of race are connected to Black youth far more frequently than ethnic traditions. For example, with all of the rhetoric about African American youth being oppositional, many social scientists and teachers have stopped even considering that such attitudes and behaviors have cultural limits. Yes, it is true that many Black youth assume oppositional postures and cool poses in response to social conditions, which I have observed at times from Kenya to Kansas, but it also happens that they continue to hold aspirations toward being successful adults and providing for their families as matters of tradition. Similarly, Black parents are often distant toward their children's schools as a result of their own empty or demoralizing experiences there, but they still value education and want the best for their children.

Recent scholarship focusing on African American students actually reveals that many of the youth value education and see school as viable. As Cokley and Chapman (2008) stated, "Contrary to popular depictions of African American students," participants indicated that they value academic success, and do not endorse anti-White/anti-intellectual stances in efforts to assert their self-worth (p. 360). Young African American men in Stinson's (2011) study expressed that they excelled in high school and resisted negative racial perceptions by retaining positive ethnic identities and staying focused on making Black community members proud. Rather than placing their focus on any supposed threat to their success, they blazed a trail of high achievement through school by focusing on the strengths in their heritage and role models in their community. Certainly, social and political changes underscore the need to reexamine theories such as Ogbu's (1993) oppositional identity and Major & Billson's (1990) cool pose as they relate to developing healthy, academically thriving Black children. What were accurate descriptions of Black youth in the specific sociopolitical context of the 90's may not be so in the 21st century.

We must ask new questions and pose new theories if we are to understand changes in Black student development and assist in their achievement. Stinson (2011) related a participant's response to Fordham and Ogbu's '90s literature (e.g., Fordham, 1993) and concluded that Black student achievement is not altogether a win or lose, White versus Black dichotomy. A participant in Stinson's study "acknowledged that an internal conflict between choosing social success or academic success did exist for some African American students," but he felt that "this conflict did not exist in his schooling experiences because of his participation in athletics (a coping strategy identified by Fordham and Ogbu) and the type of high school he attended"—a predominately African American high school where teachers and students spoke of Black history and experiences proudly (p. 55–56). Sankofa, Hurley, Allen and Boykin (2005) have also found results contrary to the rhetoric of oppositional identities and devaluing of formal education as acts of resisting racism.

A central question for educators and psychologists today is how to increase African American engagement with education through school as customary to African culture, despite a nearly 500-century long European imperialist stronghold on schools. Since they experience so much contradiction and lack of fulfillment in Eurocentric schools, many African American students begin to channel their determination elsewhere, such as toward the streets or the military (Asante, Jr. 2008; Williams & Baron, 2007; U.S. Army, 2010), thus all too often fueling the so-called "school-to-prison pipeline."

Many African American students begin to lose sight of their abilities and cultural wealth during elementary school. As they grow they feel a lack of options because neither school nor the larger society welcomes them. They remain suffocatingly marginalized in spite of their efforts. Too often the academic potential of African American youth is masked by lies and stifled under hidden memories. They know little about their history, so they rarely realize the extent of their abilities and they are left unclear about where they should be headed. The contours of their ancestral journeys have become too blurred for them to see the reality of their heritage and the promise in their futures. They lack SigHT.

And yet, there are those who shine where there is little sun. Under conditions of racism, poverty, intergenerational blues, and uncertainty of future, some Black children keep their dreams, plant dream seeds and water them as they grow. They are the silver clouds sought after by Ama Mazama (2007), taking hold of hope and winning against countless odds. How do they do it? Can we replicate their methods to create sunlit patches in our communities, and even brightly lit skies in our nations? My study participants—Ture, Talib, Kwame, Assata, Kenya, and Aisha—not only have special abilities, but they exude hope by channeling and developing the best within themselves, their family and community to win in school. I only hope that I have asked the right questions to get at what contributes to their young African agency.

Using Hope Theory to Understand Black Youth

SigHT describes the results of a study I conducted with six African American junior high school achievers in 2010. The students were asked a total of 52 questions, notwithstanding a few clarifying or improvisational queries. Their responses are reported and analyzed throughout this book. Insights from the study will inform the work of teachers, school administrators, psychologists, legislators, and parents about some of the essential factors that contribute to the development of high-achieving and self-determined African youth. I believe this work will resonate with adults who work with or parent Latino and Indigenous American children as well.

My interest in posing questions that tap into the (1) goals, (2) motivating factors, (3) racial-ethnic identity, (4) degree of self-cultural knowledge, and (5) attitudes toward school of Black student achievers was borne out of sincere and serious intention to answer the very question of what must be understood about the internal ingredients found in the cognitive and philosophical network of Black students in a continuously racialized and disparity-ridden 21st century world. To be clear, what is sought after here are outcomes of school achievement and completion, not enjoyment of, or connectedness to school.

In conceptualizing and completing this study, I brought to the task certain knowledge and skills that enabled me to elicit meaningful responses from the achievers spotlighted, insightfully analyze the narratives, and communicate the outcomes in a way that can be used by others to develop more empowering programs for Black youth. As teachers, parents and other invested readers should always consider the merits of research and interpretations presented, it is important that the source be cross-examined for personal position and skills. This is especially true regarding research discussing African children and achievement. Consider the following:

Child development. As a school psychologist, I understand how changes in brain development effect cognitive development, mood, and behavior across the life span. Especially during the early adolescent years, brain development in the prefrontal cortex motivates gradients in sensitivity to self-concept and understanding of social factors. Accordingly, middle schoolers are bound to proffer an initial response that may not be their last or final answer. They may be expected also to profess humor or carelessness in their anxiety over serious topics, while in actuality caring much and feeling confused about their feelings.

To accurately decode the students' responses, it was important that I understood not only basic child development but also *Black* child development. The air of coolness exuded by most African youth is unique to them, with additional subtleties between subcultures within the global ethnic group. I understood that the initial responses of my African American participants to some questions during the SigHT study were sometimes those that they found to be ideal to harmonious or cool positions rather than their honest reflections on the state of things, so, I rephrased the questions and waited patiently as some of their cool dissipated. Fragile as adolescents sometimes are in serious discussion, I frequently reminded the participants that their answers were confidential through anonymity and character unjudged by me. This reassurance helped to elicit more honest reflections.

Finally with regard to child development, it was important that I understood the cognitive limitations of my participants. Although smart, high achieving students, they sometimes wrestled with articulating their experiences and perspectives on provocative topics smoothly. Analysis can be difficult when you are living an experience. Even we adults struggle at times to discuss controversial and conflated issues such as race and culture. Nowhere is confusion regarding race and ethnicity more prominent than in segments of African communities, where wrestling with self-hatred, assimilation, and the like are realities too often. Here again is where knowledge and understanding of African peoples and experiences is important in conduction of research.

Cultural decoding. My ability to have critically meaningful dialogue with the Black children in this book comes only through my position as an Afrocentric woman. When the study participants broke from Standard English or communicated through African American gestures, such as the lip-perched facial expression that says, "yeah right" or "man, please," I understood them and carried on the dialogue fluidly. If my philosophical alignment were with Europe, I would not have allowed their cultural realities and expressions space to exist (Ladson-Billings, 1996). The Afrocentric Inquiry (AI) model as described by Dr. Molefi Kete Asante in his *Kemet, Afrocentricity and Knowledge* (1990) was essential in guiding the process of uncovering the narrative meanings and imaginations of my young participants (Asante, 2008, p. 35).

In addition to understanding the importance of centering major African American cultural traditions, such as communication styles and general African philosophical beliefs like collectivism, focused social awareness of African America was also critical. For example, my awareness of the contemptuous role that racism has played within the Black community up to the present day made me sensitive enough during interviews to know when to move on and return to a question later, or when to ask follow-up questions to reticent responses. Where my intra-cultural knowledge was less or off skew, I might have accepted reticent responses as complete ones and missed important information for Black youth's achievement processes.

Therapeutic Techniques. When the study participants became nervous during discussion of what they perceived to be controversial issues, such as their thoughts about Africa or whether they had ever experienced racism, I was able to stabilize the discussion before their anxiety turned to distress. As a school psychologist with interests in qualitative research and competence in multicultural practice I have taken an interest in motivational interviewing techniques. Skills in motivational interviewing help to present questions that allow respondents to guide the discussion or solve their own thought problems (Cormier & Nurius, 2003).

I have also been trained to observe body language for nonverbal communication and voice fluctuation indicating changes in mood (e.g., Merrell, 2003). Even as my African-centered awareness prompted me to gather more information on race and culture questions that the students felt di-ease about, for example, I knew when the students' mood had altered and it was time to move on entirely or break and return to a question later. These skills served me well during the interviews presented here. I offer the information and recommendations found with great care and confidence of accuracy.

As you will read in Chapter 1, theories for terms that we frequently use in colloquial conversation, such as optimism, resilience and hope, have become legitimate fields of study in the social sciences. For researchers interested in helping others understand what makes people successful and satisfied in life, subfields like positive psychology are gaining interest. The usefulness of positive psychology has been limited in scope and depth, however, by monocultural bias toward serving Europeans. The time has long come that the worldview and experiences of all the world's people be included and given space to pursue happiness. *SigHT* begins inclusion of Africans in hope theory discourse, with a platform given to youth and posterity first. The question is not whether Black children can achieve, but whether or not they will be given opportunity to develop determination to achieve. Let us remove the veil from over our eyes to begin to see the truth about the legacy and needs of Black youth to then increase their hope. Then we might begin to truly educate and develop the best in them.

Both the Cleveland Metropolitan School District and University of Wisconsin's Institutional Review Boards (IRB) for research approved the presented study. IRBs in educational institutions such as public school districts and universities examine research proposals for safety and appropriateness for participants.

Part 1:
Laying the Foundation

Chapter 1: Hope Theory Reviewed

The word "hope" or a sentiment like it is used in many cultures around the world. Regardless of the language, the emotional tenor of the term is typically one of prayerful intent, an urging or calling up to the divine or the universe to bring a certain something to pass. You may "hope" to receive a raise or promotion at work, or you might "hope" to pass a class. Often, we "hope" for things even when we know we have not performed to the best of our ability.

This is not how the term is used in the social sciences. While the colloquial term is an adjective that describes an emotion felt during dire straits, hope in the social sciences is a noun that refers to goals and plans to pursue them. Colloquially, you experience hope in your feelings and thoughts, which may or may not lead to planning. From a social science perspective, however, hopeful thinking stirs self-motivation and strategizing. Going a step further, hope in my perspective is both a noun and a verb denoting intentions *and* actions that are clear of cultural and social delusion. Each and every one of us is a cultural being operating in social environments filled with people who are either within or outside of our cultural group. With this, hope is not merely emotional and abstract, but rather concrete and action-oriented in human experiences seeking to prosper and maintain balance in life. In the SigHT perspective, we can say that we hope for something when we have dedicated thought power and activity toward our desires and personal development.

Understanding the difference between hope as a cognitive or emotional adjective and hope as a noun and verb will determine how useful this work will be for you. I often use the terms hopeful thinking and hopeful acting rather than simply hope in my research and practice to help others understand the important difference between hope as a dream (often deferred) and hope as an action (ultimate reality).

Hope theory is an area of psychological study that aims to help children and adults alike realize mental health and achieve success. Yet researchers have neglected to explain how hope theory can be used to help non-Europeans. In this chapter I will explain historical aspects of the most widely discussed hope theory led by C.R. Snyder and colleagues. In Chapter 2, I will move the discussion toward the establishment of a hope model relevant to the Black community.

Distinguishing Hope from Resilience

When discussing hope theory it is important to differentiate it from resilience as many people, social scientists included, often conflate the two. Where hope is described as proactive and ongoing, resilience is reactive and dormant. For instance, a person is decidedly resilient in their facing "adversity" (Abelev, 2009, p. 14), overcoming "serious threats to adaptation or development" (Masten, 2001, p. 228), or "coping with environmental challenges" and trauma (Maluccio, 2002, p. 596). Resilience

1

is characterized by the ability to overcome extraordinary obstacles. For resilience to be demonstrated, some threat to physical, emotional, or psychological health, or to prospects of upward mobility, must be present.

Typical resilience research therefore focuses on perseverance over poverty, teenage pregnancy, single-parent upbringing, and living in disadvantaged neighborhoods—all of which are typically considered to constitute harmful or negative situations. Children raised in these contexts are categorized as "at-risk" for dropping out of school, engaging in criminal activity, failing academically and professionally, living in future poverty, etc. (Abelev, 2009, p. 115). Ironically, although the Black community has been significantly excluded from hope research, which is far more positive, we have been disproportionately included in resilience research (e.g., Abelev, 2009; Hines, Merdinger, & Wyatt, 2005; Li, Nussbaum, & Richards, 2007).

In my opinion, heavy focus on resilience theory is problematic because it breeds preconceptions about who people are, what their life experiences have been, and how far they can achieve based on demographics and laboratory prescribed "risk-factors." Are there no households at the poverty level (i.e., $14,060–$44,380 for households of two to nine people or more; U.S. Census Bureau, 2009) that have loving families, scholastic appreciation, and produce healthy, successful people? Have there been no people raised in poor households and high crime neighborhoods who did not endure "serious threats to adaptations or development" during their upbringing, and who turned out to achieve in life (e.g., Abelev, 2009, p. 121)? The answer is yes such people exist. I know many people who fit this mold.

Resiliency is inherently positive, however, resilience theory and research are seriously flawed, as problems are too often the focus, and especially for African populations. Resilience research often diminishes human agency with a sort of risk ratio between the person and challenge(s), for which most often the person is hypothesized to have the lesser odds (Lagana, 2004; Li et al., 2007; Newman, 2005). Most resilience theorists appear to fall in line with Ruby Payne's "poverty theory," which only increases the dreadful culture- and color-blind orientations of the mainstream with the idea of class and income trumping all other personal and social factors (Payne, 1996/2005). Money is no antidote to racism or discrimination (Kunjufu, 2006). Under these deficit models of individuals at-risk, many African children (and Latino and Indigenous Americans too) have the equivalent of "a shot in hell" for succeeding in high school and college. In other words, they should have very little hope.

Snyder's (e.g., 2002) hope theory is brighter and more useful given his attention to personal will and developmental mechanisms. With hope, your child does not have to wait around for obstacles. Instead, he plans before and beyond them. With hope, your student might give very little time and energy toward "overcoming" racism, as her focus is on being prepared for opportunities when they greet her so that victory is her

Chapter 1: Hope Theory Reviewed

revenge. The mantra therefore becomes "I am the decider today" rather than "we shall overcome."

However, as I waive the hope flag, where Snyder failed is in recognizing that *cultural context and social impetuses matter* greatly. In neglecting cultural diversity, Snyder and his colleagues have relegated hope theory to the low rank of Eurocentrism. More specifically, popular hope theory fails to consider that family support, role modeling, community inclusion, and school effectiveness will look different in development and action according to ethnicity and culture. Similarly, in neglecting the social contexts of contemporary society, popular hope theory assumes that family, community, and school resources are the same and exist equally for everyone. Those subscribing to Snyder's theory and research presume to fit every child into this neat, simplistic, one-size-fits-all hope model. The corresponding assumption is that children who do not fit are deficient, and hopeless. To this end, hope has been just another mainstream, racist benchmark to measure all children with European yardsticks in a culturally diverse world.

The Current Theory—Hope in White
In short, hope theory has its roots in the field of positive psychology, which seeks to discover and study the processes of human strengths (Sheldon & King, 2001). The underlying assumption of positive psychology is that all human beings have virtues that may be developed to enhance psychological well-being and manifest functional behaviors. Whether studying resilience, self-efficacy, optimism, or hope (all of which are theoretically different), positive psychology researchers seek to understand how people prevail or succeed. Explaining the need for an alternative to the traditional pathology focus in Western psychology, Gable and Haidt (2005) stated that, "one cost of focusing resources solely on the treatment of those who are already ill may be the prevention of these very same illnesses in those who are not ill through research on the strengths and circumstances that contribute to resilience and wellness" (p. 106). Or as Snyder (1995) stated, a "benefit of measuring hope is that we can identify high-hope people and see what they do naturally to achieve their advantages in living…we can learn from high-hope people about how to help others…" (p. 73).

Snyder conceptualized hope as an affectively regulated cognitive interplay between self-motivation and problem-solving to achieve goals (Snyder, 2002). For the last two decades, researchers have documented the positive effects of hope among study participants using Snyder's conceptualization. Outcomes with focus on educational achievement and mental health have been included (Parajes, 2001; Snyder et al., 2002; Snyder, Lehman, Kluck, & Monsson, 2006). At first interested in why people offer excuses after failing to meet performance expectations, Snyder (2002) began to study adaptive processes of adult behavior in the workplace, with the assumption "that human actions are goal directed"

(p. 250). Early in the conceptualization, he hypothesized that goal-pursuit must involve significant forethought since "the purpose of the brain is to comprehend and anticipate causal sequences" (p. 249)—e.g., if I do "A," then "B" will happen, and then maybe even "C."

When a person "hopes" that something will or will not happen, then he has, at some point, thought about how to realize his hoped for end—which brings us back to the difference between the layperson's definition of hope (emotion-focused) and social scientists' theoretical definition of hope (cognitive process with conative implications). Both are affected, but not dictated by emotions. According to Snyder's theory, hope is comprised of agency cognitions, which supply willpower to meet objectives, and pathways thoughts, which are premised to deliver routes to derive at goal attainment (Snyder et al., 1997). A person may be characterized as highly hopeful if she has the self-confidence that she can achieve her goals, and also takes the extra measure of producing a plan to achieve her goals (Shorey, Snyder, Rand, Hockeymeyer, & Feldman, 2002). Low agency and high pathways thinking or high agency and low pathways thinking prevent hopefulness and reduce chances for goal attainment.

Determination without appropriate planning would stagnate even a strong-willed person if he lacks the how-to necessary to exercise his motivation. Similarly, a person full of ideas about how to reach a goal but who lacks the mental energy required to self-motivate toward action is unlikely to achieve his goals. Consider two students. One thinks, "I know how to produce a winning college application, but I can't decide where to apply under so much pressure." The other thinks, "I am the worst writer in my class and I loathe writing, but I know exactly which schools I want to apply to and where to begin with these college applications." The first has high agency and low pathways thinking, while the second is low in agency and high pathways. Both are likely to have a difficult time completing their college applications independently and timely.

Hope is both dispositional and task dependent, meaning a person might be highly hopeful overall but less hopeful regarding his ability in a particular area. Conversely, a person might be generally unhopeful except for her ability in a specific area or two (Snyder, Lopez, Shorey, Rand, & Feldman, 2003). The highly hopeful person, even if insecure in one area or another, will experience happier emotional states and more successful life experiences than the low hope person whose general outlook on life is more negative than positive (Snyder, 2002). Reserves of hopefulness serve to push us through our negative thinking and enable us to plan and move beyond the roadblocks of life. Hopeful thinking has the capacity not only to elevate emotional states, but also improve experiences through personal will and planning.

Developing Hope
Snyder et al. (1997) have asserted that hope develops through two core phenomena, one of a primary and intrinsic nature, and the other of

Chapter 1: Hope Theory Reviewed

a secondary and external nature. Internal development of hope, which Snyder considered to be a far greater determinative, occurs through the self-appraisal of personal abilities to achieve goals. These can easily be thought of in terms of Albert Bandura's self-efficacy theory (e.g., see Magaletta & Oliver, 1999). External development of hope occurs through experiences that teach how to self-motivate and create pathways, such as through observation of role models. Externally, children learn to be effective hope actualizers by watching "critical role models" especially, such as their parents, teachers, and siblings (Snyder et al., 1997, p. 402).

Hopefulness is said to begin developing in the minds and spirits of children during the toddler years, and lessons of hope are reinforced throughout childhood and adolescence (Snyder et al., 1997). However, it should be obvious that parents, older siblings, teachers, etc. can also impact a child's internal development of self-confidence and problem solving skills in negative ways depending on a number of key variables, such as parent personality factors, teacher expectations for certain children, positivity of a child's family dynamic and peer group, the list goes on. An underlying assumption in Snyder's theory is that every child's home and school environment is caring and high functioning. This is a bogus assumption regarding social realities on many levels under conditions of rampant race, class, gender, and education inequality. Shortsighted by their Eurocentric orientation, Snyder and colleagues paint in their research a picture of equity that in fact does not exist at all.

In response to this, Snyder et al. (1997) seem to have attempted to neutralize social differences by placing concern of external factors beneath personal needs and value judgment, in effect stating that hopefulness is almost solely up to the individual. The gravity of self-appraisals during goal pursuit, for instance, is said to depend on the value level individuals place on goals. Further, positive experiences of meeting goals would lead to higher goal-setting, with one success experience encouraging the second, third, and so on. The fact remains, however, that forces outside of the physical self can have significant influence, good or bad, on hope development especially for people in collectivistic and/or marginalized communities. Even should the development of hope be viewed as a largely individual process for all, it matters that people from different backgrounds and experiences have different values or may value the same things somewhat differently. So, here we have another bogus assumption, this time more so on cultural than social grounds.

In the end, "I" is expected to hold greater value than "we" in Snyder's hope theory (wherein opportunities and systems reflect the "mainstream" White individual and provides an unwritten power collective of course; e.g., Wilson, 1998). The real crux in this conceptualization is personal goals, which are set, achieved by children (and adults), and assessed based on the satisfaction of the individual. Among children from cultural groups with a collectivist tradition of placing the needs and reputation of the entire family, and even community group at par or above personal desires and image, the experiences, beliefs, and plans of parents and community members holds far greater significance than what Snyder's theory and corresponding interventions suggest. The idea that people experience positive emotions and heightened motivation from winning, so to speak, is a basic one. I can certainly agree that Black children benefit from experiences of achievement, praise from parents and teachers, etc., however, school psychologists, educators, and parents should be mindful not only to ensure that Black children have increased experiences with personal success, but also that their family and larger community be included in their programming for success.

Theoretically, the lack of contextualizing in hope research is especially perplexing in that Snyder (2002) placed "developmental lessons" at the beginning of his conceptualization of hopeful thinking. Yet he made no attempt to study Latin developments in psychology and education, African developments, Indigenous American developments, etc. Neither did he attempt the minimal work of citing possible differences in goal orientation based on sociopolitical realities other than to state that differences in hope scores between children and adults across ethnic groups implies that "Caucasians may have fewer obstacles" (Snyder et al., 2003, p. 127). So, the moral of the story, according to Snyder, is that Europeans are more hopeful because the system better supports their achievements. This is quite a half-hearted and incomplete theoretical model for such an important topic.

Snyder and colleagues (e.g., Pedrottie, Edwards, & Lopez, 2008; Snyder, 1995; Snyder, 2002) have suggested interventions for instilling and enhancing hope. The guiding principle behind positive psychology constructs like hope is that adaptive traits can and should be developed within people to improve life experiences. Before this can be realized for Black children, however, we must first demonstrate the reliability of the constructs for them. Their beliefs, values, and culture *must* be included in the conceptualization of theories used in directing their instruction and intervention.

The overwhelming majority of participants in hope studies have been of European descent (e.g., Snyder, 1995; Snyder et al., 1997; Snyder et al., 2002). Snyder et al. (1997) noted themselves that their standardization work for the Children's Hope Scale (CHS) included only two samples out of seven that had "sufficient numbers" of non-European children to claim validation for other child communities (p. 405). African children constituted about 3% of the entire standardization sample (all seven studies), compared to European children at 91%. Other hope studies fail to mention the racial-ethnic demographics of their participants, inferring that their samples meet the typical American background of Whiteness or mainstream norms (e.g., Cheavens, Feldman, Gum, Michael, & Snyder, 2006; Snyder et al., 1991; Snyder, 2002). Unless intercultural knowledge is included in psychological and educational programming we will fail in our mission of educating children and miss important shades and styles of hope and success.

Chapter 2: Toward An Afrocentric Hope Theory

Q: ...Do any of those goals come from you being African American?
A: I think a few of them do.
Q: Which ones?
A: Like takin care of my granny. I don't see much, I don't see a lot of White people actually thinkin of that...just like takin care of my family and payin people back. White people don't think about that. Not the White people I know...not most of them. —Assata, 7ᵗʰ grade

Hope theory is only as useful for all children to the degree that intracultural truths and social realities are included. Psychological theories must be humanized if they are to be effective in helping people achieve their goals and live fruitful lives. It is for this reason that I refer to a strength-based model that may act as a kaleidoscope paradigm functional across cultures and contexts. For the purposes of my work with Black youth and the study described in this book, I have broadened the scope and framework of hope theory to include Afrocentricity, or better stated, I have included the idea of hope in Afrocentricity.

> Thus, it will be contended that Black psychology is something more than the psychology of the so-called underprivileged peoples, more than the experience of living in ghettoes, and more than the genocidal atrocity of being forced into the dehumanizing condition of slavery. It is more than the "darker dimension" of general psychology. Its unique status is derived not from the negative aspects of being Black in white America, but rather from the positive features of basic African philosophy, which dictate the values, customs, attitudes, and behavior of Africans in Africa and the New World. (Nobles, 2006, p. 5)

SigHT, and in this case Afrocentric SigHT is a strength-based model that centers Black history, culture and experiences for action that free from cultural and social delusion to produce optimal success. The point of Afrocentric SigHT is to recognize the beliefs and practices that lead to goal achievement and health for African peoples. In this chapter, I will discuss how hopeful thinking and acting can lead to lifelong achievement for Black children. I believe there is such a thing as hope in various cultural shades, and in this chapter we will put this position to the test. We will also deal with other issues in African psychology, namely identity, race, and philosophy, as they relate to the meaning of hope for Black student achievement.

My objective is to construct a theory of hope that is relevant for Black student school achievement, from preschool to college. The theory is based on Black students' unique perspectives and achievement experiences as they themselves define and describe them from their cultural and social locations. Thus, Afrocentricity succinctly defined as "placing African ideals at the center of any analysis that involves African culture and behavior" (Asante, 1998, p. 2), serves as the methodological and rhetorical foundation of this study. Furthermore, Asante's (1990) framework for Afrocentric Inquiry, defined as "a method [that] pursues a world voice distinctly African-centered in relationship to external phenomena," is employed in the study's implementation and analysis (p. 8).

Afrocentricity
Early in the 20th century, Du Bois (1903/2003) posited that any discourse of United States history must take into account African American experiences. Correspondingly, the social sciences must attend to cultures and sociopolitical experiences across racial-ethnic groups in order to produce relevant theories and effective programming. In as much as European perspectives on history, thought, and pedagogy have permeated all colonized systems, culturally centered scholarship has been seldom undertaken (Allen, 2004).

At the very same time, Black people originate from and continue to share strong commonalities with the same cultural source and therefore operate through near identical fundamental philosophical and spiritual principles. Near identical but not exactly, it may at times be ineffective to treat us monolithically. In truth, both the forced and voluntary migrations that characterize the Black experience have tested our ability to adapt in various environments, and with adaptation often comes change. Afrocentrists understand this phenomenon of collectivity in the midst of variability because we understand how epic memory (or blood memory: Cose, 1997; Sharkey, 2004), cultural binding, and kinship work to liven our spirits and enable our survival.

As a researcher, I am intrigued by the refusal of K–12 schools from North America to Europe, and now parts of Africa, to teach historical and cultural information about non-Europeans. Within this environment of curricular neglect, a battle is underway against Black youth developing conviction for their worth and ability to set and pursue goals. Rather than focus on the wagers of war, we Afrocentric scholars must excavate and analyze first person narratives, archeological artifacts, anthropological, historical, and political data with the objective of channeling Black peoples' inner strength, cultural patterns, and individual and collective needs toward truth and achievement. In doing so we will gather information useful to our families and communities in correcting miseducation and building institutions that suite our needs and make it

8

impossible for racism and misdirection to lead our way. Guided by literature, intellectual discussion, and observation of human social and political activity, we must continuously evolve consciousnesses of victory and methods of inquiry in the interest of our self-determination.

More than a theory or claim, Afrocentricity is a paradigm developed through and for the complex spiritual and cultural factors that support the Black experience—an experience that may constitute local nuances across global locations but is yet borne from common cultural roots and social dilemmas (Diop, 1981/1991; Walker, 2001). Contrary to "mainstream" belief, Afrocentricity is not an inconsequential aberration to "conventional" rhetoric and methodology. It is not a mere reaction against past transgressions of racism. After years of rigorous study and development, Afrocentricity has evolved into a potent model for capturing Black existentialism, self-determination, and purposeful action. Asante's (1980/2003; 1990; 1998) conceptualization of Afrocentricity and analytical frameworks have "introduced fundamental referential changes in the African community," and its impact has reverberated throughout many fields and in a number of nations (Mazama, 2001, p. 387). As such, the utility of Afrocentricity for analyzing and interpreting the thought processes and behaviors of African people is unquestionable.

Research continues to demonstrate that ethnic identity and racism are critical in the lives of Africans everywhere and of significant discussion in the United States (Gamst, Dana, Der-Karabetian, & Kramer, 2004; Rivas-Drake et al., 2009). Research also continues to demonstrate the relevance and validity of Afrocentric principles and methods across subcultures of the global African community (Phelps, Taylor, & Gerard, 2001; Sankofa et al., 2005). While variants of Afrocentric terms may be used, or some scholars opt to employ African Worldview or African-centered terminology, intellectuals invested in the experiences and achievement of Black people have supported the view that research pertaining to the community should be conceptualized and interpreted based on the unique experiences of the people (McDougal, 2011). Let us remain on one accord.

Almost Doesn't Count

Michael Jackson was wrong—it *does* matter if you're Black or White. The idea of cultureless people is one of many lies that has been propagated throughout America and Africa. African American identity without reference to Africa is humanly impossible. Such an idea is akin to being born without an umbilical cord. Since "an analysis of African American culture that is not based on Afrocentric premises is bound to lead to incorrect conclusions" (Asante, 1998, p. 11), I do not divorce my participants from their expansive history. African American history predates European imperialist excursions into Africa beginning in the mid 1400s and slavery "on the main land" beginning in Virginia 1619 (Asante & Abarry, 1996; Walker, 2001).

The impossibility of Black-is-same-as-White is evident in education research and practice when theories and interventions are tried with success in one community, but failure in another. If race and culture truly do not matter, then there would be no supporting evidence that the Children's Hope Scale (CHS) is a poor predictor of achievement among African American and Latino children. If race and culture truly do not matter, then Black children would also be considered more often in positive, strength-focused research studies, such as this one. Instead, positive psychology research that *does* include Black children is preoccupied with undesirable circumstances, including physical illness, pathology, or violence (e.g., Hagen, Myers, & Mackintosh, 2005; Hinton-Nelson, Roberts, & Snyder, 1996; Kliewer & Lewis, 1995).

At least one other study, Elliott and Sherwin (1997), has addressed the individualistic nature of hope theory. Edwards, Ong, and Lopez (2007) set out to validate the CHS with 135 Latino children and found that some items required adaptation before reaching an acceptable validity score. They also asserted that hope theory in general requires reconceptualization in order to have predictive power for Latino children.

Kaylor and Flores (2007) tested the effect of two interventions among 46 Latino students and one African American student using the CHS. Like Edwards et al. (2007), they found that many of their participants had difficulty responding to CHS items, requiring the researchers to explain or reword items "in terms they appeared to understand" (p. 84). In neither of the studies did hope significantly predict affect, behavior, or achievement. Valle, Huebner, and Suldo (2004) found significant differences in CHS scores between African American and European American adolescents in their reliability study across groups.

My research experience with the CHS also suggests cultural and psychometric invalidity. In a study including 33 African American children, the CHS yielded poor internal consistency and inconclusive information regarding the prediction of math and reading achievement (Chandler, 2008). Specifically, whereas Snyder et al. (1997) reported coefficient alpha scores for the CHS of .72 to .86, my African American sample indicated reliability at only .62, or 62% of the time. Multiple regression correlation analyses revealed that hope scores predicted academic achievement only 4% of the time for African American fourth and fifth graders. Snyder and colleagues have found better results with all White samples, one with a sample size of just 29.

Overall, these findings suggest that hope as conceptualized and measured by Snyder et al. (1997) does not fully encompass or measure hope in diverse children, especially African and Latino. The key difference in our studies has to do with all European versus all African and Latino samples. Since our ultimate goal is a brighter future for all

10

Chapter 2: Toward An Afrocentric Hope Theory

children, certain epistemological and axiological limitations in hope theory must be addressed so that psychologists might advance the late C.R. Snyder's hope of a more positive world for all. Receiving "almost" the same positive outcomes for Black and Latino children does not pass the 21st century litmus test for justice and reciprocity.

Changing Positions—Hope in Black

In the abstract of a 2002 article, Snyder defined hope "as the perceived capability to derive pathways to *desired goals*, and motivate oneself via *agency thinking* to use those pathways" (italics added, p. 249). Hope theory, conceptualized and treated as a globally applicable concept, further contends that there are "grand goals that have enticed people throughout history" and that we all essentially want the same things. According to hope theory, we not only want the same things, but if we exert enough mental and physical energy, we can achieve any goal equally. Herein lay several problems.

First, goals are value-laden, and values are culturally determined (Kaplan & Maehr, 2007; Klein, Wesson, Hollenbeck, & Alge, 1999). While a woman born and raised in America would inevitably share some aspects of American culture irrespective of race or ethnicity, it is illogical to presume that her national cultural similarities supersede her racial-ethnic values and traditions. In fact, because racism has been so institutionalized across America, we may be more certain that her racial-ethnic culture is the leading determinate for her values and goals (Asante, 1990; 2005; Du Bois, 1903/2003; West, 2001).

Indeed, Cokley and Chapman (2008) used a path analysis model to study the direct and indirect links among racial-ethnic identity, academic self-concept, and academic success values of African American college students and found that racial-ethnic identity significantly impacted academic self-concept and valuing of school success, both of which had direct and significant impacts on the students' GPAs. "In other words, students with more positive ethnic identities had higher academic self-concepts which were predictive of higher grades" (p. 360).

The authors explain that the indirect impact of racial-ethnic identity on academic self-concept was so strong that once it was removed from the pathways analysis, academic self-concept no longer had the significant impact that it did on academic achievement:

> Specifically, when the paths from ethnic identity to academic self-concept and devaluing academic success were removed from the model, fit index values indicated a significantly poorer fit to the data. This suggests that ethnic identity is an important component in a model of academic achievement for this sample of African American students. (p. 360)

The results of Cokley and Chapman's (2008) study support Afrocentric understanding that positive ethnic identity among Black people should be developed such that Black people are able to view themselves as having (a) a history and cultural perspective worth asserting (subject term of Afrocentricity) and (b) the determination to do the asserting (agency term of Afrocentricity). And yet, we are all too aware that few schools today incorporate African or African Diasporic history, let alone encourage Black students to learn and take pride in their heritage.

Oppressive conditions such as institutionalized racism and misconstruction of African history create two critical psychosocial realities in public schools: dissonance between groups, and namely Blacks and Whites, and a lack of self-cultural awareness and agency within the Black community (Asante, 1998; Woodson, 1936/1968). In as much as hopeful thinking and acting toward goal attainment requires self-confidence, racism and oppression in schools serve to obstruct goal-setting and pursuit among Black children. As Snyder et al. (2003) themselves had to note, there are certain social and environmental obstacles strewn about the paths of Africans that Europeans have heretofore never had to face. It seems to follow that racial-ethnic demarcations result in heightened cultural segmentation between Europeans and Africans, further reinforcing differences in value systems, goal sets, and processes toward goal-pursuit.

The likelihood of Africans sustaining hope in societies where we are marginalized depends on the degree to which we view our race and culture as meaningful and positive, regardless of the racism and oppression that we face. What are the confounding or supporting variables that strengthen the emotional and cognitive resolve of African people in the face of continued racial discrimination in employment, police profiling, judicial sentencing, educational content, etc.? Standing theories and empirical studies seeking to answer this very question point to intracultural awareness and healthy racial-ethnic identities as major strengths (Cokley & Chapman, 2008; Dei, 2006; Ellison, Boykin, Tyler, & Dillihunt, 2005; Hughes & Chen, 1997; Shealey & Lue, 2006; Stinson, 2011; Vandiver, Cross, Worrell, & Fhagen-Smith, 2002). The keys to our success reside in our spirits, minds and memories.

Factoring in the Historical Element
One of the biggest errors that educators can make when working with Black children is to reduce their history and culture to post-16th century colonial composites. Black children viewed through a mere 500-year, slave-era lens become cultural and historical dependents, capable of neither intelligence nor agency without the support of others, meanwhile, all other children are treated as operating from a much longer and colorful history and culture. Black children are rendered Black Sambos and Topsy-type picanninies (e.g., see Pilgrim, 2000), "Miss

Chapter 2: Toward An Afrocentric Hope Theory

Watson's nigger Jim" (Twain, 1999, p. 10), or the violent and sex-crazed subhumans of D.W. Griffith's *Birth of a Nation* (Griffith, 1915). These caricatures were promoted by the media during the height of colonization and continue to permeate national and global psyches. It is through this post-16th century to present scope that Axum becomes Ethiopia and Kemet becomes Egypt, fading out from Black to White. It is also through this narrow scope that it becomes possible for Black children to receive more severe and frequent punishments for the same behaviors as all other children (e.g., Blumenson & Nilsen, 2003; Jordan, 2005; Skiba et al., 2008). In actuality, Black children come from a long line of achievers and civilization builders, and it is through this line that they interact with the world around them, to the extent that they are silenced or coerced into states of confusion or self-hatred.

Carter G. Woodson referred to Africa as "the cradle of all humanity" (1936/1968, p. 3). Indeed, Africa is "the oldest and most enduring landmass in the world," extending more than 300, 000, 000 years (Pitcher et al., 2007, p. 33). Many great examples of the wide and deep ranges of African intelligence, skill, and dignity can be found in Van Sertima's (1976/2003) *They Came Before Columbus: The African Presence in Ancient America*, and Asante and Abarry's (1996) *African Intellectual Heritage: A Book of Sources*. Van Sertima's research in anthropology, linguistics, and history provide a synthesis of staggering evidence showing that Africans traveled beyond the continent to far western, southern and eastern regions of the world, including Mexico, the Caribbean, and China long before Christopher Columbus was even born. The ancient Olmec Heads, pottery and rock carvings in modern day U.S., Mexico and Ecuador speak to the significant influence that Black people had in these regions many centuries ago (Van Sertima, 1976/2003).

First hand accounts of those who bore witness to the precolonial state of Africans abound, and they should be noted for the development of African children today. As Lugard (1906/1997) stated, although in the racist language of early 20th century writers,

> When the history of Negroland comes to be written in detail, it may be found that the kingdoms lying towards the eastern end of Soudan were the home of races who inspired, rather than of races who received, the traditions of civilization associated for us with the name of ancient Egypt (p. 17).

Homer (800a, BC) writes of Greek gods and kings feasting with the Axumites (Ethiopians) in *The Iliad*. He describes Kemet as "the richest city in the whole world," in *Odyssey* (Homer, 800b, BC, book IV). He further describes Kemet as the favorite nation of the gods, thereby receiving such blessings as "the heaven-fed stream," referring to the Nile River (book IV).

Herodotus (440, BC) documented that Kemet was filled with people of "black skin and wooly hair," or who were "black with the heat" (book II). European nations, Herodotus said, believed that the people of Kemet "surpassed all other nations in wisdom" (book II). For example:

> Now with regard to mere human matters, the accounts which they gave, and in which all agreed, were the following. The Egyptians, they said, were the first to discover the solar year, and to portion out its course into twelve parts. They obtained this knowledge from the stars. (To my mind they contrive their year much more cleverly than the Greeks, for these last every other year [and] intercalate a whole month, but the Egyptians, dividing the year into twelve months of thirty days each, add every year a space of five days besides, whereby the circuit of the seasons is made to return with uniformity.) The Egyptians, they went on to affirm, first brought into use the names of the twelve gods, which the Greeks adopted from them, and first erected altars, images, and temples to the gods, and also first engraved upon stone the figures of animals. (Herodotus, 440 BC, book II)

Herodotus also informed us many thousand years ago that,

> [Egypt] projects into the sea further than the neighbouring shores, and I observed that there were shells upon the hills, and that salt exuded from the soil to such an extent as even to injure the pyramids, and I noticed also that there is but a single hill in all Egypt where sand is found, namely, the hill above Memphis, and further, I found the country to bear no resemblance either to its borderland Arabia, or to Libya- nay, nor even to Syria, which forms the seaboard of Arabia, but whereas the soil of Libya is, we know, sandy and of a reddish hue, and that of Arabia and Syria inclines to stone and clay, Egypt has a soil that is black and crumbly, as being alluvial and formed of the deposits brought down by the river from Ethiopia. (Herodotus, 440 BC, book II)

While today Kemet and much of northern Africa are colonized by Arabs, Herodotus explained that the Black tribes of Axum "appear to have formed culturally and racially" Kemet and Ancient Nubia as one land (as cited in Woodson, 1936/1968, p. 25). His historical account in 440 BC agrees with modern science naming Axum, which the Kemites knew as Kush, the eldest known location of human life (e.g., Pitcher et

14

Chapter 2: Toward An Afrocentric Hope Theory

al., 2007). As a "child to Axum" (Woodson, 1936/1968, p. 179), the Egypt that so many around the world revere today provided the religious, academic, artistic, and ethical foundation for the world beginning around 4, 000 BC (Browder, 1992). Africa's history runs deep and while dates and names may be debated, the fact is that it was clear to ancient wisdom that the earliest people and civilizations extend from parts of Africa that lie to the south of modern day Egypt. The builders of the greatest civilization looked like Ture, Talib, Kwame, Assata, Kenya and Aisha, the children informing this book.

The first written languages, with the oldest known being Mdu Ntr (or Medu Netcher) are African and date to ca. 3400 BCE (Asante, 2007). Mdu Ntr (the hieroglyphic alphabet) formed the basis for several African, European, and Arabic languages (Asante, 1990). Poetry, and the performing arts are also talents that were described as supreme among Africans (Woodson, 1936/1968). Philosophy, the word itself deriving from the Kemetic term *seba,* meaning wisdom, has found a home among Africans continental and Diasporan at least since Ptah-hotep of the 5th Kemetic dynasty (Asante & Abarry, 1996).

Though some might discount the intellect and wisdom of Africans constructing clay and mud houses that are harmonious to nature where there was previously no concept of a dwelling before, certainly the intelligence in discovering the power of chemistry with the creation of antidotes for physical ailments, arrow-head poisons for war and hunting, and embalming fluid for corpses is evident (Woodson, 1936/1968). The establishment of Axum and Kemet as great empires required skill in geometry and irrigation for agriculture along the Nile. Mathematical precision was necessary for the building of the Pyramids and the Sphinx at Giza. Indeed, the great pyramids, temples and Mdu Ntr and Meroitic languages in Kemet and Sudan remain largely indecipherable wonders (Asante & Abarry, 1996; Pitcher et al., 2007).

We realized the abundant natural resources of Africa, including the use of iron, gold, salt, and cotton early in human civilization. Europeans first saw cattle tamed in Africa. Many of the ancients were evidently master hunters and athletes, as food and animal skin were abundant. The art of horseback riding, with the use of the bit, stirrup, and saddle was also first seen in Africa. Ancient Africans were adept at sewing and weaving a variety of cloths (Woodson, 1936/1968). So industrious and organized in blacksmithing, the arts, weaving, hunting and farming were African empires like Axum, Bantu, Nubia, Kemet, Kumbi (Ghana), Diara, Soso, Galam, Senegalese Futa, Manding or Mali, Songhay, and Mossi that the Greeks, Asians, and Semites vied for trading agreements with them.

Today we are afforded rare exemplification of custom Kemetic and Adinkra jewelry made of silver, gold, brass and copper in the fashions of this legacy by Per-aa Heru Ankh Ra Semahj Se Ptah through his Studio

15

of Ptah in New York. His works centering the ankh, which is the preeminent religious and spiritual principle that came to inform the Semitic religions of Judaism, Christianity and Islam symbolizing veneration of life through the union of man, woman and child as well as the connection between the celestial and terrestrial, may be seen on the likes of artists and entertainers Erykah Badu, Wesley Snipes, Andre 3000, Ben Vereen, Keith David, and Sun Ra, master educators and practitioners Dr. Yosef Ben Jochannan (whose work discusses the association of world religions to Kemet as the eldest and longest lasting human civilization), Dr. John Henrik Clarke (whose work also informs us about world religions and cultures), Alma Nomsa John (first known African American registered nurse), Ra Un Nefer Amen, Baba Isshangi, Dr. Maulana Karenga and his wife Tiamoyo Karenga, motivational speaker Les Brown, New York Judge Bruce Wright, Essence magazine's Suzanne Taylor, and many others continuing in the legacy of The First Time. Historical records reveal the reverence that the people and principles of Kemet garnered.

Not only were traders and rulers of less developed nations eager to replenish their economies through African trade, but they delighted themselves in observing the "black race," who they recognized to be "the most beautiful and long-lived" of all humans (Lugard, 1906/1997, p. 221). The power of African art and activity lay in the spirit of the things and the people that create them. More than beauty in the physical sense, what Lady Lugard may also have been referring to over a century ago is aesthetics and rhythm. Thompson (1974) and Gottschild (2002) have noted that to persons of African descent, physical aesthetics and maintaining a sense of cool during task completion is almost as important as task completion itself. From the creation and traditional use of tattoos and body piercing amongst African civilizations to the emphasis on stylistic fervor in communication, Africans have been both intellectual and artistic pioneers. The continuation of artistic, rhythmic, and industrial talents may be seen in the pluralistic music, fashion, and business expressions of Black people in contemporary history.

The cool is an African aesthetic tradition. It has been perhaps best defined as "an all-embracing positive attribute, which combines notions of composure, silence, vitality, healing, and social purification," and "a strong intellectual attitude, affecting incredibly diverse provinces of artistic happening, yet leavened with humor and a sense of play" (Thompson, 1974, p. 43). Woodson (1936/1968) seems to have observed the cool in action when he noted of the 8th century Songhay empire, "there was much gaiety…dancing and looseness could not be stopped, the emperor had been loose himself from the Western point of view. Yet there was much learning" (p. 71).

"The cool" is alive in young Black people today. Just as the Western point of view qualified Black culture as "loose" centuries ago, Western-focused teachers still over-qualify Black youth's natural exuberance, playing of *the dozens*, *clownin* or *jonin* as problematic behavior that detracts from, rather than stimulates learning and togetherness (e.g., see Kunjufu, 2011b). The assumption made is that Black children have no culture other than acting disruptively, and certainly no African cultural ties on which to base any expectations of excellence and intelligence. African history, however, quickly shows us that Black people have a remarkable ability to balance work and play, excelling intellectually while simultaneously paying much attention to aesthetics and energy. The numerous and widespread African kingdoms spanning ca. 3500 BC to all the way up to19[th] century 1896 further supports Woodson's assertion that "the usual story about the nomad in Africa has been much exaggerated" (1936/1968, p. 149).

A powerful truth is that the most remarkable contemporary achievements made by African Americans in business and community development have occurred during the 1950s and 60s prior to desegregation. In even the most politically red, meaning Republican and White conservative regions of the country, such as Texas and Oklahoma, Black people developed successful and wealthy communities unto themselves. A section of Tulsa, OK, for example, became known as Black Wall Street until it was destroyed with fire in 1921 (e.g., San Francisco Bayview, 2011). In 1930, Blacks in Texas alone outdid *all other states in the country* in total sales revenue, and between 1930 and 1935 Black farmers owned over 1, 000, 000 acres of land with a value of over $90, 000, 000 (Hall, 1936). Over one billion dollars of Texas state revenue was made by Black people in just a five-year span, and during the height of American racism!

There were countless tailoring businesses, Black owned and Black-operated newspapers and magazines, book publishers, insurance companies, electrical companies, salons and grocers to speak of in Dallas alone prior to 1960. *The Negro Business bulletin* was a monthly magazine devoted to better business among Blacks of Dallas in the 20th century, not in ancient history (African American Museum [AAM] Dallas, 2011). The Daily Metropolitan was a Black newspaper in Texas running a monthly subscription. True Life was a "Negro fiction magazine" publishing "the stories and poems of any colored people" whose quality work would otherwise go unpublished (AAM Dallas, 2011).

African Americans also excelled in the north and east. After droves of African Americans left the southern states during the period between 1900 and 1930, referred to as the Great Migration (Smithsonian, 2007), cities like Cleveland, Detroit and New York grew exponentially from their businesses, artistry and industrial labor (Harley & Middleton, 1994, Jackson, 2008). The Harlem Renaissance, centered in Harlem, NY, is the most often cited success of this time period. Major African American influence in areas ranging from literature, music, dance, painting, politics, education, and religion occurred in the United States and around the world during the Harlem Renaissance (Cartwright et al., 2012).

Although the Black population in the U.S. west has been historically small in comparison to the North, South and East, historians have found that African Americans were entrepreneurs and successful business men, women and farmers there too. John W. Templeton outlines much of the musical and business history of Blacks in California in his *Cakewalk: A Novel about the Untold Creators of Jazz Music*, and also his series, *Our Roots Run Deep: The Black Experience in California, 1950-2000*. In California, African Americans are to be credited for co-developing the mining, lumber and agriculture industries prior to 1940 (National Park Service [NPS], 2004). The era dubbed the California Gold Rush included so much Black participation that at least three regions in the West bear prior names or references of the community: Negro Bar, Negro Flat and Nigger Ravine (NPS, 2004). The African Methodist Episcopal (A.M.E.) Church of California opened the first schools that taught Black children in Sacramento and San Francisco, where most African American people lived during the 1850s. The bottom line seems to be that African Americans managed steady progression in line with their lineage within the protective confines of their community (NPS, 2004). What does this mean for Black people, and especially Black children today?

Factoring in the Sociopolitical Element

We cannot discuss hope without including agency. The sense of community agency that Africans in America held before the 1960s has been gravely demoralized. Post-60s desegregation has failed because of reluctance of those in power to change and grow in understanding of marginalized communities in combination with political fragmentation within African America. Groups that have been forced into second and third class positions economically and politically must set and pursue their goals through proaction and reaction in their own interests. Ogbu (1993, 2004) wrote extensively on the volatile relationship between what he called involuntary minority communities and the (passive) aggressive majority community. Often educators, and even parents, do not understand the thinking and behavior of involuntary minority status youth and this creates many problems for hope and achievement.

As Black children grow research indicates that their developmental lessons are very likely to be characterized by higher discipline rates and lower achievement recognition in school (Blanchett, Mumford, & Beachum, 2005, Skiba et al., 2008). African American boys are disproportionately diagnosed as having Attention-Deficit Hyperactivity Disorder (ADHD) and Oppositional Defiant Disorder (ODD) (Ford, 2011; Kunjufu, 2011a). In the U.S. and France African children learn that they can expect unemployment in adulthood despite their employment qualifications based on the discrimination that their adult family and community members experience in their homes (Demby, 2012, Oppenheimer, 2008). For Africans in a world that knows no reciprocity, hard work in school or work does not always result in pay off. For example, while Black male college graduation rates in America increased by an estimated 7% between 1990 and 2005 (Journal of Blacks in Higher Education [JBHE], 2006), the rate of imprisonment and police brutality grew to genocidal proportions (Chandler, 2010). During the same period, Black female college graduation rates increased by 12%, creating significant within group differences and difficulties in African American families.

When setting basic goals, such as graduating from high school, Black students may first have to confront the social and political situations into which they are born. What additional goals must a student who has to help with the light and gas bill or cooking and cleaning set in their pursuit of college graduation? The fact is that African people find themselves having to over-produce just to receive the same level of respect and opportunity as people from communities with less racially burdened histories. Given this reality, African children are more likely to have both direct and indirect experiences that involve stress from political disenfranchisement and social apathy. This is true whether their role models are successful in life or not (Asante, 1998; Thompson & Akbar, 2003).

To demonstrate, Rivas-Drake et al. (2009) found that African American middle school students report significantly higher instances of discrimination from both peers and adults in school and significantly lower public regard than do Dominican American middle school students. The same study found that discrimination experiences predicted perceptions of public regard, and peer discrimination predicted private regard (how positively one views one's own cultural group). The authors noted, "[a] troubling implication of this finding is that youth who consistently report lower public regard or feeling devalued because of their race or ethnicity may ultimately experience less positive psychological and academic outcomes" (p. 578).

Indeed, theories of Black racial-ethnic identity pay particular attention to the issues of racism, oppression, collectivism, and concern for cultural integrity, which, in combination, characterize the post-Kemetic or colonial African experience (Sellers, Rowley, Chavous, Shelton, & Smith, 1997; Thompson & Akbar, 2003; Worrell, Cross, & Vandiver, 2001). Such resources as health insurance, food, school supplies, and harmonious home and school environments are taken for granted in Snyder's conceptualizations of hope—perhaps in his White world there is less need to consider them. Further, it is not enough to simply take note of social and political issues faced by Black communities. Hope theory should consider how Black people themselves perceive the issues they face in order to improve community achievement.

Taken together, African children in America are more likely to receive life lessons that encourage collective rather than individual thinking and acting. Sociopolitical need for collectivism only compounds the already existent collectivist orientation that African peoples have held historically. As a result, African children are likely to undergo self-*and* group-appraisals (Asante, 2005; Obama, 1995; Tatum, 1997). All African Americans, whether low, middle, or upper class, assimilationist or Pan-Africanist, live in highly racialized environments because they attend school in America, shop for food and cosmetic products in America, watch television or listen to the radio in America, and/or attend religious and entertainment venues in America. Race and racism are omnipresent. Africans everywhere, individually and collectively, must tap into their creativity to find ways to cope with racist conditions permeating pedagogy and consumerism, the nightly news, and local housing and service options (Chandler 2010; Este 2004; Ladson-Billings & Henry, 1990; Loewen, 2007). In the theoretical realms of Snyder's hope theory, many African children, ill fitted for the theory as they are, would be assumed failures and targets for special education "intervention." However, rather than conclude that Black children are hopeless and doomed for poor futures, we as responsible adults must help see them through the matrix toward a model of hope that fits their social and cultural reality.

Factoring in the Cultural Element

Individualism contradicts African ethics and disregards the heightened communal approach to life that Africans use to protect themselves against sociopolitical oppositions, such as employment discrimination (Chandler 2010). Hurley, Boykin, and Allen (2005) found a significant difference in mean post-test results when African American 5th graders were provided with individual mathematics materials versus one collective set. In this case, the students were still expected to demonstrate personal learning through their individual work, but the mode of instruction and materials were communal. Needless to say, the children evidenced mastering the skills taught far better through their collectivist tradition.

The authors cite several studies demonstrating the similar results with lexical tasks, such as vocabulary and typing. Hurley et al. (2005) concluded "inclusion of Afrocultural themes in learning contexts can support learning by providing opportunities for African American children to use existing competencies in the service of attaining new ones" (p. 515). Any psychological model applied to Africans in America, and South Africa, and Europe, and the Caribbean, and the UK, etc., must consider the community's Pan-Africanist orientation and our predisposition toward reclaiming our cultural identities from European strongholds (Asante,

Chapter 2: Toward An Afrocentric Hope Theory

2005, Vandiver, Fhagen-Smith, Cokley, Cross, & Worrell, 2001, Walker 2001). This is true even when considering ideological differences that sometimes stem from discrepancies in income and political orientation (Asante & Hall, 2011; Cho, Hudley, Lee, Barry, & Kelly, 2008; Consedine, Sabag-Cohen, & Krivoshekova, 2007).

We see the close connection between Black student achievement and degree of Black community welfare in the U.S. when during the racially and culturally contentious 1960s the national high school graduation rate peaked but then began its progressive decline by the second half of the decade with the greatest decline being among Black students (Heckman & LaFontaine, 2010). Immediately following the murders of Medgar Evers, the four little Black girls in the Birmingham, AL church bombing, Malcolm X, and Martin Luther King, Jr. Black student participation in high school dropped significantly. Our community was under serious attack, we recognized it, and we acted (although perhaps not in the best way for our long-term benefit).

Given the African emphasis of community over the individual and the interconnectivity between the physical and spiritual (Asante, 1998; Karenga, 2002), the agency component of Afrocentric hope theory must include community agency as well as universal African values. Further, since many Africans consistently exhibit high determination and resilience as they pursue their goals *despite* sociopolitical oppositions and cultural dislocation, it makes conceptual sense that successful Africans undergo processes of reconnaissance regarding their goals in light of their African existential realities. In other words, Black people who are healthy and successful consider and understand the social and cultural positions that they are in. Resultantly, we think frequently and carefully about our actions in relation to our personal, family and community progression. Rather than deny or ignore racism and anti-African conditioning, we find ways to reconcile opposing sociocultural forces and cultural dislocation by creating psycho-emotional stress buffers that are channeled to maintain internal harmony and progression as needed. More importantly, we embrace our natural, precolonial values and energies.

A recent example showing the connection between personal and communal agency was President Barack Obama's political victory in 2008. Not since the 1990 release of Nelson Mandela, a former political prisoner, has the world witnessed such a powerful illustration of personal and communal African agency than during the Pan African celebrations for President Obama's victory. As a young man, he buckled down in school and work in pursuit of his goals (goals = personal agency). More than this though, as he revealed in *Dreams from My Father: A Story of Race and Inheritance* (1995), he also felt a strong sense of appreciation and responsibility toward the African community (intracultural awareness = collective agency). Not only did President Obama and a young Mandela

21

feel communal responsibility, but Africans across the Diaspora shared and rejoiced in the victories of these two men as their own. Although the achievers in my study were too young to understand the victory felt by Black people around the world when Mandela was released, they were well aware of the significance of the first African American President, a man with an African name, for them and the rest of the Black community in 2008.

Unlike the European idea of agency as a purely individual construct, the African idea of agency is both personal and communal; it is *part-of*, not *part-and-parcel-to* community concerns and community action (Elliott & Sherwin, 1997). The successes and failures, and joys and pains of one community member are often embraced as that of the entire community. The African cultural reality of collectivism is primarily what makes self-knowledge from ancestral and historical standpoints so important to achievement—one cannot support or counter, nor revere or discount what one does not know. Some African American parents have been found to educate their children about African cultures, racial discrimination, and cultural mistrust (or carefulness during White-Black interactions) as early as four years old (Hughes & Chen, 1997). Of these three areas, lessons on what it means to be of African descent culturally were most frequent. These lessons increased in frequency with the children's age. While some of us appear to "get it" even in the midst of Western confusion, most of us have not yet restored our consciousness and traditions of teaching our children who they are and where they come from in order that they will know what they should be doing and where they should be going as African people.

Reassessing and Realigning

Quintana and colleagues (2007; Quintana, Castañeda-English, & Ybarra, 1999) have demonstrated that children begin to understand the implications of racism early in childhood. Though the American system has evolved from an explicitly legal racist one into a more implicit and less brute form, racism continues to dictate assumptions of who can do what, when they can do it, and how far they can go with it today. Many people believe that much growth has taken place in the world and issues of race and opportunity are outdated. The inauguration of President Obama would strengthen this position if one believed it true.

What Black youth believe about the social conditions of their time is perhaps the single most important factor in understanding world progression with race and justice, and their insights alone are the best indicator of the necessary procedures for perfecting their education and increasing their achievement. Were Black student achievers surprised by President Obama's victory, and if so, what does this say about American democracy in the 21st century? Does President Obama's victory carry any import in the hearts and minds of aspiring Black youth, and if so, what does this say about their sense of community and racial pride? The answers may surprise you.

Black youth in America constitute approximately 17% of the student body, but Black adults are only 6% of the teaching field (Curriculum Review, 2005). Despite significant educational gains, the Black community remains pigeonholed into menial and trade professions (Chandler, 2010). Even worse, 33% of the total 17% of African students are labeled mentally retarded (MR, National Research Council, 2002). Nearly 100% of the children bused to schools outside their districts and neighborhoods are African (Kunjufu, 2006). What is happening locally in Black communities matter far more than what is discussed nationally. Again, how and when do African children learn about their right and ability to pursue and achieve goals in America? How do the cultural and experiential distinctions of African children affect the types of goals they set? When they resist the system for cultural preservation, how does this affect their conscious or subconscious approach toward hopefulness in school? These are only a few of the questions that scholarship and praxis must address before claiming to have conceptualized a theory of hope for African children.

It is possible that some of the tenets in Snyder's hope theory are basic cognitive truths for all people, and some of the existing interventions might be applicable to African children. In all likelihood though, a thorough and Afrocentric study of hopeful mental and behavioral processes among Black children will produce a hope theory that is as unique as the community itself. In 1992, Allen and Boykin argued that the reason for African Americans' difficulties with school progress in the United States, despite the vast historical strides we have made, is cultural discontinuity between community and home life on the one hand, and school culture and pedagogy on the other. Cultural centeredness rather than cultural dislocation is a central tenant of Asante's Afrocentricity paradigm (1980/2003, 1998, 2007). Focusing on African American students' academic experiences, Allen and Boykin (1992) reported observing nine "afro-cultural" belief systems that are based on traditional West African culture, which itself stems from Kush and Kemet:

1. Spirituality – as ritualistic and constantly employed rather than mechanistic
2. Harmony – among humans and between humans and nature
3. Movement expressions – with emphasis on rhythm, music, and dance
4. Verve – meaning sensitivity to sensate stimulation and creation of high energy
5. Affect – being free displays of emotions and feelings
6. Communalism – as in a commitment to social connectedness to the degree that individual privileges are minimized

7. Expressive individualism – being development of a distinct personality and creativity within the group, rather than individualistic beliefs in separation from the whole
8. Orality – referring to preference for and skill in oral modes of communication
9. Social time perspective – indicating orientation toward time that exists in a social space rather than a contrived material one that one must be controlled by.

How we think and view ourselves in the world directly dictates our effectiveness in negotiating the various locations and situations of life.

Having articulated the African-American's basic cultural system, researchers are currently focusing on the cultural discontinuity created in settings where aspects of the afro-cultural and mainstream experience are put at odds. Basically, it is argued that since pedagogy in the United States is founded upon mainstream ideals, the traditional classroom lacks outlets and vehicles for expression of afro-cultural behaviors. Such a constraint in learning and performance experiences reduces the chances that many black children have to exercise existing competencies, as well as reduces the chances that the classroom will provide the contextual conditions necessary to sustain and enhance the motivation of the student to engage in required tasks (Boykin, 1991). Moreover, the absence of afro-cultural factors within the classroom lends the perception that the most salient aspects of these children's lives are neither valued nor relevant to the academic arena. In the end, the school experiences of these black children fail to tap what they have the ability to do, and ignores what they value as important and therefore are motivated to do. (Allen & Boykin, 1992, electronic copy)

School psychologists and teachers are positioned to be, and should serve as, assistant developers of hope for students (Snyder et al., 2003), alongside parents. Without question, a new definition of hope that considers the culture and experiences of diverse people is needed. The present "SigHT study" begins a new page in education and positive psychology wherein the voices of children of African descent who are living their purpose will be heard and received as valid and critical to their success and that of their peers. Now we lift the veil to see the light of the sun.

Chapter 3: Context, Participants and Methodology of the SigHT Study

Much of what is presented in the social sciences as qualitative research, and certainly quantitative research, are but snapshots or sound bites of a much larger or deeper situation of existence. Very often, researchers provide readers with a list of demographics intended to paint a full contextual picture of people, such as income, household membership, race, and age. The scope of the SigHT study attempts to dig deeper in order that the participants and the people that they represent in culture and context will be more fully understood. The central aim of this study was to solidify a theory of hope from the narratives of African youth in America. Based on a thorough review of African-centered literature as well as my own understanding of life as an African American person, I have identified hope in the Black community as goal-driven action grounded in culture and conscientiousness about social phenomena. To better understand how hope is operationalized in the Black community, I decided to study a group of junior high school achievers in the U.S.—six sixth, seventh, and eighth grade African American students whose achievement scores met or exceeded state requirements, and whose attitudes and behaviors received favor from teachers. In this chapter I will describe my method and methodology, meaning how and with whom I actually designed and conducted the study. The actual research questions used during interviews are also provided.

Context
At the time of this study, which concluded in the spring of 2010 I was working as a clinical and school psychologist in Cleveland, Ohio. After working and living there I can say with confidence that Black youth succeeding in the Cleveland Metropolitan School District (CMSD) are among the best participants for this type of study given the depressing conditions of the city. Historically, Cleveland was one of the few major cities in America to have been a leading business, farming, manufacturing, and mining center in the development of the "new world," and it has a rich history of success (Wright, 2009). Additionally, Cleveland is one of few U.S. cities with a history of racial-ethnic diversity. Over the past century the city has consistently lost residents to more economically promising locations, but still, the current population is estimated to be 51% African, 41% European, 7% Latino, and 1% "other" (Wright, 2009). Social, political, and economic changes at national and local levels have dealt Cleveland, among other northern cities, significant blows to its infrastructure.

From 1796 to the mid-20th century, the city boasted successful commerce and a population that exceeded 2 million. The opening of the

Erie Canal in 1825, trading through Lake Superior beginning in 1855, and mass manufacturing and mining employment during the Civil War reaped huge economic benefits for Cleveland residents (Wright, 2009). However, spikes in racial hostility with declines in industrial work during the latter 19th and 20th centuries progressed steadily, resulting in increased unemployment rates, heightened school problems, and a lower quality of life mostly for Black citizens (Collins & Smith, 2007; Wright, 2009). Today, Cleveland has less than a quarter of the population that it held during its 20th century prime, and about 115,700 of the 445,000 households in Cleveland are living below the poverty line, with just as many near the line (U.S. Census Bureau, 2009). Twenty percent of Cleveland residents, a significant number, are youth between the ages of six and 17 (U.S. Census Bureau, 2009).

Compared to Ohio state trends, Cleveland is characterized by median household incomes and median home values that are below the state average, and a significantly lower than state average number of residents holding bachelor degrees or higher (Cleveland Live Census, 2009; The Relocation Professionals, 2009). These conditions complement the city's above state average unemployment rate and age of homes. Such poor conditions might explain Cleveland's rank as third in the nation for population loss, with an estimated 60,000 people leaving the city between 2000 and 2008 alone (Cleveland Live Census, 2009). The fact that Cleveland has some of the poorest living conditions and the largest Black population in the state speaks volumes about the chances of hopefulness among residents so unsupported by the city and state.

CMSD is an important institution to consider for any plans of uplifting Cleveland. Some 50,364 students attend CMSD schools today, 70% of whom are Black (CMSD, 2009). Amid increasing de-enrollment, largely unanswered calls for aid to support school restorations, threats of school closings due to underachievement, and safety concerns against a backdrop of school shootings and prison-school modeling (e.g., the 2007 Success Tech Academy mass shooting), CMSD CEO Dr. Eugene Sanders, along with staff and community members, set forth to implement many rebuilding efforts (Ott, 2008).

Some of the many efforts that Dr. Sanders has implemented since assuming his position in 2006 include enforcing a dress code, combining some middle schools with elementary schools so as not to "warehouse" and isolate mid-level students, converting several K–8 schools to single-gender academies, updating schools with more rigorous curriculum and contemporary technologies, extending the school day and school year in many schools, and creating preparatory programs in partnership with local colleges (Ott, 2008; Sanders, 2009). Among many indicators of improvement are the standing 92% attendance rate—nearly meeting the state's attendance requirement of 93%—and 60% graduation rate—the highest graduation rate in CMSD since 1995 (CMSD, 2008). School accountability and community partnerships have become increasingly important in Cleveland. For example, teacher quality has received special attention, and professional development is now factored into the 10-week on, three-week off schedule of some schools. Additionally, Governor Strickland and Mayor Jackson have worked closely with Dr. Sanders to award college scholarships and support for programs fostering cross-teacher coaching to improve some of the district's "hard-to-staff" schools (Sanders, 2009).

U.S. Education Secretary Arne Duncan under President Obama's administration held meetings with Dr. Sanders and other urban school district leaders to align education agendas and distribute funds for improvement programs around the time of this study (WKYC, 2009). The horizon of opportunity and achievement for CMSD students appears near, perhaps to degrees never before seen or felt by the past two generations (Michney, 2006; Ott, 2008). However, the road ahead for Cleveland and many other American cities remains unpaved and uncertain. The troubling history of racial and class inequity in Cleveland schools that current enthusiasts are treading was poignantly illustrated by Chief Justice Rehnquist in the recent Supreme Court case over the fairness of Cleveland's school choice voucher system:

> There are more than 75,000 children enrolled in the *Cleveland* City School District. The majority of these children are from low-income and minority families. Few of these families enjoy the means to send their children to any school other than an inner-city public school. For more than a generation, however, Cleveland's public schools have been among the worst performing public schools in the Nation. In 1995, a Federal District Court declared a "crisis of magnitude" and placed the entire Cleveland school district under state control...Shortly thereafter, the state auditor found that Cleveland's public schools were in the midst of a "crisis that is perhaps unprecedented in the history of American *education*"...The district had failed to meet any of the 18 state standards for minimal acceptable performance. Only 1 in 10 ninth graders could pass a basic proficiency examination, and students at all levels performed at a dismal rate compared with students in other Ohio public schools. More than two-thirds of high school students either dropped or failed out before graduation. Of those students who managed to reach their senior year, one of every four still failed to graduate. Of those students who did graduate, few could read, write, or compute at levels comparable to their counterparts in other cities. *(Zelman v. Simmons-Harris, 234 F.3d 945, U.S. 2002)*

Note that the latest roster of CMSD students dropped from the approximate 75, 000 noted by Justice Rehnquist in 2002 to 50, 000 in 2010. CMSD continues to be under state control, one of eight out of Ohio's 613 school districts to lose its functional independence (Newark Advocate, 2009). Sadly, but necessarily, CMSD students are well aware of the stigma of attending a failing school district. It seems likely that the Black youth in CMSD today are as aware of the proverbial veil between them and their majority White peers in nearby districts and cities as Du Bois was in the early 20th century. And just as it was the case more than a century ago, many Africans today live on the side of the veil that either blinds them from or frustrates them about any promise for opportunity in school and life success. The insight, or rather SigHT, that the achievers here will lend to the world informs us of how and why they see and live effectively beneath the veil that they are forced by society to peer through. How is it that they refuse to let the veil block their vision of and action toward success? As Du Bois (1903/2003) so eloquently described it:

> Then it dawned upon me with a certain suddenness that I was different from the others, or like, mayhap, in heart and in life and in longing, but shut out from their world by a vast veil . . . I held thereafter no desire to tear down that veil, to creep through, I held all behind it in common contempt, and lived above it in a region of blue sky and great wandering shadows. That sky was bluest when I could beat my mates at examination time, or beat them at a footrace, or even beat their stringy heads. Alas, with the years all this fine contempt began to fade, for the worlds I longed for, and all their dazzling opportunities, were theirs, not mine. But they should not keep these prizes, I said, some, all, I would wrest from them. Just how I would do it I could never decide: by reading law, by healing the sick, by telling the wonderful tales that swam in my head—some way. (p. 8)

Participants

At the time of this study, Ture, Talib, Kwame, Assata, Kenya, and Aisha attended a combined elementary and middle school in CMSD, fictitiously referred to as Justice Academy. Pseudonyms are used to ensure confidentiality and protect the children's anonymity. It is for the same reason that limited family and demographic information is offered, but also because the study is student- rather than family-focused. The unveiling of these six, bright and hopeful African American achievers is enough for two studies alone.

The chosen age group for this study was middle school, grades six through eight for two important reasons. From a biological sense, significant development of the prefrontal cortex during adolescence marks changes in cognition and behavior that are unobserved during any other life stage (Feldman, 2003). From a psychological sense, children begin to spend time thinking critically about their future during this major transitional period (McCabe & Barnett, 2000). It is during the ages of about 11 to 14 that youth begin to come to terms with who they are, choose who they will be as adults, and manifest in their behaviors any hope, despair, or frustration that they feel during their trek toward adulthood.

At the very same time, social developments are occurring for adolescents at school and home. Teachers, for instance, begin to have higher expectations for student independence and decision-making once children enter junior high, potentially adding extra stress to adolescent students' lives (Scruggs & Mastropieri, 2005). Also for Black youth, issues of race, mis-education, and cultural memory loss can further complicate those age-typical questions of identity and life purpose. The middle school years are a pivotal crossroad between healthy, functional citizenship and a life of confused, dysfunctional delinquency. My quest to find a cohort of hopeful Black students in the middle school years led me to three African American boys, and three African American girls born and raised in the northern states of the USA.

Justice Academy was undergoing restoration in the 2009-2010 and 2010-2011 school years. A dress code was being enforced, for example, and students attended a temporary building while the main facility was being renovated. Most of the rooms in the temporary building had windows, however, the majority of them were so high that the students could not look out of or open them. The lunchroom doubled as the gym with the preschool and kindergarten classrooms in a small annex behind the main building, therefore older students had to walk to and from buildings for lunch and Physical Education class. Several classes were provided in the basement of the main building, with dim lighting and exposed pipes along the ceiling and walls. While the district deemed the temporary building to be in better condition than the facility undergoing renovation, it was old and dilapidated by most "industrialized nation" standards.

Each of the participants qualified for free and reduced lunch, and one of the students lived in the "projects" neighboring the school, while another lived very nearby. Interestingly, none of the six achievers were friends with one another, instead their friendships tended to be spread out amongst their many classmates. Two of the participants, Ture and Assata, were cousins, but they did not live together or socialize closely. The students lived in both single and two-parent households, single and mixed generation households, and with immediate and second- or third-degree relatives. Some were the only child in their immediate families while others had siblings.

In order to qualify for participation in the study, students had to have met or exceeded Annual Yearly Progress (AYP) standards sanctioned by the U.S. Department of Education in both reading and mathematics on the previous year's Ohio Achievement Test (OAT). The Assistant Principal identified students who met standards on the previous exit exam. Teachers' opinions were also considered through nominations of students based on their history of observing positive interpersonal relationships and high grades. To minimize subjectivity, however, teacher recommendations were not weighed as strongly as exam scores.

Additional information about the youth's personality types and personal experiences are presented in the chapters detailing their narrative responses. For now, what is important to consider is that they exuded hope and appreciation for life through their school achievement, and in the hostile and hopeless context of their location. The highest levels of the 2008–2009 OAT were *Advanced* and *Accelerated*, meaning, essentially, superior and above average, respectively. The level of *Proficient,* meaning average, was next, and it was followed by *Basic,* indicating below average performance. Finally, there was *Limited,* which indicated elementary level skills. In the year of this study, less than 50% of the students at Justice Academy scored at the *Proficient* level in both reading and math—meaning most scored in the below average and elementary ranges. A very small minority reached *Advanced* or *Accelerated* in one or both of these areas: two of them were male students selected to participate in this study.

Methodology
Afrocentric Inquiry in Practice: In the epilogue of his *Papers in African Psychology*, Na'im Akbar (2003) humbly discussed the challenges that Afrocentrists have faced in implementing Afrocentric studies. In the spirit of *Lendo Kiandiakina* (giving healing power; Nobles 2006, p. 357), Akbar placed the onus of creating implementation processes of Afrocentric studies on the younger generations of Black scholars. Standing on the steady foundation of theory and scholarship that elder Afrocentrists and social justice activists have toiled to provide, I offer here a potential implementation framework for Afrocentric research studies (see Figure 1). The overarching goal of all Afrocentric studies is the development of Pan Africa and the advancement of universal harmony. Therefore, researchers must enter into the research process equipped with knowledge of African people and intentions of critiquing human interconnections for victory and accord if they hope to complete their study well. It is for this reason that Africological study is listed as the first step in Figure 1.

Presented by Asante (1990) in *Kemet, Afrocentricity, and Knowledge,* Afrocentric Inquiry (referred to here on as AI) is an intimate and holistic research-to-practice methodology for understanding, critiquing, and assisting African communities. Seeking to discover "in human experiences, historical and contemporary, all the ways African people have tried to make their physical, social, and cultural environments serve the end of harmony," AI requires grounding in the cosmological, epistemological, axiological, and aesthetic traditions and experiences of African people (Asante, 1990, p. 8). These four pillars constitute the conceptual composites of AI, designed to encapsulate the vast philosophies, traditions, and experiences of African peoples in a clear enough form that culturally centered studies may be conducted.

As expounded by Asante (1990), cosmological issues include those concerns that are essential to the African experience across virtually all study topics, such as historical cultural foundations, race in contemporary society, and gender.

Figure 1. Framework for Implementation of Afrocentric Inquiries

1. Literature Study in Africology (+ Cultural and Social Immersion)

2. Formulation of Study Using AI Composites (Cosmology, Epistemology, Axiology, & Aesthetics) and AI Paradigms (Functional, Categorical, &/or Etymological)
Always With Africans as Subject and Agent

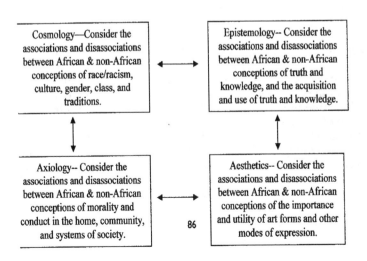

31

3. Continuously Analyze, Synthesize, & Separate Data by Coding Responses, Grouping Observation Patterns, & Referencing Aesthetics (including speech & dress) Within & Across Participants. Continue to Code, Group, & Reference Data Until No New Data Emerges.

4. Articulate the Continuities & Developments of Contemporary Africans (including needs, for studies using the Functional Paradigm) to the Classical Referent of African Knowledge, Traditions, & Experiences.

5. **Interpret the Supports & Barriers to Universal Order & Harmony According to Topical Area & Paradigmatic Approach**

The cosmological component of AI is what drives my questions of me versus we in goal-setting and agency, and what drives me to consider the affects of cultural centeredness on Africans' search for internal and external harmony in places of dislocation. It is from this aspect of AI that I raise such questions as whether African American youth experience feelings of cultural dislocation or rejection in school.

The epistemological component of AI addresses questions about the truths Africans consider necessary to know, rather than what constitutes knowledge for everyone. African beliefs about truth and knowledge find their sources in language, myth (e.g., religion), ancestral memory, the arts (dance and music especially), and science (Asante, 1990). The importance of hip hop and Ebonics as tools of resistance and life-promoting creativity are part of the epistemological foundation for African Americans. It is from this aspect of AI that I raise such questions as whether self-knowledge affects hopeful thinking and acting among African American youth. In the follow up interviews, African epistemology is also a part of what drives me to ask about the achievers' hobbies and engagement with music, along with aesthetics below.

Axiology in AI was conceptualized by Asante (1990) to be important in guiding researchers toward understanding of African value traditions that are critical to our beliefs and actions. As he stated, "the question of value is at the core of the Afrocentric quest for truth because the ethical issues have always been connected to the advancement of African knowledge which is essentially functional" (p. 11). Philosophy, proverbs, spirituality, and a strong work ethic are all "good" and "right conduct" within global African culture. For the present study, analyzing data from the Afrocentric viewpoint while considering acculturative processes is critical according to the axiological domain. For example, it was important to understand why a community that values education would have such a high failure rate in modern schools. Without understanding the axiological truths within the African worldview, the very research questions driving my study would be flawed and subject to misinterpretations of the youth's responses.

The fourth AI composite, aesthetics, considers aspects of the African tradition that have historically received great attention in the West: the arts. In conceptualizing how the African emphasis on dance, music, orature, and poetry factor into empirical inquiries of the community, Asante (1990) used the seven "senses" of the African aesthetic conceived by renowned African dance choreographer and theorist Kariamu Welsh: polyrhythm, polycentrism, dimensional, repetition, curvilinear, epic memory, and wholism. By definition,

> Polyrhythm refers to the simultaneous occurrence of several major rhythms. Polycentrism suggests the presence of several colors in a painting or several movements on a dancer's body occurring in the context of a presentation of art. Dimensional is spatial relationships and shows depth and energy, the awareness of vital force. Repetition is the recurring theme in a presentation of art. The recurrence is not necessarily an exact one but the theme or concept is presents as central to the work of art. Curvilinear means that the lines are curved in the art, dance, music, or poetry—this is normally called indirection in the spoken or written forms. Epic memory carries with it the idea that the art contains the historic memory that allows the artist and audience to participate in the same celebration or pathos. Wholism is the unity of the collective parts of the art work despite the various unique aspects of the art. (Asante, 1990, p. 11-12)

Aesthetics are complex and fundamental to Black life. Art is not simply art for art's sake or the interests of the artist. Everything is for the sake of something else in the African cosmological frame. The contradictions of life, the things that could counter harmony or goodness, are also exemplified in African art. The natural combining of dialectical forces through the arts is a matter of complex simplicity in the African frame, and it is in large part the magic that has allowed our continual innovation and fortitude to make Black Lemonade with the sourest and driest ingredients in our respective colonial locations (e.g., coined by Dr. Patricia Ackerman, Dr. Portia Hunt and Michelle Walton in their Black Lemonade Project).

The practical impacts of the aesthetics tradition are many. Gottschild (2002) described African aesthetics as an amazing ability to "laugh and cry simultaneously," or convulse inside while maintaining the cool outside. She referred to the African aesthetic tradition as "embracing the conflict" (p. 6). In my study, I anticipated that aesthetics, especially dress, music, and dance, would surface as important sources of inspiration, expression, and even coping amongst the young achievers. Also, Black people are global drivers of physical and artistic expression, our physical agility and creative abilities in athletics and music often exploited (Tully, 1994; Ventura, 1985; Walker, 2004). The centrality and exploitation of aesthetic ability in the African community and global marketplace prompted me to query the achievers about their hobbies and coping strategies.

Seeking Ontology, Axiology and Epistemology: A number of questions that speak to my Afrocentric orientation were posed throughout the first half of this text. They have included, for example, what prevents successful Black children from quitting their academic and positive behavior goals despite demeaning schooling experiences, low staff expectations, curriculum biases, etc. especially after second grade? With 33% of the total 17% of African children categorized as being MR in the United States (National Research Council, 2002), how and when do Black children receive positive messages of their right to feel capable to achieve goals? How do Black children's cultural and social distinctions affect the types of goals they set?

The answers to these questions will help us understand the salience of struggle in today's African community, does it continue to exist or be necessary in consciousness or have developments like the election of the first African American President in 2008 removed all or most concern of racism as a reality in modern contexts? If Black youth today continue to view race and culture as important areas for restoration, then the strategies that they employ to balance their concern with academic progress during the turbulent junior high school period will be essential for educators, social scientists and parents to know. The following four research questions guided the SigHT study:

1. *Does self-cultural awareness affect African youths' processes or levels of hopeful thinking and acting, and if so how?* Many researchers have asserted that Black people who have high self-cultural awareness are psychologically healthier and achieve greater than those who are self-culturally unaware, confused or self-hating (e.g., Bass & Hardin, 1997; Chavous et al., 2003; Kunjufu, 2006; Merry & New, 2008; Sellers, Caldwell, Schmeelk-Cone, & Zimmerman, 2003; Worrell et al., 2001). Following these conceptualizations, higher self-cultural awareness in this study should result in more positive beliefs in personal and communal ability to achieve goals, even if environmental barriers exist. Is cultural centeredness important to hopeful thinking in the African student community?

2. *Given the tradition of collectivism in the African community, and given the reality of racism that Africans uniquely*

experience, do Black youth today engage in hopeful thinking and acting from a community orientation, or has their sense of collectivism been worn out by time and dislocation? This question is specifically important in terms of motivation and personal agency. If African youth tend to embrace the collectivist orientation toward achievement, that is for example "I work hard so that I can go to college to get a good job *and* represent my community well," special education and therapy services like positive behavior supports (e.g., behavior interventions in schools or counseling) would need to be tailored for this orientation to be most effective.

3. *Do African youth face pressures in- or outside of school that force them into roles that oppose the existing order?* If achieving Black youth realize problematic social or cross cultural situations in school or society, then one of two things must occur in order for them to be successful, they either employ some defense against the negative forces, or somehow internalize the forces they face so as to assimilate with them and give up some of their power. The goal of psychologists, educators, families, and others vested in the health and success of Black youth must be to equip them with the necessary tools to achieve. If defense is necessary for Africans to succeed in Eurocentric school systems, then what forms of resistance help Black students reach their goals without losing their identity or disrupting harmony? My contention is that "defense" in this case is in fact a strategy of pro-action rather than reaction in the common sense of the word.

4. *How and about what do African youth tend to set academic and life goals?* In as much as goal-setting and goal-commitment are considered by psychologists to be thought processes first, theoretically speaking there must be a cognitive process by which goals are conceived and aspired to. One of the research questions of this study on hope then must inquire about what motivates young Black achievers. What concerns or desires factor into their goal-setting, and what pushes them toward goal attainment?

These four major queries were broken down into shorter, more basic ones in order to ask clear and specific questions that the children would understand well enough to answer fully (see Table 1). The achievers were first asked 35–37 questions, depending on the need for "if so, then why" questioning. Special care was taken to modify the interview questions for understandability and validity. The initial interview questions were largely open-ended and opinion or behavior-seeking so as not to lead or constrain the participants' responses.

Table 1: Research Queries and Corresponding Interview Questions

---

1. ... Do African youth today engage in hopeful thinking and acting (i.e., goal-setting and goal-pursuit) from a community orientation, or has their sense of collectivism been worn out by time and dislocation.

---

3. What does a successful life look like?
4. What makes someone's life a success story?
5. What do you hope for?
6. What do you want to be when you grow up?
7. What are the values and beliefs that you live your life by?

---

2. How and about what do African youth tend to set academic and life goals?

---

8. How did you come to choose to be a _____?
9. I am interested in how you work to make your hopes come true. How do you work toward being a _____?
10. How confident are you about reaching your goals?
11. What makes you confident/unconfident?
12. What are some things that might stand in your way?
13. How will you overcome these challenges?
14. Do you get support from someone or someplace to reach your goals?
15. How do you get social or moral support?
16. Do you have any role models, people you look up to? Who are they/where are they?
17. Do your family and school influence each other/do your family and school ever come or work together?
18. Do any of these goals come from you being African American?
19. What about being a boy/girl?

20. Do you think you have a different type or amount of hope to reach your goals because you are a boy/girl?

3. Does self-cultural awareness affect African youths' processes or levels of hopeful thinking and acting, and if so how?

21. What does it mean to you to be African American?
22. How does being African American influence you?

23. How does being African American affect what you hope for?
24. When you think about Africa what comes to your mind?
25. Let's pretend that I am only 7 years old and I have a 2nd grade homework assignment to learn about Africa and African American history. If I asked you to help me, what are some things that you would you tell me?
26. What would we do?

2. Do African youth face pressures in- or outside of school that force them into roles that oppose the existing order?

27. What is it like for you to go to your school?
28. What do you like about your school?
29. What do you not like about it?
30. If a dislike is offered, "How do you keep hope about _____ even though _____ is bad/challenging?"
31. Have you experienced racism?
32. Do you think you will experience racism in the future? Why or why not?
33. When _____ happened to you what did you think about it? What did you do about it?
34. How do you still think positively about yourself even when things like _____ happen?
35. How do you go about reaching your goals when you experience racial stuff?

The goal was to allow the students to share their own stories and convey the messages they deemed important. Further, the order in which the questions were asked was important for the participants' well being and to the validity of the data. I began with neutral, safe questions. More controversial questions about race, culture, etc., were asked once a safe space and level of trust was established. When the participants appeared to be uncomfortable or cautious with a particular question, I offered verbal support and encouragement so that they could feel free to speak their minds. I also reminded them that their answers would be held in confidence. When the youth signaled with their intonations, facial expressions, or other cues that they had completed their response(s) to a question, I tended not to ask them follow-up questions. I believe their narratives, shared in Part 2, are honest reflections of their personal perceptions and experiences.

Rounding Up the Study: During a second interview, the achievers were asked an additional 15–19 questions in order to clarify initial statements or confirm interpretations of initial responses. Qualitative research, meaning the study of substantive properties in human thinking or phenomena (versus a statistical study), often requires multiple attempts before one can confidently draw conclusions. One question could easily lead to additional questions as responses are not always clear, and new information builds fresh concerns. Multiple interviews are often conducted so that a question can be probed more deeply and confusion or disagreement may be put to rest. The students of SigHT in fact presented clear and consistent information in response to my questions, however, I know that readers will be inclined to their own interpretations, and there may be controversy over my analysis. This is common in qualitative research, but also indicative of the great controversy over effective pedagogy and psychological service delivery to Black children and families.

Supplementary questions included the following. Where two questions are listed for any item, the second only represents an alternative way of asking the same question:

1. What are your hobbies? What do you do for fun?
2. Do you listen to music? How often would you say, e.g., every free chance you get, everyday, whenever someone else plays it?
3. What kind of music do you listen to? What's your favorite type of music?
4. Who is your favorite music artist?
5. Do other kids in school make fun of you for doing well in school? If yes, what do they say or do? How does that make you feel? What do you do about it?
6. Do you think that your future success affects other Black people (in a special way)? How so?

7. What does Barack Obama represent to you?
8. Did you think that there would ever be a Black President before President Obama?
9. Does knowing about President Obama make you feel differently about your own life? Do you feel more hopeful, or about the same? Why do you think that is?
10. What helps you learn?
11. Do you think Black people represent a unified group? Are Black people together as a community today?
12. Do you think they should be?
13. Do you think Black people used to be more together than they are today?
14. What happened to Black people?
15. Walk me through a typical weekday for you.
16. Do you plan your days? Do you plan for school?
17. I hear a lot of teachers at this school yelling at kids all day. What do you think about teachers yelling at kids at school? Does that bother you?

The purpose of the follow-up questions was not necessarily to extend the themes found, but rather to confirm or supplement the data from those questions that represent the major research queries. The follow-up questions, if posed well, will address any issues that appear to be missing or somehow lacking from the original set. For example, the long held notion that achieving Black students face bullying or ostracization from their lesser performing Black peers and are negatively impacted by it is an important one that has yet to be clearly tested through data-driven research. Additionally, many of the activities or beliefs said to be important to the culture and resilience of the Black community, such as appreciation for and use of music and dance, have rarely been studied among *achieving* Black students. Several of the students referenced significant nuisances in their school experiences, as well as connectedness to family who sometimes struggle that could create stress for them as young strivers. Understanding their stress relieving activities is meaningful. Finally, asking the achievers directly whether they held special concern for unity in the Black community during the initial interview would surely have been leading. The initial questions on culture and motivation, for instance, did not address these concerns specifically although students often touched on them in their responses willingly.

Analyses: Data were collected for this study through multiple mediums, including face-to-face tape recorded interviews, observations, and participant observations (referred to as a "means to obtaining meaningful information about individuals [from] within the communities being studied" by Suzuki, Ahluwalia, Mattis, & Quizon 2005, p. 206). Interview narratives were analyzed using a constant comparative coding and grouping approach (e.g., Rennie, 1994). To verify the legitimacy of the codes applied to participant responses, a Professor of Counseling Psychology and a PhD student also in the field reviewed and discussed with me the accuracy of my interpretations of the students' words and intent.

Classroom observations were maintained for additional qualitative information regarding how the students successfully navigated their instructional and school environments to manifest hopefulness. Observations were important to describing the students' affects and personalities in relation to the narrative analyses. For example, in considering what the essential meaning of a student's response to a question was, observation data for that student were useful in supporting or refuting interpretations. I believe the full method outlined in this chapter to be consistent with the Afrocentric objective of acquiring and analyzing data that considers the dynamic African experience holistically. Using this method, I believe that many will find the views and stories expressed by the following six African American achievers to be extremely useful for all Black students and families.

Part 2: Black Student Achievers Speak

Chapter 4: Ture

Achiever 1, Ture (pronounced tour-ay)

A seventh grade male being raised in a two-parent household, Ture was the highest ranked student in his grade, and possibly the top in the entire school. With excellent grades, classroom behavior, and post-graduate ambitions that reflected both high intelligence and discipline, his teachers were unanimous about him being a model student. His English and language arts teacher especially spoke highly of his writing skills, stating that his performance was well above his local and statewide peers. Ture's professional goal was to be an architect. His scores on the OAT placed him in the Advanced range in reading, and Accelerated in mathematics. Despite the critical acclaim he received from teachers, however, Ture tended to be blasé about appealing to them or receiving their praise. His approach to school was matter of fact, resolved, and serious. As we talked, I soon discovered some of the primary reasons why Ture was so resolved about his school and life achievement.

In my observations of Ture outside of interviews I noticed that his behavior was always controlled and responsible. He was rarely observed in horseplay with peers, never disruptive during instruction. In the hallways, Ture almost always walked with his hands in his pocket, which made it impossible for him to be accused of intruding on another student's space or causing trouble. At the same time, his manner was relaxed and easy going. Sometimes he would smile silently or talk quietly to a peer while in class or at lunch tables. Ture appeared to be very mature, but also socially well adjusted for his age. He seemed to naturally strike a balance between kid and scholar, child and budding young man.

With staff, his demeanor was reserved and typically sober. He often averted eye contact with teachers, especially in the hallways. It was evident that Ture took his education seriously and understood that there was a particular decorum that went along with being in school. He wore glasses almost daily and usually had a pencil behind his right ear. Staff never seemed to notice when Ture's pants sagged or when he chewed gum unlike most other boys in the school.

Research Question One

Paying attention to the teacher during instruction and completing schoolwork "wasn't a big thing" for Ture. These were actions that kids should take as modus operandi. He understood that there was a time to play around, and during school hours was not it. In his words, "it ain't a big thing just to pay attention to 'em [the teachers]. All you gotta do is do the work ... I mean, playin is good but, like, sometimes it take your attention away and then you really don't get what's goin on." The essence of Ture's stance on what kids need to do to do well in school seemed to be, quite simply, act studiously.

Ture believed that working hard at making good grades increased his chances of becoming "rich" and escaping the life of "just a regular person workin at McDonald's or something" else less rewarding. Going a step further, school success was the path not only to material wealth, but also, and more importantly to psychological health and communal esteem.

> Q: What does a successful life look like?
> A: Maybe two or three cars, a nice house, a good job, not many worries. Success is to be able to have all the things in life that you always wanted and not really have to turn them back in after a month or something because you didn't pay your bills. It's like where you can do everything and anything that you like...as long as it's in the law, that you could really do, that you felt like you wanted to do for a long time.
> Q: Ok, what makes someone's life a success story?
> A: When they have something that they could live for, like, after you die, I mean you want something that you could look over back on the years and don't wanna just have something, like, where you just own something and then when you die there's really no record of it.
> Q: Like a legacy?
> A: Yeah.
> Q: What would you like your legacy to be?
> A: I'd like to have something named after me, or something, like, for a lot of people to remember.
> Q: For what?
> A: Just for me doing something great.

While his initial response highlighted monetary wealth, as the discussion progressed Ture's responses increasingly reflected the nonmaterial, including peace of mind, stability, making a universal contribution, and leaving a legacy. By performing above federal, state, and district standards, Ture believed that he was making a down payment on freedom, life satisfaction, and very Kemetically, a proud life in the afterlife. His response during the first question calls forth the very legacy from which he comes. One might think of the countless tombs and rituals to venerate and keep alive the souls of the deceased in Egypt.

In addition to having a building or park named after him, Ture hoped to go to college with scholarships, stay healthy, and "live life, like, [he] could do what [he] want[s] to do without really havin to face a lot of consequences." Ture's responses indicated that one, he values life, and two, he has been influenced by the fact that his family lacked financial security and, therefore, the ability to live freely. Rather than try and distance himself from them, he used his family experiences to motivate him in school. To the question of what he values in life, Ture responded that he values family and education more than anything else. He appreciated his family's high expectations for him to make good grades and his grandmother's "extreme" belief in Jesus Christ. Both his family's scholastic expectations and religious foundation influenced his general belief system, including faith in the promise of school achievement.

Ture's reasoning for exerting effort in school, as he described it, went beyond personal gain or individual interests. His family strongly influenced his motivation, as he stated for example, "I mean family's awesome, and it's [about] getting good grades and stuff, cuz then the family dumps on you if you don't get good grades." His persistent referencing of family members and his desire to leave a mark on his community and the world indicate a collectivist orientation. Already, by answering the first seven questions of the interview, Ture has shared significant information regarding his cognitive leanings toward school and life.

Research Question Two

Ture's approach toward choosing a career was simple and practical—do something that pays "good money" and that will keep you interested. In this respect, architecture seemed to be a good fit for him since he liked to draw and architects tend to make enough money to live securely and freely in America. In order to achieve his goal, Ture saw the importance of practicing his trade, so he drew "quite a bit," and he found pleasure in it. However, he stressed that his primary goal was to earn a living wage and that architecture, like school, was but a means to that goal: "Architect[ure] is, like, one of those things that, like, if I can do it I will, but if it doesn't come to that I guess I'm gonna have to think of something else, [and] I will." His point was that he was flexible in his career choice, and his loyalty stood with quality of life and use of his skills rather than a particular career path or college, etc.

Ture's confidence in a high probability of his future success through multiple career avenues stemmed largely from his belief in the promise of school to assist him in acquiring the quality of life he wanted. He a put forth a conscious effort to be practical and realistic in his goal-setting, even using famous African Americans as guideposts:

> *Q: How confident are you about reaching your goals?*
> *A: I really wanna reach 'em, cuz I'd probably be greatly disappointed if I didn't reach 'em, so, I try not to aim 'em extremely high, like Lebron James rich, but I think I wanna get rich. Like, I wanna have a nice amount of money...and stuff.*
> *Q: How confident are you about getting all that money?*
> *A: I think I could do it, if I keep doin school like I do now.*

Ture focused on school achievement as *a tool* in building the life he wanted. As he expressed under the first research question, his goal was to make high marks in his classes for a better life, not to receive praise from teachers, connect with school leadership, or even be a "model" student. School did not define his identity or determine his choices. He spoke of the need to go to college to help secure general well being and to make his family proud, but not of an idealized view of what formal education has taught him about knowledge, citizenship, or even success. He saw himself getting rich through school achievement, but his vision was tempered by his real life experiences (e.g., of family "dumping on" him if displeased with his grades) and not the celebrity images of wealth promoted by schools or the media (e.g., superstar athletes).

Ture possessed a controlled determination to be successful in life *by using* American education in the pursuit of peace and happiness *rather than embracing* it as a part of his self-worth. Reminiscent of Malcolm X's infamous lesson of progress "by any means necessary" (Shabazz, 1999), Ture understood that school could be made useful to him and his family even though his was a largely failing one in a failing district and a generally failing city.

> *Q: What makes you confident?*
> *A: Well, once you see your report card you get more confident after you see it and it's not ugly, like D's and F's and stuff, and you get confident. So, as long as I keep stayin on that path, with A's, B's, maybe one or two C's, I'll stay good.*
> *Q: What happens if you get a D or F?*
> *A: Bring it up. Work harder.*
> *Q: Do you go, "I can't do this"?*
> *A: Nah, I ain't gone say I can't do it. I'm just gone try harder.*
> *Q: What are some things that might stand in your way?*
> *A: As long as you went to school and you got an A and stuff, you'll still have your mind. As long as that doesn't leave—I mean not much. If I wanted to go somewhere I'll go there. Nothing can really stop me from going there if I really wanna go there.*

Work hard, and look good while doing it. His expression of viewing his report card as "ugly" or "pretty" and basing his "goodness" on his deeds in school bears a striking resemblance to the African cultural belief in the beauty of a person or thing being contingent upon the quality of the person's actions, decorum, or functionality—do good to be considered good, and be good to be considered beautiful in the truest sense of the word (e.g., Asante, 1998).

Complementing Ture's determination, and perhaps even instilling it, was the family guidance and support he received. When asked who supports him in his school efforts, he named his family as his only source of encouragement. By expressing interest in his school behavior, expecting academic excellence, and praising him for high marks Ture felt consistently supported through the achievement process by his family. Ture's parents consistently, but not necessarily daily, asked about whether or not he had homework. They reviewed his report cards and offered ideas if he asked for help on projects.

Further, referring not only to his mother and father but to his "entire family basically," Ture's support came from an extended family network. More specifically, his support came from "a lot of cousins, a lot of aunts, a lot of uncles, two grandmothers, a dad and mom, and sister," each of them berating him for at least "the next two weeks" if he brought home "a bad grade." His family may not have directly participated in his schooling, but they cared about his life and future, and they showed caring through indirect participation. Regardless of their own achievement or social status, the family had high expectations for him. Their expectation for Ture was always excellence.

According to Ture, no one in his extended family network were "big people" making a lot of money or having fame, but they impressed upon him that he could be and do anything he wanted to. They expected him to see his goals through to completion and be successful. It is perhaps for this reason that, in spite of having a "lower class pedigree," Ture maintained a mental list of millionaire role models who inspired him to reach his fullest potential; yet he understood the difference between success and fame, happiness and financial wealth—although one can surely come with the other.

Ture named superstar athletes Lebron James, Michael Jordan, and "Kobe" as his role models, if for no other reason than "they came from just regular people and became mega millionaires and stuff." Of course "regular" is relative to one's background and experience, just as being "rich" is. Born and raised in Cleveland, Ohio (on the Black side), Ture placed Lebron James at the top of his role model list. In doing so, Ture articulated a need for *self-identifiable* role models. As an African American male "from the hood," his role models were just as likely to be superstar athletes as family members. Interestingly, he did not want to be a professional athlete or celebrity himself, but he was inspired by the fact that he and his role models came from the same type of community.

During the second half of research question two, Ture described very clearly the distal relationship that he and his family have with school. For just as his self-identifiable role models were Black men who rose from the bottom to the top outside of college, and in the same way that his family members monitored and supported his academic progress from afar, Ture understood that, for him, home and school were largely separate entities between which school was a means to an end for him but not necessarily a part of him. In other words, school achievement itself was not critical to Ture as an African American boy, for many African Americans were faced with finding success through other means. Indeed, many African Americans are disaffected with American schools. Alternatively, what was critical was finding a viable option for success in his context or conditions, and for Ture who had a clear understanding of his skills and definition of success, school was very achievable. School success was in his line of SigHT. His vision was so clear that he could see the full reality of American schooling—both fallacy and opportunity. The trick was making it work for him. Ture had mastered the art of what may best be described as *conscious acculturation*—it is the know-how or agency component necessary to Du Bois' (1903/2003) concept of double consciousness.

> *Q: Do your family and school influence each other, [or] do they ever come/work together?*
> *A: Are you saying, like, do my family influence my grades?*
> *Q: Sort of. Do your teachers, classes, all that school consists of, do your family and school affect the other?*
> *A: I mean yeah, they affect the other. But, it's like kinda one of those medium situations. They don't largely kinda mix together, but they're there. It's like a bridge.*
> *Q: What's the bridge?*
> *A: I mean grades and stuff. My paperwork that I bring home. That's basically the bridge.*
> *Q: Do they ever work together?*
> *A: Yeah, on projects and stuff, yeah.*
> *Q: Do your parents come here?*
> *A: Nah, they don't come here. I take the projects home, and we brainstorm stuff.*

For Ture and undoubtedly many of his peers, community-home life and school are two different worlds that sort of coexist but never quite seem to merge. In his reality, home and school diverge at the intersection of Black and White, Afrocentric and Eurocentric, care and apathy. Ironically, Ture himself serves as the very point of these intersections. He has learned how to speak two languages and see through the hypocrisy and hopelessness of or between his school, neighborhood, and family experiences. Somehow he has managed to be successful by home *and* school standards, two vastly different places in many ways.

In his determination to succeed as a man, Ture has learned by the young age of 13 to acquire aspiration from both worlds, trailblazing toward a career, financial security, health, a happy family, and a legacy in the midst of contradictions evoked from his own African American culture and his school and country's European privilege, 'just like Lebron

James and Kobe', but through the promise of school achievement. At face value, one might argue that Ture's belief in the promise of American education is an indication in itself that he feels a connection to his school, and his identification of his family as his source of support is commonplace, perhaps as it should be. However, this argument seems more a delusional American epithet of national ethos than a critical analysis, lacking in any real excavation of race relations and the importance of heritage and culture.

For example, Ture perceived his goal of being an architect and a financially and psychologically secure adult to be far removed from what he was used to seeing among "the little people," having achieved, and given that the majority of the people that he knew were African American, logically, African American becomes associated with abject poverty rather than achievement. He works hard in school with this reality in mind, not in spite of it. And yet, so ingrained is his complex sociocultural reality, with all of its race-ridden and race-hidden American disparities that Ture assumed that the goals he had set for himself by the seventh grade had nothing to do with his race or heritage in any concrete sense (he responded that being African American had no influence on his goals). Having identified African American male role models whose background closely resembled his, and having expressed the presence of such a strong African American family influence on his academic resolve, it is obvious that the impacts of race and heritage are significant to Ture. At his age, he had not yet connected the multi-sized and multicolored dots that shape his spirit, thinking, and behavior, but he seemed to be closing in on the puzzle.

Reading with cursory eyes, it seems that Ture espoused the same notion as Snyder (2002) with regard to the race-less or monocultural conceptualization of hope. That is that race and culture matter not to goals or goal-pursuit. A closer look, however, corrects this hasty interpretation.

> Q: *Do any of these goals come from you being African American?*
> A: *Not really. But, I mean I wanna get rich and famous, but it's not always gonna be easy because I'm Black, but...*
> Q: *How come?*
> A: *I mean it's like a lot of racist people out there, but I know that's not...everybody's not racist, so I know that everybody won't sit there and ridicule me because of my color.*
> Q: *How do you know?*
> A: *Because if you look at history, history's basically nothing but racism and anger and stuff.*
> Q: *Example?*
> A: *Uhhh, the Ku Klux Klan, like, you see them on the history channel and stuff and how angry they were just for basically nothing.*

Q: You think racism still exists today?
A: Yeah it still exists.
Q: How do you overcome it?
A: Just gonna have to live with people. I mean, you can't stop
somebody from thinkin that about racism. It's always gonna
be in the back of their mind.

While becoming a successful architect may not obviously connect
to his being African American and male, for surely kids of other ethnicities
have the same interest, for Ture, the goal to become an architect is
inseparable from the reality of racism, discrimination and his desire to
give back to his family and community. Ture's point of view based on
his historical knowledge and experiences was that he could become
anything that he wanted to in life, but his "becoming" meant additional
self-resolve, racial awareness, and ethnic pride, all of which he describes
in more depth below in response to Research Questions Three and Four.

Contrary to the issues of sexism or gender bias, Ture viewed race
as a central problem in the world. While he recognized sexism as a
potential obstacle for some females because of historical oppression, it
is an issue that might allow him just "a small glimmer more [of hope]
than a female" since the world is not as much of "a man's world" anymore,
what "with all these female things, like organizations…females can get
into things real easy." Racism, however, is a major historical *and*
contemporary problem that he would have to combat increasingly as a
Black teenager and man in order to reach his goals.

Research Question Three

Ture's determination to complete college, have financial security,
peace of mind (or freedom), and make his family proud was matched by
his level of self-cultural awareness and pride. He described his racial-
ethnic identity in various terms: through natural attributes (e.g., having
rhythm), through culture, and having a shared history with other Black
people. Interestingly, and perhaps mirroring the sociopolitical importance
that race has taken over ethnicity, Ture defined his racial-ethnic identity
in terms of color first and ethnic and cultural characteristics second—
"uhh, to be brown. I mean have rhythm…" Ture's Blackness, much like
his dichotomous world of home and school, was shaped both by racial
notions from the larger society and a heritage and culture unique to
African people.

Q: What does it mean to you to be African American?
A: To be brown…I mean, have rhythm…just a person, yeah. And
a lot of heritage and culture and stuff.
Q: How does being African American influence you?

A: *It lets me know where we came from cuz if we didn't get out of slavery and stuff... Yeah, you look at history. We came through a lot so...just wanna be successful cuz we came through it. Now we can [be successful] so what's the point of not takin a opportunity to become successful?*

Q: *Do you think that because you're Black your success would be something different or special?*

A: *eah a little bit cuz, like, if you get a job, a major job over somebody who's Caucasian I mean, it wouldn't really matter if they weren't racist, but you know that you still got that job over somebody...over somebody of a race that maybe runs the country.*

Racism has had a big impact on Ture, enough that even in middle school he considered the implications of racism on his future success. As much as he wanted to view himself as just another person with ordinary hopes for his future, Ture could not escape the potential consequences of his existence in a world overrun by racism and Eurocentrism, nor did he seem to try to. Black people have for a long time been subjected to racism and continue to live in a world institutionally dominated by their subjugators; he would be wise to consider this reality. Neither beaten nor broken, however, the tone of Ture's self-expressions, and the grades and test scores that he achieved as a consequence of his attitude toward school, espoused a sense of determination that outweighed any subjugation. Just 13 years old and in the seventh grade, he perceived that racism was a reality but not necessarily a barrier. This perception helped to maintain and even fuel his motivation in school rather than kill it.

Still, the impact of race as a modern social construct borne out of Eurocentrism has real and negative effects on kids like Ture. Case in point, negative and stereotypical images of Africa continue to exist in the minds of Black children worldwide, even alongside notions of strength, beauty, and philosophies of cultural pride.

Q: *When you think about Africa what comes to your mind?*

A: *Umm, a lot of people helpin it. It's kinda poor, and the buildings are tattered, and...yeah. Then you kinda think about wild animals and stuff, but then you kinda go back to the poor parts of it and it's not straight just like the little wild shows [on television] try to act like it is because they don't show all the people in poverty and wit' all the diseases. They just show the animals so it's not like you seein all the people sufferin around there.*

Ture was aware that the media's images of Africa were half-hearted and incomplete. However, he did not reference any contemporary alternatives or correctives for unfair portrayals of the huge continent and the many people on it—most likely because he did not have any contemporary substitutions or remedies to offer. Although with a sense of activism toward "seein all the people sufferin," his only other images included disease and poverty. Importantly, the discontentedness with which Ture spoke of racism and negative portrayals of Africa indicates that he somehow knows better. He knows that there is more to Africa and his African roots than what he has been taught or shown by American schools and media.

Q: *Let's pretend that I am only seven years old and I have a 2nd grade homework assignment to learn about Africa and African American history. If I asked you to help me, what are some things that you would you tell me?*

A: *Well....I'd tell you that Europeans tried to take it over, but it didn't work as well as they thought it would. But Africa was a very beautiful place. Yeah. And then, like all of a sudden people tried to start takin it over, then started tryna use Africa's beauty, like all their diamonds for, just to sell and get money off of, so they started shootin people and stuff, so Africa kinda turned from a good story to like a bad nightmare or something.*

Q: *Anything else you would tell me? What about African American history?*

A: *We had a lot of great leaders, a lot of great African American leaders, a lot of tragedies. But through it all we've gotten over it...and can still get over a lot of the problems that we still have today.*

Q: *What would we do? Where would we go?*

A: *Just go over, a quick skim of the most important things in African American history, from Africa, from slavery all the way to now, in the current day.*

Q: *Would we go anywhere?*

A: *The library (laughter). A computer, that's like the best thing to get quick information without having to go there and go through every single book.*

In spite of stereotypical portrayals of Africa and the absence of African and African Diasporic history within K–12 history books, Ture demonstrated an attentive disposition toward African American origins and possibilities, piecing together bits of information and pairing them with his life experiences as an African American boy. He is certainly conscientious in his self-development. His awareness of Africa and African American history is truly more conscientious than most of his peers and even many adults (Chandler, 2010). For instance, key indicators of this is his use of "Europeans" to describe colonialists and imperialists rather than "Whites," which is more commonly used. He referred to Africa as having natural beauty and resources, and he recognized a pre-colonial Africa and compared it with post-colonial conditions. In general, Ture recognized a heritage of beauty and resilience among African people both continental and Diasporan, a people that he senses being both genetically and culturally connected to.

Just as he felt disapproval and agitation against racism, he felt disgruntled by the increasing fragmentation within the Black community. This further underscores his degree of self-cultural awareness, social consciousness, and sense of collectivism as a Black community member.

Q: What if I said, "That was then. What does all that have to do with today?"

A: Today is even worse cuz now it's like Black people are shootin other Black people for dumb reasons. Like, just for having like a quarter on you they'll shoot you and take the quarter or a cell phone that they can't even use. But it's even worse. Cuz now it's like, Black people aren't even together anymore. They're just doin violent things for no reason.

Q: So should I feel hopeless? I'm only seven years old.

A: No, you shouldn't feel hopeless. I mean you should feel motivated to be different, do more to be on the better side.

Q: But how do I do that?

A: Set goals for yourself. Uhh, try to complete the goals the best you can.

Go hard. Set goals for yourself. Use social challenges as fuel to achieve your goals. Work together with your racial-ethnic community to overcome social challenges that you face collectively. Set goals for yourself *without fear* of racism, but with awareness that racism is ever present so as not to fall victim to it. These are some of the messages Ture relayed to his Black peers (and their teachers and parents). These attitudes and behaviors seem to have helped him maintain his determination to succeed, even while he does not feel a connection to school.

Research Question Four

Ture's responses to the first third of the study questions present an adolescent boy who is hopeful about his own standing and his community's prospects. He is confident in his ability to achieve goals and conscientious about issues of race and self-understanding in a racialized world. He has set goals that he foresees will establish not only financial security and psychological safety from stress and regrets, but also a legacy that he, his family and community will be proud of. He has set goals in the face of racism, and against what he realizes is mis-education about the value, history, and conditions of Africa. Conscious of intra- and intercultural issues (e.g., "Black-on-Black crime", institutionalized racism, etc.) but not self-destructive because of them, his life success is more important than social assumptions and inequities, and his school success is bigger than his teachers' attitudes or school inadequacies.

Actually, he had very little to say about his school experiences except that he likes going because he values learning. He described his school as just okay, stating, "I mean it's not bad. The days are quick...most of 'em." His brief response and lack of emotionality suggests that he sees school as no more than a means to an end—the end being life achievement and making his family and community proud. The majority of Ture's comments regarding school dealt with the building in which the (so-called) learning and growing take place.

> Q: What do you like about your school?
> A: It's compact. I mean we don't have to walk all the way to another side of the building just to go to, like, one classroom then leave back out and go to the other side.
> Q: Anything else?
> A: The teachers I guess... the teachers aren't half bad.
> Q: Describe them.
> A: I mean they aren't horrible, but they're cool...I mean, they're not like just awesome, awesome...but they're nice people.

Understandably tentative in detailing his thoughts about his teachers to another staff member, we can easily draw the conclusion that Ture's interest in learning did not equate to nor stem from zeal about his teachers because either or both their personalities and pedagogy did not speak to him. He focused on the school edifice rather than the culture, for example. Ture did not like having to walk to an annex behind the main building in order to reach the lunchroom-gym area. Especially in the snowy winter months, the trek between buildings was unpleasant. Never deterred, however, Ture did not feel that having to walk between the two buildings was a major imposition. When asked how he is able to remain hopeful and focused on his schoolwork despite having to attend school in a subpar building, he responded, "I mean, it doesn't really mess with me because I ride the bus to school so I gotta get up and walk out to the corner. So it's not really anything compared to walkin to the corner."

Helping him to maintain a sense of hopefulness in school under unpleasant circumstances, Ture employed a philosophy of positive relativism. He managed daily challenges or annoyances by comparing them to greater irritations, and this helped him maintain a positive perspective. Undoubtedly, this is also a part of the strategy that he used to deal with racism.

Chapter 4: Ture

While he had not by the seventh grade experienced any direct confrontation with racism, Ture viewed it as an imminent threat given his African race-ethnicity. He clearly expressed an understanding of societal 'isms' and the impact of history on contemporary realities. Conscious of evident disparities in employment opportunities, political power ("Caucasians kind of control the country"), skewed media portrayals and cultural appropriations in education, etc., Ture knew racism existed, but he also felt confident in his ability to deal with it effectively.

Q: *Do you think you will experience racism in the future?*
A: *I'm not gonna say I'm not gonna experience it, but...I hope I won't experience it... I hope I don't.*
Q: *Why is it a possibility?*
A: *Cuz, you don't know people. You don't know who's racist, you don't know who's just sayin stuff in front of your face and might not even mean a word of it, so...*

Ture relied on his awareness of resilience in African and African American history to fight against hopelessness from possible confrontation with racism in the future. His foundation for hope was laid centuries ago, from the brilliance of ancient Kemet to surviving the Maafa to contemporary African American models of success from his own neighborhood. His philosophy was that of, 'if my ancestors and elders did it, then I can do just as much or even more.'

Q: *How do you still think positively about yourself even when things like the possibility of facing racism come to mind?*
A: *Uh, I just think about all the history we had. If they could come through it, then I could come through it too.*
Q: *What if you don't know the history? You think all the kids in this school know as much as you know?*
A: *I wouldn't say all of 'em. But I know that they probably know some information on it. They don't...[They're not] just clueless about it.*
Q: *You think it's important information to know?*
A: *Yeah.*
Q: *Why?*
A: *Because if you don't know yo history then you might accidentally repeat what history already happened...*
Q: *Ok, do you think that knowing where you come from, knowing your own history is important for you to do well in school?*
A: *Yeah, cuz, like, say you came from a poor place. You don't wanna stay in that poor place for your entire life...you wanna get money and stuff.*
Q: *I'm going to play devil's advocate...it doesn't matter, who cares, get over it.*

A: *I mean, if they said that...I mean I would care cuz I wouldn't wanna be some slave on some field workin for somebody for nothing, with no money at all. I mean I would wanna be successful.*

Q: *Now I'm gonna say, "Man please, you from Cleveland. You're not goin anywhere. You came from slaves."*

A: *Well, didn't Halle Berry come from Cleveland? Yeah, it was somebody. Well Lebron James, a lot of people, all the Cavaliers, they live around Cleveland. They play for the Cleveland Cavaliers. And Lebron, he came from Akron, or something like that, so... but they might count as a Clevelander, so it's not true that just because you come from Cleveland and you're African American doesn't mean that you can't be rich and successful...cuz it's a lot of people from Cleveland who became rich and successful... yeah, I'm still hopeful.*

Clearly, Ture derives inspiration from both his ethnic history and awareness of self-identifiable role models. Whether negative or positive, lessons and wisdom may be found in history. He made clear that his goals are set on a platform that is larger or higher than school and a career in America's job market, his platform, the very building blocks for his aspirations as an African American child entering adulthood includes a system of care for himself, his extended family, and his racial-ethnic community. Knowing that African descended people face pressures inside and outside of school, Ture was able to channel the pressures he faced (or expected to face) as an African American male into personal fortitude and scholastic achievement. Ture's response to the final question indicated his level of determination well.

Q: *How do you go about reaching your goals when you experience or think about racial stuff?*

A: *I mean, it doesn't really mess with me or nothin cuz I know that if somebody did say something racist to me, I mean, I just try to do better. Just out-score them completely.*

Q: *Out-score them in...?*

A: *Anything. Whatever they're tryna be racist on.*

Q: *So whether school stuff or...a state test, architecture...*

A: *Yeah.*

Ture echoed Du Bois' (1903/2003) statement of lifting the veil almost exactly (i.e. see Du Bois quote at the end of the first section in Chapter 3). Being Black and successful involves self-awareness and the resolve to be victorious in the face of social inequality. If the Black tax today means working harder and paying more in time, productivity, and sacrifice than others, then let your returns be great and doubly rewarded.

Chapter 5: Talib

Achiever 2, Talib (pronounced tah-leeb)

Talib was the second achiever interviewed for this study. Like Ture, he was a seventh grader living with his mother and father. Originally from an impoverished Black neighborhood in Michigan, Talib felt that Cleveland was a step up, despite its economic problems and failing schools. His mother was a college graduate who had "a good job," and his father once played either college or professional football, he was not exactly sure which one, but both were important to him. Talib was well aware that money did not come easily to his family any more than most other students in his school. He observed his parents having a hard time making ends meet, and he discussed his desire to be more successful so as not to have the same difficulties.

Talib's demeanor and interview responses reflected dignity reminiscent of older generations of African peoples. He tended to say "yes, ma'am," "no, ma'am," and "thank you" instead of the more common "yeah," "nah," or "thanks." Bashful smiles often completed his responses to compliments regarding his behavior and scholastic performance. Like Ture, Talib received glowing remarks from his teachers. Many said they enjoyed having him in class because he never presented any academic or behavioral problems. A bit more sociable than Ture, Talib still maintained a level of focus that kept him out of detention and the principal's office. Although he would openly laugh at his peers' mischievous behavior, Talib made sure to work more than he talked or laughed. His teachers often turned a blind eye to Talib's untied sneakers and sagging pants or gym shorts, which were breaches of the school's dress code, just as they had with Ture.

Research Question One

Talib's response to what kids need to do to do well in school also rested on a particular description of acting studiously. With a bit more specificity, he explained that kids "should study until they really get the questions they get asked in school." He said also that they should "make sure they finish all their work…get good grades on their tests, [a]nd get at least more A's and B's, and less C's on their report card." Talib strived for excellence in school because he believed that was the path to achieving his goals of completing college and having a successful, a well-paid job. Like Ture, Talib's expectation for himself was excellence, and his family played a key role in influencing his attitude toward school and achievement.

Q: What does a successful life look like?
A: Well, my dad told me about my mom. She umm, she went to school then kinda stopped goin to school, then she was like on

> *the streets and stuff, then she went back to school. She passed*
> *high school, and she passed college, and now she has a good*
> *job...that pays a lot of money.*
> *Q: So when you think of success, what do you think about?*
> *A: Like...someone who has success or succeeded to...pass a goal.*
> *Like passin high school, goin to college, passin their ACTs,*
> *and their college tests.*

In addition to school achievement, Talib's response reflects an appreciation for resiliency. Several times during his interview he referenced his mother's return to school and securing "a good job," despite having faced several obstacles that could have stopped her in her tracks. Talib was impressed by the fact that life had not weakened his mother's hope for completing college and that she used hardships to strengthen her resolve. Talib spoke about resilience in his immediate family in much the same way that Ture spoke of resilience as a characteristic of the African world in general.

Where rich in other communities reflects desire for exorbitant material profit, Talib's definition of "rich" or making "a lot of money" means something different. Talib's responses on this point again parallel Ture's.

> *Q: What makes someone's life a success story?*
> *A: (Silence)*
> *Q: Do you think you'll be successful?*
> *A: (Nodded)*
> *Q: So when you see yourself in...when you're 25, right, so again,*
> *you're a grown up. What do you see? What are you doing?*
> *Where are you? What's your life look like?*
> *A: I would probably be married. I would probably have at least*
> *one kid and have a job that pays enough money for me to pay*
> *my mortgage and my electric and my water bill for my family.*
> *And provide food for my family.*

Here, Talib leaves no question about what he means when he references having a lot of money after college. A successful life is one in which a man is able to achieve his goals, have a family, and have the means to support his family's daily needs. His major hope, even as early as the seventh grade, was to maintain his determination to complete high school and college and take care of his family.

Talib knew that he would succeed in school. If for some reason he "mess[ed] up in college," he resolved to go back until he finished. He also shared that he intended to get a job "in the near future," perhaps when he turned 13 or 14 years old, as a babysitter since he loved kids and his family often told him that he is good with kids. Talib felt that babysitting would be a good way to prepare himself for work at 16 years old, perhaps at a store. These work experiences, he further explained, would give him an early start on working as an adult and allow him to put money toward his college fund now. His practical thinking and work ethic in childhood rivals that of many adults.

The opinions, admonishments, and accolades Talib's family gave him played a key role in how he envisioned his future. His professional goals for the future were in part based on what he felt were his natural skills and sources of enjoyment, and also on his family's experiences and support of his decisions.

Q: What do you want to be when you grow up?
A: Well, I told my dad I wanna be a football player, but he said that's not good enough. But I really don't know what I wanna be yet.
Q: Okay, not sure, but you know you wanna go to college.
A: (Nodded)
Q: When you go to college, you want to play football for the college?
A: Yes.
Q: Would you go if you didn't play football for the college?
A: (Nodded) ...I wanna play cuz next year football season starts...so I'm finna start playin then, and I might keep playin every year, and then I will play high school football and then college. Then I wanna see if I can get into professional.
Q: How did you come to choose to be a football player?
A: Well I started playin one year. I don't really know when I started playin football, but once I played with some of my friends and I thought it was real fun. So I said to myself, I think I wanna play football cuz I'm good at football and I like football.

Talib and Ture both had families that supported their academic efforts and paid attention to their interests. Talib's family went a step further: they directly participated in helping him with his studies. Bottom line though, for both boys family was important, and education was promoted in their homes and community.

Q What are the values and beliefs that you live your life by?
A: I think that being with my family is important, and getting good grades in school, getting a good education...passin all my years of school. And getting a good job.
Q: What's so important about your family?
A: Like sometimes if I don't, like, if I would have to study for my test at home I'd ask them to help me study for it, so then, like, the next day I can get, like, a A or B on that test.

Q: So they help you, they support you in school, help you study if you need it, stuff like that?
A: (Nodded)
Q: How [exactly] do they support you doing well in school?
A: Well, they would tell me to, like, for tests, they would tell me to make sure I study, and for homework they would make sure that I do my homework, make sure that I do it right. So, like, probably the next day, they would probably give us like a pop quiz, ask us a few questions, and then I would, they would ask a question and I would just raise my hand and say, "Oh, I know it because I did my homework, and I did it all right."
Q: Okay, got it. Is there anyone else, or any place that you get support from?
A: No
Q: No. [Your] family.
A: (Nodded)

Talib's family (his parents and sister) was his first and last line of support when it came to doing well in school. Whether or not his family's influence resulted in a greater connection to formal education as more than a tool for livelihood is unclear. It is clear, however, that neither Talib nor Ture perceived being supported by their teachers or any other adult at school. This is a meaningful message to Black parents, school staff, and legislators considering the fact that all students *should* feel encouragement from their schools. If they do not, then surely their families have additional work to do in meeting their children's needs for fulfillment and success, and many schools and government officials should feel shame.

Research Question Two

Talib's determination to succeed in school and athletics is special. He did more than verbalize a general goal. He also demonstrated conscious daily effort toward his future. For example, he studied until he felt complete understanding of course material, and certainly before any exams. He read and practiced his schoolwork to be able to participate in class confidently and receive more A's and B's than C's. He practiced playing football regularly, given his goals of playing college ball and *maybe even* professional football. Even more, he practiced the specific position that he hoped to play frequently, clarifying that, "I got a few friends across the street, and sometimes I go over their house and we would play football. And sometimes their friends would come over and we all would play football [because everyone plays a little differently]." Talib practiced with different kids in order to be challenged more, since some kids are better or different at the game than others. It is clear from his responses that he welcomes challenges and sees them as opportunities for growth.

It is perhaps this attitude that makes Talib so confident in his abilities to achieve his goals. He expected that hard work would always be a necessary part of life and learning.

Q: *What makes you confident?*
A: *Because, like, I know that I always work real hard, and I know that I can pass to the next grade. Except last year, I was in danger of failing a couple things...I think it was social studies, science, and math. So what I did was, I asked my mom and dad for help and some of my friends in my class to see if they can help me, and the teacher...Now I'm in seventh grade...and I know I can pass seventh grade, eighth grade, high school, and college.*
Q: *Was it hard for you to ask for help?*
A: *Kinda sorta.*
Q: *What was hard about it?*
A: *Like (throat clearing), some of the stuff that the teacher taught us was kinda late, and I asked like a few days too late. (Throat clearing)*
Q: *So you thought that, what, the teacher would ask...why did it take you so long to ask [for help] or something like that?*
A: *(Nodded)*
Q: *But were you afraid to ask your friends for help or your parents?*
A: *(Shook head)*
Q: *No. You didn't think they'd think you were silly or, you know, not as smart or cool?*
A: *(Shook head)*

Talib seemed to be describing a motivated work ethic, meaning a work ethic that was consistently forward-focused and therefore moving ahead. He also exhibited a sense of humility in asking for help when he needed it, from family, peers and teachers. He was unperturbed by the thought of his "coolness" conflicting with his intelligence. He was no less cool for asking for help to improve his grades, and he was no less smart for needing the extra help. He was also unscathed about asking for help in school in spite of not feeling particularly supported there. He remained confident in his abilities and focused on his short- and long-term goals. Self-assured, Talib was flexible in how he reached his goals, but uncompromising about whether or not he would reach them. Much like his school mate Ture.

Q: *What are some things that might stand in your way?*
A: *No.*
Q: *No. Nothing?*
A: *Nothing.*

> *Q: Nothing. Alright (laughter), so no challenges for you going to*
> *the eighth grade, going to the ninth grade, going to college.*
> *A: (Shook head)*

With his mother and father as primary role models and influences on his future plans, and with his motivated work ethic and excellent grades, Talib's unwavering confidence was justified. I never did ask why he was in danger of failing those classes, but judging from his school record, confidence, and reports from teachers, the issue was a passing one, circumstantial rather than dispositional or psychological. Certainly, whatever the case was, he had motivating factors that were stronger. He looked up to his dad for his success in football and to his mom because "she was an honor roll student." His role models were self-identifiable, but not necessarily popularly successful or allied with his school. He looked forward to providing much of the same family support that he received to his own kids one day.

> *Q: You said you wanna go to college, get a good job....what for?*
> *A: Someone would ask me a big high school or college word.*
> *Like, say, I have a kid, and they would ask me, "What does*
> *this word mean?" and I would just stand there and stare at his*
> *face, and then I would probably be feelin real stupid because*
> *I didn't go to college, and I didn't study.*

What is profound about Talib's response here is that his seventh grade focus is obviously anchored by his vision as a father during manhood. While at first both family and school may appear to be equally valued, further deconstruction of his responses reveals that Talib values family separately and higher—noting again that school for Black youth in America does not necessarily equate to education in a philosophical or self-developing sense. As with Ture, school and home represented paradoxical and divergent coexisting entities, not allied or synchronized ones. Thus, while Talib's family may have reviewed his homework, prepped him for tests, and helped him on special projects, they went to his school or corresponded with his teachers "only sometimes, on parent-teacher conferences." Talib served as the bridge for his home and school similar to Ture.

Parent involvement, or the perceived lack thereof in the Black community, is a hot topic among teachers. African American parents are often criticized for not being involved enough in school. However, as Talib and Ture's experiences show, there is more than one way to be effectively involved. Although not establishing collaborative roles with the boys' teachers, or joining the Parent-Teacher Association (PTA), both families set the tone for valuing "education" and striving for high achievement at home. Black parents might not attend PTA meetings, but they may be creating a rigorous environment of academic excellence in the home. Talib and Ture's parents laid and enforced the ground rules for school success *at home.*

Already planning on marriage, children, and getting a good job to provide for his family, Talib's desire for future success included less attention to social factors such as race. He did not seem to connect his family's intergenerational upbringing in poor Black communities to a larger societal problem nor even to his intense desire to provide for his future family following college. On this note, Talib proved to be less contentious about social issues that could prove to be problematic for him and his family later in life. Likewise, he did not see sexism as a relevant concern to goal achievement, with the belief that boys and girls were likely to have the same degree of hopefulness without particular social concerns. Undeniably determined and family-oriented, and equally as focused and mature for his age as Ture, Talib was not as developed about social issues. As the rest of his narrative will indicate, Talib's cultural awareness was also lacking, clearly demonstrating the important linkage between cultural centeredness and clear social thinking.

Research Question Three

Questions of racial identity and ethnic influence were ambiguous to Talib. He "didn't really know" what it meant to be Black or how being African American had influenced him. His limited understanding of his racial-ethnic position meant that he also had a limited understanding of his family's values and experiences as an African American family beyond the obvious, such as valuing education and success (e.g., obvious because his parents were vehement about his completing his schoolwork.).

Whereas Ture's awareness of his African heritage created a sense of pride and determination based on a history of resilience, Talib's lack of consciousness meant almost sole focus on immediate family views and concerns. Yet, Talib was as self-confident and determined as Ture, which suggests that a lack of self-cultural awareness and pride does not have to preclude school achievement or positive ambition if Black children have a strongly connected and achievement-focused family. Said another way, if you are not culturally and historically knowledgeable as a young Black person, then you best at least have a family that demands your success and believes in the rewards of scholastic achievement if school success is the goal.

Ideal for Black children is racial-ethnic consciousness and family support in combination. The consequences of Talib having an empty or imbalanced view of his ethnicity and culture should be considered. In facing a world filled with racial-ethnic solidarity amongst non-African groups, and unjust systems predicated on the collective power wielded by others against African people, Talib's strong family focus but weak communal position as an African American man with a wife and children will put him and his family at a huge disadvantage? Consider his response to what he thinks about Africa and what he believes with regard to African and African American history:

Q: *When you think about Africa what comes to your mind?*
A: *(Throat clearing) Umm, sometimes when I think about Africa, I think about like (throat clearing), the different things that they wear than us Americans wear. Like, they wear different colors, they do different activities than we do.*
Q: *Okay. Anything else?*
A: *No.*
Q: *Let's pretend that I am only seven years old and I have a second grade homework assignment to learn about Africa and African American history. If I asked you to help me, what are some things that you would tell me?*
A: *(Throat clearing) Umm, I would probably say that...in Africa there are many different things that they have and do than us in America, and umm, they listen to different music, they dress differently (throat clearing)...they do different activities, they umm ...... (Looking down)*
Q: *Okay, you're doin good.*
A: *Sometimes I think they hunt for food. They make their clothes out of different animals, like coats. And that's probably all I would say.*
Q: *Okay, what about African American history?*
A: *Ummm...*
Q: *What would you tell me? What do you think I would need to know?*
A: *I think you would need to know that (throat clearing), I would ask you if you notice how...I would ask you if, did you ever wonder how the African Americans and other different color people got together, and then if you would ask how, I would say, well Martin Luther King, he brought all of us together. He brought the Blacks and Whites together, and that's how we got mixed...the Blacks and Whites combined. And that's how we started getting mixed, and then...umm...that's about it.*

These responses suggest that Talib views Africa as distant from his African American existence, both physically and philosophically. His understanding was that African people are entirely different from him. His "us" and "them" orientation was that of Americans and Africans. He held a national American identity that is far more salient than a racial-ethnic identity. Yet, this observation must also include reflection of the extremely stereotypical and gravely limited knowledge that he held with regard to his ancestry and cultural reality. Talib's low social awareness of systemic inequalities and disparities is not a mere coincidence.

Talib held Eurocentrically clichéd views of Africa. He made no connection between Africa and African Americans or the history of slavery in America that created the existing African American community. He understood African American history as a component of the Civil Rights Movement, personified only by Martin Luther King, Jr. By his expressed knowledge, the most important thing, and perhaps the only thing for a student to learn about African American heritage was that Black people are now able to mix and mingle with White people. He suggested a single source of completing Black history research—a search of "African American history" on the Internet, which makes sense given his understanding that there is but one thing to learn about his heritage, and it is only that we have the great fortune of "mixing" with Europeans.

Research Question Four

A striking reality about the state of racism is that conditions are so severe that even Black children like Talib with low levels of self-knowledge and social preparedness recognize that it continues. In fact, he has not only learned about racism from the media, he has already heard the voice of racism in his middle school.

Q: *Have you experienced racism?*
A: *Well, my friend Bob, in the other seventh period class, he said that, I think it was his cousin or his brother that's racist to Black people.*
Q: *How does that make you feel?*
A: *(Throat clearing) Well, I'm not really offended by that.*
Q: *Okay, because...what? How do you feel?*
A: *I don't really know.*
Q: *You don't really know. So you said you've never experienced racism, but you do think it exists, stuff you see in movies, stuff you hear, people talk about it around you.*
A: *(Nodded)*

With little-to-no cultural awareness or reserve of self-cultural esteem, Talib was left dumbfounded when insults were made against Black people like himself and his family members. A troubling thought is how he will fare in the future if he is indeed confronted with racist provocations, as he expressed believing he would be.

Indeed, even for Talib, racism remains an imminent threat. As unsure as he was about what being an African American person meant to him, how his ethnicity and culture influenced him, and why he was unmoved by racist remarks against him and other Black people, Talib was sure that racism continues as "there are new people being born, and their parents might not raise them right." Thus far, his motto was to "just ignore it and keep goin on with [your] learning."

Like Ture, Talib enjoys going to school because he is "learnin a lot," and he is "still [there] with all of [his] friends." He dislikes when students are noncompliant, such as when a teacher tells them to be quiet but they continue to talk. Student disruptions and issues involving racism did not impede Talib's achievement thanks to his level of focus. Although his consciousness paled in comparison to Ture's and undoubtedly impacted his confusion toward his own feelings regarding racism, both boys indicated that they had mastered the skills of managing frustrations and concentrating on the task at hand.

> Q: *How do you keep hopeful about school? How do you stay motivated when people are doing the wrong thing?*
> A: *Well, what I would do is, I would just ignore 'em, cuz they keep talkin about the same thing, and they keep doin the same thing, so I would just ignore 'em, and just keep listenin to the teacher so I don't miss anything that might be important.*

Race, racism, peer disruptions—none of these issues seemed to be even remotely as important to Talib as his opportunity to learn and achieve for the comfort and security of his family. Based on his responses, no facet of life superseded his family values or determination for life success as a college-educated, self-sufficient husband and father. While his family focus is admirable and should be reflected in more African American males, his self-determination leaves much to be desired. His ignore and move on motto may very well have been effective for him up to the seventh grade, but we are left to wonder about his stability in the long run.

Chapter 6: Kwame

Achiever 3, Kwame (pronounced quah-may)
Kwame was a sixth grade boy at the time of this study, living with his mother and maternal grandmother. The school principal expressed that his mother and grandmother had corresponded with her and other staff during the school year regarding his academic progress. This suggested to her that they were "very supportive of his education".

Kwame was strong in mathematics, he scored in the Advanced range in Mathematics on the OAT exam in the fifth grade. Teachers remarked that he "caused no problem" in class. I observed that he was typically quiet and spoke only when spoken to. His reticence was also detected during the interviews. His responses were much more succinct than the other students, requiring that I dissect what he did offer more carefully.

Despite his reserve, Kwame sometimes smiled and chuckled under his breath at comments or antics made by his peers in class. He obviously found humor in the interactions between his peers and teachers. On occasion, I observed teachers redirecting Kwame to the task in front of him, not because he was being rude or disruptive, but because his attention was turned toward peers in amusement. I sometimes wondered if the teachers were simply peeved about one of the few "good students" musing at the lack of order in their classrooms, as Kwame's name would be the only name called for redirection, although he would be the quietest student musing.

Kwame's smiling and laughing appeared to be both part of his sense of humor and mechanisms for coping with nervousness when someone looked at or talked directly to him. During the interviews, Kwame could become bashful easily. He was especially timid during research questions three and four when Africa and African American experiences were discussed. Smaller in frame than the first two boys, Kwame's pants fit his hips and waist, but he was often seen with his shirt halfway untucked, although the school dress code required students to have their shirts tucked into their pants at all times. He also tended to wear his shoelaces untied and of different colors than his shoes. He wore "fat laces" rather than the more traditional "skinny laces." He often wore black undershirts, to offer a contrast to the white, yellow, or light blue top shirts prescribed by the school uniform code. A thick, silver chain necklace lay on top of his shirts. While one may have overlooked Kwame because of his low profile personality, he had a sense of style that indicated that he had opinions and a direction of his own. His personal aesthetic made him easily visible.

Research Question One
Several running themes from Ture and Talib's narratives continue through Kwame's. Kwame believed that kids must "listen and stop actin

up" to do well in school. Acting up to him meant talking and playing around in class while the teacher was talking. Acting studiously in class meant behaving in ways that enabled students to master instruction— listen and focus on the tasks given. Like Ture and Talib, Kwame believed that acting studiously would lead to "a good job" in manhood, such as being a doctor. In turn, having a good job equated to being "rich and livin in a big house." As previously found, being rich in cash and material things had a quantitatively and qualitatively different meaning for Kwame than that assumed by traditional American views.

For example, Kwame's very definition of life success was "havin a good family." Like Ture and Talib, Kwame expressed that he valued "getting a good education" mostly for the return of a career and means to have a happy family and life. Though he had not yet settled on a career goal, he understood that completing high school and going to college would open doors to multiple options. The promise of school investment for him and his family and the belief that "as long as you have faith in God all things are possible" served as Kwame's daily primers for acting studiously.

Research Question Two

Kwame had belief in a higher power (name unknown), but he did not rest on his spirituality by "putting everything in God's hands" or "waiting on God to show up" and deliver a career to him. While spiritual grounding was a source of resiliency for Kwame, he held a philosophy *and* method that included working hard to secure a future life of stability and happiness. True, his sole response to what he valued and believed in was about having faith in God to make possibilities realities, but we can see from his school behaviors that he also valued personal agency. For Kwame, faith in God and self-accountability were interconnected, simply a way of life, assumed and not necessarily spoken—do good to be good. His faith in God *and* his exercising of personal agency made him confident about reaching his goals.

> Q: You said you work hard in school to get good grades... Anything else? You can talk all day long. (Laughter)
> A: No.
> Q: How confident are you about reaching your goals?
> A: A lot.
> Q: What makes you confident?
> A: Thinkin about bein rich.
> Q: Okay, thinking about bein rich. That makes you wanna work harder at it?
> A: (Nodded)

Kwame's motivation appears to be even more strongly fueled by his vision of his future self and life than Ture and Talib, who referred more to their family and community's immediate influences on their work ethic. Remarkably, Kwame exhibited achievement behavior despite not having specific goals or plans for his future. According to typical social science research, however, this would be an impossibility. Instead, he held firm to a broad objective of living comfortably, his plan was to make it, and for him it was apparently plan enough.

Like Talib, Kwame expressed feeling displeased by disruptive peer behavior. He felt that his classmates' talking to him during instruction might impede his learning and achievement. However, contrary to popular theories regarding Black peer dynamics, none of the boys (or girls) in this study isolated themselves from their lesser achieving peers, and neither did their peers oppose or ostracize them. Rather than feeling isolated, smarter than, or attacked by their peers, these students kept their eyes on the prize in order to keep their school behavior in check *as a member* of the student body and larger community. As Kwame stated, "Just don't talk back to them," and "Keep gettin good grades."

Like Ture, making good grades was important to Kwame because it impacted him, his family, and the Black community.

> *Q: Do you get support from someone or someplace to reach your goals?*
> *A: My mom.*
> *Q: How does your mom support you?*
> *A: She just tells me to keep doin good so we can, so I can get a good job.*

Subtle but telling was Kwame's use of "we" in the above response. Kwame accepted the "we" orientation that supplanted or at least supplemented any individual ethos that he might have acquired outside of his home and community. Thus, if he gets a good job, then so does his mother because their efforts and victories are one for the other. Further in the interview, he extends his family bond to the rest of his racial-ethnic community.

Although his response to the question of his role models was simply to shake his head, indicating that he does not feel consciously inspired by anyone, we can conjecture that he was indeed thinking locally inasmuch as he was determined to become "rich," and no one in his home or community had an abundance of money. He could not think of any way that his family and school worked together or collided in thought or action, and his support for school came from home. His orientation was home and community. Kwame perceived school as a means to an end in much the same way as Ture.

Yet, like both Ture and Talib, he viewed his goals as unaffected by race-ethnicity, having not come to a comprehensive understanding of how his background has influenced his thinking about goal-setting and pursuit. He did, however, have a more mature sense of social issues alongside Ture, recognizing that males "can get more jobs" than females in general, based on gender roles (e.g., construction or manual labor positions). Still, to him, people of all races and ethnicities, and both males and females, could be equally hopeful as long as they worked hard and "got a good education." With awareness and determination, any social issue, whether race or gender related, could be surpassed.

Research Question Three

Like Talib, Kwame was hesitant to answer questions about racial-ethnic identity and racism. He only smiled after being asked what it meant to be African American. Eventually he graduated to shaking or nodding his head in response to questions, and even then these responses came after long pauses. He concluded that he was unsure of what his race-ethnicity meant to him. He was sure, however, of how being of African descent might affect him in America:

> Q: How does being African American influence you?
> A: Cuz a lot of African Americans don't get good jobs.
> Q: So, if a lot of African Americans don't get good jobs....but Kwame works hard [in school] to get a good job. How does that happen?
> A: You do well in school.

Kwame learned more about the negative connotations associated with being of African descent in contemporary society before learning about the positive aspects of African culture and history—and in his case African American. He reacted as if self-defining questions about ethnicity and culture were unsettling, taboo, or controversial. Yet, the fact that he excelled in school despite recognizing that African Americans face social oppressions like employment discrimination suggests that he was at least subconsciously aware of his community collective, and of the importance of social awareness. In other words, he recognized that Black people were his people, and his people were mistreated by a predominately White society or political power. He held a belief in the promise of school achievement to help him be the victor over social inequalities. Unfortunately, he lacked the level of intra- and intercultural awareness needed to critically understand the conditions of his community and importance of his identity.

Case in point, his only thought about Africa, which he recognized as the genetic source of African American people in reference to slavery, was, "All the people living in there and being poor." Interestingly, Talib recognized African Americans as having high experiences in poverty and unemployment, and associated poverty with Africans on the continent, yet failed to see a clear connection between the two groups politically. He recognized African Americans as enslaved African descendants, but did not connect the communities in any way culturally.

Race-ethnicity and social experience were at once obvious and obscure issues for him. Apparently, his social studies and language arts classes did not help him to make sense of these vexing social and ethnic concerns. They were meant for training, not educating.

> *Q: Let's pretend that I am only seven years old and I have a second grade homework assignment to learn about Africa and African American history. If I asked you to help me, what are some things that you would you tell me?*
>
> *A: About...*
>
> *Q: Africa and African American history.*
>
> *A: About how they were slaves and about Martin Luther King and, and Rosa Parks and Harriet Tubman.*
>
> *Q: What would you tell me about slavery?*
>
> *A: That they made the slaves work hard and if they didn't then they would hit them with a whip (eyebrows raised, nervous smirk).*
>
> *Q: What would you tell me about Martin Luther King and Rosa Parks?*
>
> *A: Martin Luther King helped go against slavery and wanted everybody to be equal.*
>
> *Q: How does that affect you?*
>
> *A: (Confused facial expression)*
>
> *Q: Or does it? No? So I'm seven, and I said, "So what. That was then." What would you tell me?*
>
> *A: What if you were born back then?*
>
> *Q: What would you tell her about school?*
>
> *A: That she need to be good and get a good education, or she gone end up workin at Burger King.*
>
> *Q: And what's wrong with workin at Burger King?*
>
> *A: You don't get paid a lot of money.*
>
> *Q: And why do you need a lot of money?*
>
> *A: So you can...help your family.*
>
> *Q: Help them what?*
>
> *A: So they won't be poor.*

Kwame's only awareness of Africa was of victimization experienced as a result of the European slave trade. So under-informed was he regarding his African American community's history and culture that he credited Martin Luther King, Jr. for opposing slavery, as if Africans were still legally enslaved during King's lifetime. He named only widely recognized African American activists as historical figures, those typically named in mainstream history books or during Black History Month in American schools. Further, he saw these activists and protests against subjugation as necessary "back then," when African Americans were affected by slavery and de jure segregation, not today, although a lot of African Americans still "don't get good jobs." He has simply come to expect that he must work harder in order to become a doctor as a Black man, because Black history is summed up to hard work and fighting for freedom and jobs.

Certainly less culturally knowledgeable than Ture, but seemingly more intraculturally versed and socially aware than Talib, Kwame did at least indicate a degree of pride in African contributions, resilience, and collectivism (i.e., Ancestors' opposition of slavery, appreciation for legal freedom today, working hard in school to support your family, etc.). These levels of consciousness and conscientiousness are likely to position him in safe and healthy psychological and social positions as an African American teenager and man. Congruously, his higher level of scholarship resembled Ture's, in that they both surpassed state standards for achievement, reaching the Advanced and Accelerated levels. Both boys, having greater self-knowledge and cultural esteem, referenced multiple sources of information to learn about Africa and African American history (i.e., the internet and books). What we find is that when knowledge of self and ambition come together, Black kids' motivation and determination are increased, and so is their propensity to improve their academic performance.

Research Question Four
That self-cultural awareness and family connectedness are more imperative for Black children's academic performance than school-connectedness is again demonstrated in Kwame's responses to questions about his liking to school.

Q: What is it like for you to go to your school?
A: I don't know.
Q: Think about it. You come here every day, right? So what's it like?
A: You just work.
Q: What do you like about your school?
A: The teachers.
A: What do you like about them?
A: They help us with our work.
Q: Anything else?
A: (Shook head)

Like Ture and even Talib, school is a means to an end for Kwame, a place to work. It is an essential tool used to build a better life of security, health, and happiness (and for Ture a legacy) for himself and his family. It is not, however, a place to learn about yourself or build relationships or work together with your family and teachers to help your community. To the contrary, these three African American youth understood that their giving back to their families and community would be done after, or

72

through school completion and achievement of a career. Teachers serve only to "help [them] with [their] work," but not to shape their thoughts about themselves or society, which is what compulsory schooling was intended to do as the national process of building up the citizenry (e.g., Fagan & Wise, 2000).

Rather than association with quality curriculum or great teacher relationships, what should be the real substance of schooling, Kwame's responses about what he likes and dislikes about school demonstrate disassociation of his cultural values from his American school culture.

Q: *What do you not like about [your school]?*
A: *We gotta wear dress code.*
Q: *Anything else?*
A: *(Shook head)*
Q: *Just the dress code. Why don't you like the dress code?*
A: *I don't like it.*
Q: *Because what?*
A: *Just don't.*
Q: *You'd rather choose what you wear yourself?*
A: *(Nodded)*
Q: *How would what you choose be different than your dress code?*
A: *I wouldn't wear tan pants and a white shirt like this (facial expression of "obviously").*
Q: *Why not (laughter)? Tell me why not. Pretend that I'm our superintendent. I'm Dr. Sanders, and you have the chance to convince me to remove this dress code rule. You gotta convince me now. So what's wrong with it? Why wouldn't you wear tan and white?*
A: *Cuz it's a lot of other things to choose from.*
Q: *Okay, then I would say, but you come to school to learn, so why does it matter?*
A: *(Exasperated facial expression, sigh) Cuz the clothes...cuz being creative helps you be better in school.*
Q: *How?*
A: *People feel better about theyself.*

Almost directly out of Asante, Welsh, and even Ladson-Billings' work, Kwame expressed the notion that his aesthetic sensibility was important to his dignity, creativity, and intellectual performance (e.g., Ladson-Billings, 1994). He connected his appearance to his personal dynamism, and his dynamism to his scholastic performance, each positively affecting the other. Here again, Kwame expressed the importance of connecting the exterior to the interior, in this case looking good aesthetically to shine in his classes. In the African worldview, we should be on the inside what we appear to be on the outside and vice versa.

Kwame maintained his academic resolve despite feeling aesthetically bored by the school uniform through strong focus, just as Ture and Talib focused on their school goals in spite of class disruptions. Interestingly, though, more closely resembling Ture's response yet again, Kwame's answer to racism was not simply to ignore it but to make a judgment about it and continue moving forward.

Q: *Do you think you will experience [racism] in the future?*
A: *Maybe.*
Q: *Maybe, why?*
A: *Cuz a lot of people still are racist.*
Q: *How do you know? You've never experienced it.*
A: *Cuz people told me about it.*
Q: *People like who?*
A: *This lady, umm, at my, at the daycare for my sister.*
Q: *Anybody else?*
A: *My mom.*
Q: *What did the daycare lady say? What did she talk about, or what was the racism that happened?*
A: *It was this White lady. She was walkin, and she was talkin about these little girls, the lady's daughters, and she was talkin about they was White and we was Black, and they was better than us.*
Q: *What did your mom say?*
A: *Don't be like that, she said because without Martin Luther King we would probably still be slaves.*
Q: *Alright, when you hear stuff like that, like what the daycare lady was saying and what your mom says about racism still happening and stuff, what do you think about when you hear that?*
A: *That it shouldn't be like that. It's wrong. Just because we a different color.*

Kwame's perception of racism more closely resembled Ture's in that he assumed a deeper role in responding to it than simply walking away or turning a blind eye. Not only did he maintain his hopefulness by "not caring about what they say," he also believed that racists are wrong in their thinking and discrimination against others, and decided that they should act differently. Having learned about racism from his mother and others, Kwame began to conceptualize racism and the effect it might have on him (e.g., underemployment). Like the boys discussed before him, Kwame was wise to racism and discrimination existing, and, unlike Talib who was less conscious, if and when the issue arose he knew what his position about it would be. The reality of racism to Ture, Talib and Kwame all the same is one that they hope to claim victory over through their scholarship and family stability as men.

Chapter 7: Assata

Achiever 4, Assata (pronounced uh-so-tah, short 'o')

The narrative of the first female student interviewed, Assata, sets the tone for what is to come from the other two female achievers. The girls demonstrated more impassioned opinions and cadences than did the boys. The girls also communicated with more body language toward teachers, peers, and me during interviews. Significant differences were also found in their perceptions about gender roles and sexism, with the females being more concerned for girls' freedom and boys' responsible actions. Still, given the shared locale and culture of these children, the girls' opinions, feelings, and actions align closely with their fellow male achievers.

Assata, a seventh grader who received high academic and behavioral marks from her teachers, also believed in the promise of school achievement, importance of family, existence of racism, and the need to have determination above and beyond external distractions or stressors. Like Ture and Kwame, she believed that self-awareness and respect for the Black community is key to her values and life success. Full of humor and independence, she expressed her opinions and feelings with more flare and frequency in school. Assata lived with her mother and siblings at the time of this study (two or more siblings, as indicated by Assata's use of the plural tense). Her mother worked often and was available to her for short periods of time at night—that is if Assata was awake to visit with her.

She and Ture were first cousins, which was in many ways helpful to the study as Assata elaborated on influential family beliefs and traditions that Ture only touched on. The two children did not live together, and both expressed that they tended not to get along or interact with each other much. Their estrangement was partially due to strong personality differences, with Ture being more introverted and Assata extroverted. Assata also felt that their family compared them and praised him more. Ture was much more serious or mature, and studious (e.g., having higher grades, stricter work habits, maintaining firm boundaries with teachers, etc.), while Assata was more flippant and concerned with how her family perceived her. Similarities in their responses are evident, but so are differences.

Assata's teachers scolded her regularly for her quick-wit comebacks and calculating rhetorical questions. Sometimes bordering on bothersome and near surpassing the line between smart and insubordinate, Assata often engaged in debate with her teachers; or rather the teachers engaged her. A precocious and intelligent girl, Assata was able to maintain balance between respecting her role as a student worker (as the students viewed school as a place to work for vested returns) and living out her truth regarding the absurdities of American society and schooling.

Her "say it plain" attitude did not afford her the same rule-bending allowances from staff that was afforded the more deferential or muted boys above though. Teachers were often caught rolling their eyes at her quick responses. Fortunately, Assata was usually able to check her body language and verbal responses before reaching the point of punitive action, such as detention or mockery from teachers in front of the class. A fervent follower of school rules such as the dress code, class, and work schedules, her teachers praised her more often than not. She was simply bent on maintaining her integrity and being clear about her identity en route to achieving her goals. For this, she is a Black student achiever.

Research Question One

When asked what kids need to do to achieve in school, Assata's thoughts turned to teacher and parental influences on student achievement as well as students' independent roles.

> Q: *What are some things that kids need to do to do well in school?*
> A: *Their work, listen to their teachers, ignore their teachers' rude comments….umm, and I guess listen to their parents if their parents aren't ignorant.*
> Q: *Two things you just said there make me wanna ask some other questions. What are some examples, what do you mean by rude comments by teachers?*
> A: *I mean when they try to be sarcastic, and they think it's funny when it's not really funny...They try to get away with it you know, but you always feel it, you always feel it.*
> Q: *And by ignorant parents, what do you mean by that?*
> A: *Like, if they just aren't good parents and they just do dumb things for stupid reasons. Like if you bring home a bad grade and you show a parent and they don't do nothin about it, they're ignorant.*
> Q: *So good parents check on their kids' grades...*
> A: *Yeah.*
> Q: *And if they have bad grades then they do something about it.*
> A: *Yeah.*
> Q: *What?*
> A: *Like, nothing, not violence or whatever but you know like normal stuff. Like they take away their phones and computer and all that stuff.*

Similar to her achieving peers above, Assata believed that students are responsible for acting studiously and that studiousness meant completing their schoolwork, getting good grades, and listening to their teachers. However, her response went beyond the will and behavior of students to achieve to pointing out that teachers and parents sometimes subtract from student achievement when they are degrading or passive. Assata understood that permissive parents and rude, irritable, or sarcastic teachers can undermine student achievement. Therefore, young people must be assertive in separating the good from the bad in the adults around them.

While kids should be studious and mind their elders, kids should discount bad authority as they pursue their goals, even if it means noncompliance in school. Adults should be able to see the merit in Assata's position. Teachers *should* be positive and supportive of students, and parents should set high expectations and be firm with their children about them. Poor grades should not be accepted without lecture and/or punishment from parents. Parents of Black children especially should set the expectations and rules to be followed in school, and teachers should help children meet the expectations and guidelines set at home.

Q: Why do you work hard to make good grades in school?
A: Because...well, I don't like to be compared to Ture, and Ture gets good grades, so I feel that I have to get good grades. That way I'm not compared to him in a bad way.
Q: Ture of course is your cousin and he gets good grades too.
A: Yeah.
Q: So people compare you to him, and so it sounds like what you're saying is people say negative things about you and positive things about him.
A: Yep, yep.
Q: And your grades are an area that you can sort of be good [in], too.
A: Yeah.
Q: People, who compares you?
A: My family compares me a lot.
Q: So is it important to you what they think?
A: Somewhat, like, some parts of the family, but some parts are just being ignorant so I just don't listen.

Living up to family expectations and being viewed positively by them was the most salient factor in Assata's daily school experiences. Her hopefulness and contentment were deeply connected to her family's happiness with her. A successful career, legacy, and riches ranked second to her personal and family joy. As she stated, a successful life is apparent when you are "doing what you want to do, and what you're happy doing." Although she was unsure of her exact career choice, Assata did know that receiving favorable impressions from her family made her happy, and she valued peace over money or fame.

Q: *What makes someone's life a success story?*
A: *Well, a successful person...like people that look happy and that actually are happy, not people that act like they're happy just because they want people to talk about them.*
Q: *So people who grow up, or adults who are happy...and are doing what makes them happy. You mean like in work?*
A: *Yeah.*
Q: *Their job, okay. So it's not like, "ugh," you roll out of bed and go "ugh, I gotta go to work. I hate my job."*
A: *Yeah, yeah!*

While it may be assumed that these achievers have expectations of compensation following years of high school, college, or graduate training, Assata made no mention of material possessions or monetary wealth in her definition of a successful life, and the boys interviewed before her also viewed "rich and successful" as a phrase encompassing far more than money. Assata espoused a sense of graciousness toward life and its many blessings. She was conscientious about the fact that tomorrow is not promised and therefore focusing only on physical conditions or luxuries would be incomplete. Each of achievers so far presented understood that success is determined by qualitative conditions such as stability, harmony, happiness, career satisfaction, family pride, and peace of mind before material comfort. Assata in her feminine wisdom seems even clearer on this point, however.

Q: *What do you hope for?*
A: *I hope to be able to, like, live to actually get a successful life or whatever, and I hope that all my plans work out.*
Q: *What are your plans?*
A: *Well, I'm not sure how I'm gonna get rich or whatever, but I wanna be rich and well known. I don't wanna be rich and famous...cuz paparazzi just won't even let you go to the bathroom. (Laughter) So, I just wanna be rich and well known, and I have to fulfill all of my granny's plans...So I have to have two kids, a boy and a girl...and then...Yeah, yeah.*
Q: *Why is it important to be rich?*
A: *Cuz, like, I don't wanna be necessarily rich, but I wanna have money so I don't haveta, like, struggle and go check-to-check.*
Q: *Okay, got it. Why is it important to be well-known?*
A: *Because, like, if I'm not well-known, and that, like depending on what choice, or what career I choose to take, then that might cut down on my whole "I wanna have some money" thing, so, like, I wanna be well-known so, like, you know, if I just appear on, like, some little bench on this corner or whatever, people will actually know me.*

Notable is Assata's consideration of social esteem for professional promotion. By the seventh grade, Assata had figured out that being a successful professional requires social capital or prominence. She wants to be eminent so as to maintain a clientele base and stable income, not necessarily to impress the world with celebrity status. Assata simply hopes to escape a life of struggle in adulthood, not to be the most materially rich in the nation. The family connectedness that Assata feels is linked to her goals and values, as she refers to fulfilling her granny's plans.

Q: *What do you want to be when you grow up?*
A: *Well I've narrowed it down to a few choices, like a doctor, a lawyer, a judge, or a chef.*
Q: *So a well-known lawyer, a judge, or a chef.*
A: *Or a doctor, yeah. But the other night I was thinking that I really wanna be a chef, but I'm not sure my granny would be okay with that because she thinks that it's a waste of my brains, but I'm like, I don't know yet...doctor sounds nice right now so I'm not sure yet.*

Assata wants to make her family proud, and like her male counterparts, she also wants to have and care for her own children one day. As early as the sixth, seventh, and eighth grades, these African American youth living at or close to the poverty line are expressing an advanced understanding of social capital and the qualities of life that school success and money in the modern world can bring. Their values, goals, strivings, and beliefs stem from multiple sources, predominately family, racial-ethnic identity, and cultural values.

Q: *What are the values and beliefs that you live your life by?*
A: *As far as values go I think, like, I treat others the way I wanna be treated. I don't [always] do that but I think about it. And, like, beliefs...I believe in God or whatever, and I believe that people should, that you shouldn't judge people you know, and if you have something to say to somebody don't just say it behind their back. Like, say it to their face.*

As her answers to the first research question reveals, Assata knowingly or unknowingly embraced many African cultural values, such as those deeply embedded in Maat principles (Asante, 2000). Assata's belief that people should be transparent, honest, and considerate of the rights and feelings of others calls forth the principle of reciprocity and closely resembles the purpose of the Anubis scale in the Kemetic Judgment Hall of Ausar (called Osiris by the Greeks), in which the amount of iniquity in the heart of the dead should weigh no more than a feather lest it be barred from the paradise of the afterlife. Not one to be easily dejected, influenced, or hoodwinked, Assata was more conscious of African American cultural influences on her thinking and acting than her peers above, as the rest of her narrative shows.

Research Question Two

Although her grandmother was not especially keen on Assata's desire to be a chef, the career goal was actually born from watching her mother and grandmother cook. She began to cook "once [she] got old enough" to try out her family's recipes. She enjoyed that her food "started to come out pretty good," although not as good as her granny's food. She also liked the trial and error that came with making food taste good. Like Ture and Talib, Assata's career choice was based on skill, enjoyment, and the interests of family role models. Unperturbed by challenges, like Ture and Talib again, she noted areas that needed improvement, such as staying focused on cooking despite distractions from television, and she worked at it. She was determined to master the culinary arts. As she stated, "I'm very confident. I think I can do it. I think I can do whatever I want if I put my mind to it." With her family bonds, career goal linked to her personal talents, and sense of determination, Assata was right to feel confident.

> Q: *What makes you so confident?*
> A: *Well… if I think about it, I think I can be like a lawyer or a doctor or a judge or a chef cuz I'm good at those things…I can be a judge because, like, I don't let…I don't like to let the bad guy go. And I can be a lawyer because…if I know somebody's tellin the truth then I'll defend that person. I don't want them to just be gettin in trouble for somebody else's mistake. And like I can be a chef because I'm just good at cookin. I'm just good like that.*
> Q: *So you think that you just sort of naturally have these gifts.*
> A: *Yeah.*

Assata's confidence was heightened after she identified personal strengths and linked those strengths to potential career choices (that suited her and her family). In turn, she was further motivated to perform well academically, resulting in a psycho-emotional cycle that spawns her school confidence and achievement. When asked whether anything could stand in her way, she referenced her mother's identifying impatience as a potential barrier to her goal achievement. Assata's respect for and connectedness with her family enabled her to consider personal weaknesses they pointed out. Humbly, Assata expressed that she "didn't believe [that she could be impatient] at first, but [she has] grown to believe it." As a result, she began to consciously work on being more patient, using irritations with her siblings as practice.

Her mother, grandmother, and family friends supported her academic efforts. Like Ture, Talib, and Kwame's supporters, Assata's family and community elders expected her to "reach high goals" and do well in life. Their support was indicated frequently and in multiple settings, such as within the family and at her "granny's job" where coworkers cheered her on. Unsurprisingly, Assata named her "family members" as her role models. Her top role model, Auntie Mijiza, was selected for the following reason:

> *Cuz... she's a good parent and stuff, and you see that she takes care of her kids and they're, like, well-disciplined when she's around and stuff. She works hard and...her job sucks, but she stays there to get the money...She does what she has to do.*

Assata was impressed by the agency and resiliency her aunt deployed to provide for herself and her children. The idea that it is sometimes necessary to accept dissatisfying work as a means to an end was evident in her response. Assata also respected the fact that her aunt disciplined her children. She not only provided for them, but she was developing them as good people. Assata's paternal and maternal grandmothers were also ideal role models to her.

> *Q: Why do you look up to those two people?*
> *A: I look up to my grandma Lorean because she, like, she understands and she keeps her...even though she's all sick and whatever she still keeps going and whatever. So she never really gives up and stuff.*
> *Q: And granny?*
> *A: And I think I look up to her because like...she's outspoken, and...if something's wrong with her and whatever she doesn't like to keep it bottled in. She likes to tell people.*

Like her Aunt Mijiza, Assata views her grandmother and great-grandmother as role models largely for their resilience. She looked up to her great-grandmother also for her courage and voice. Despite having a difficult job and being sick and elderly, Assata's auntie and grandmothers have remained mentally strong, disciplined and above the high waters of their rainy days. The women have also contributed positively to their family. The family scenarios that Assata was most impacted by were congruous with her tenacity in school as she continuously progressed in school while maintain her dignity despite sometimes-discouraging teachers and a depressing school building.

Much like her male counterparts, her family's influence was extended to the school setting through her, as "the bridge." Assata's mother checked to make sure homework got done but had no relationships with her teachers or school administrators.

Q: *Do your family and school ever come together?*
A: *Somewhat, I guess...when she's not too tired from work and them nasty kids at her job, [my mom] tries to, like, help and ask if I have homework and how my day has been and stuff like that. So that's all.*
Q: *But not really coming here, or...*
A: *No, she threatens to come up here, but then like something gets fixed so she doesn't.*
Q: *So only when it's something, a problem...*
A: *Like, not [only] when it's a problem, but just because, just to show up, just because.*
Q: *You mean like a surprise to you, to check-in and see what you're doing sorta thing?*
A: *Yeah, she likes to do that, but, like, she'll call and then they'll call me down to the office and that'll be all scary and then it'll just be her like, "Oh, how's your day going so far?"*

The support given by Assata's mother depicts a constructive parent-child relationship that did not include a parent-school connection. An interesting addition to the boys' expression of their parents checking on their homework or sometimes helping them with school projects at home, Assata's mother also took preventive measures by checking in on her in school. As far as she and her family were concerned, though, home and school were entirely separate realms, with school being a distant, often incongruent place from community activity, family beliefs, and personal attitudes. Beyond monitoring her academic progress and behavior, Assata felt her mother had no reason to visit her school or bond with school staff or administrators as she preferred not to associate with them herself unless necessary. School for these families is connected to the student and family only through its utility in the students' goal-pursuit.

Whereas her male counterparts seemed unaware, or perhaps subconsciously aware of the ways in which being African American had influenced them, Assata was more awake. Interestingly, school as the primary institution for personal growth in American society had done little to shape their goal-setting, values, or beliefs. Racism as a social construct, school as a hotbed of institutional racism, and culture as a living process had significantly shaped their understanding of the world around them.

Q: *Do any of these goals come from you being African American? The goals you said earlier, family [having] a boy and a girl, [being] rich, [having] a good job that makes you happy, and be[ing] well-known...*

A: *Yeah, and I have to look out for some people, but that's probably not important.*

Q: *Who are those people?*

A: *Well, my old hairdresser. She said that every time she did my hair I owe her $25, and I lost track...*

Q: *(Laughter) So you wanna pay some people back.*

A: *So when I get older she says that I need to buy her a live-in maid, which I don't think's gonna happen, but I mean I might have to send somebody over there to go clean up once in a while.*

Q: *Well that would be nice of you. I'm gonna guess she was jokin though.*

A: *Yeah, no she wasn't (laughter). And I have to keep track of my granny because she said she'll go to a nursing home, but I gotta come get her every single weekend...just cuz. And she said she want me to do some pop-up visits in there to make sure they changing all her sheets...make sure stuff's clean.*

Q: *Sure, sure. Do any of those goals come from you being African American?*

A: *I think a few of them do.*

Q: *Which ones?*

A: *Like takin care of my granny. I don't see much, I don't see a lot of White people actually thinkin of that...just like takin care of my family and payin people back. White people don't think about that. Not the White people I know...not most of them.*

Q: *Okay, so you think your...valuing family so much, and lookin out for each other and things...*

A: *Yeah.*

Q: *That really is a sort of a hallmark of the African American community?*

A: *Yeah, yeah.*

Being African American means having extended family networks, having a sense of family connectedness, honoring obligations to family, and giving back to the community through the profits of your work. As Assata made lucid throughout her interview, her African American cultural orientation is key to understanding her success in school.

Assata believed that being both African American and *female* significantly shaped her family values. She expressed for example, "I think that the whole family thing is mostly for girls. Like, I mean guys want families, too, but I don't think they actually think about it." Assata, and perhaps many others, would be surprised to learn that her achieving African American male counterparts also envisioned their current and future families benefiting from their success. Taking care of business was important to the boys in this study because *family business* was central to them. Nonetheless, Assata placed boys and girls in specific gender role categories in which girls are believed to be more family-oriented than boys, and boys, or at least Black boys, are stereotypical sports lovers with limited intellect.

> *Q: Do you think you have a different type or amount of hope to reach your goals because you are a girl?*
> *A: Nooo, I mean boys have their little amount of goals and whatever, but their goals are dumb. Like, "Oh, I'm gonna go be a basketball player." I'm, like, alright, soon as you break your leg I'm gone see you on the corner askin for a dime, alright, so yeah...*
> *Q: (Laughter) Well, wait a minute though, because your answer kind of is yes, you think you have a different type...*
> *A: (Laughter) I guess, but, like, I just think that my goals are more realistic than boys'. Or some boys, because my cousins they're smart (smacked lips).*

Assata viewed most African American boys as lacking vision and common sense. Black boys, according to Assata limited their potential for success to professional sports. Her male cousins were exceptionally "smart" for their use of mental prowess and goal-setting—and actually multi-goal-setting. According to Assata, realistic goals are those that limit reliance on physical stamina and offer greater probability of occurrence—therefore professional sports as a single goal is ineffective and "dumb." Smart future planning includes multiple professional options. True to Assata's statement of her male cousins, Ture expressed to me that arthritis could be an obstacle to his career goal, and that possibility was reason enough for him to have multiple career ideas rather than rely solely on becoming an architect. Assata of course, was considering four different options, each in line with her values and skills.

The attitudes that these achievers carried were instilled in them almost exclusively by their families and community, not through positive school experiences.

> *Q: What is it you think about you and your cousins that even the boys have smart, realistic goals?*
> *A: Well...it's like the bloodline, and...knowing each other and knowing our parents and knowing how things are.*
> *Q: Things are...like what?*

A: *Like I can talk to my [older] cousins and they'll be realistic and whatever. They won't just lie and whatever. Like, we can joke around and whatever, but when you actually wanna have those serious conversations I can actually talk to them.*

Without question, all of the participants thus far had strong family connections, and in turn family members were major sources of academic motivation outside of their own fortitude. Family values have been underscored as each achiever talked about their own beliefs and values of spirituality and "getting good jobs," for example. Naturally the achievers had received developmental lessons from their families and communities that encouraged them in school, but also "hipped them" to social and cultural issues that might effect them. Based on her previous expressions of distinct African American values, Assata's last statement likely refers to family discussions of critical social, family, and professional issues. Undoubtedly, Assata and Ture's self-cultural awareness and social conscientiousness came largely from elder family members talking to younger ones, and the younger family talking cousin-to-cousin.

Not to be forgotten, their larger ethnic community also inspired them. The Afrocentric family structures described by the participants is noticeable. In addition to two-parent households, some lived within an extended family network, where close relatives, friends of the family, and neighbors took part in raising and encouraging them. Ture and Assata especially referred to their entire family equally, without emphasis on so-called biological degrees of closeness. They also understood their connection to Africa and the general African or Black community in a way that the other achievers seemed not to as yet. Importantly, Assata and Ture's higher levels of social and self-cultural knowledge correlates with the fact that they were two of the highest achieving students in the school, and among the most articulate regarding their identities and life goals.

Research Question Three

Even with a higher level of ethnic consciousness than many youth her age, self-identity for Assata as an African American child focused first on dispelling the validity of racism. Her initial response to what it means to be African American had far less to do with ethnic history and culture than it did with reaction against racism.

Q: *What does it mean to you to be African American?*
A: *It means that your skin is colored. That's it. Honestly I don't think there's much of a difference. It doesn't really matter what color you are and whatever. I mean I just think that some people are better than other people and that has nothing to do with what color you are.*

Q: Well, I'm not asking you to compare yourself to anyone, but just what it means to you to be African American.

A: Well to me it means that you've suffered. Like your culture has suffered, and that you should try to be better just because you're like...African Americans have suffered so much that you should try to be better just because.

So enthralled in discourses and lived experiences involving racism and oppression are Assata and her peers as African American youth that their first impression of their racial-ethnic identity is either confused or defensive against racism, rather than ones of pro-culture, traditions, interests, etc. It is true that Black people have endured oppression and struggle, but it is also true, and important for Black children to know that there has been achievement, global contribution, traditional customs, and beliefs in their community, in both ancient and recent history. Despite having a greater sense of self than Talib and Kwame, Assata's identity development remains peripheral because she has been trained in a Eurocentric society and school system. Even her high achieving and rather conscious cousin Ture defined himself first by color.

Most of the achievers were gravely uncomfortable in their identity, confused as to how to perceive themselves. The outcome can never be positive when culture and racial-ethnic identity are lost in an effort to downplay race or assert an anti-racist position (e.g., "Being Black doesn't mean anything because we should all be treated the same."). This is not to say that antiracist ideologies are wrong for Black youth to have, but rather that reactionary stances toward racism and Eurocentrism cannot be their primary or only foundation for which to stand on if health, lifelong achievement and peace of mind is the goal.

On a more hopeful note, the definitions thus far offered have at least combined physical and cultural descriptors of what it means to be African American. These responses, along with the social issues of racism raised, indicate ideas of racial-ethnic identity that are primed for growth amongst these junior high school students. In this there is reason to hope even more as these youth strive to complete high school and college, and withstand any obstacles in the job market. Analyses of the first four interviews alone indicate that the more nuanced the self-definition response has been, the more positive and influential culture has been named. And the clearer the students have been about their self-concepts and appreciation, the more comfortable they have been with themselves in their decisions and responses to difficult issues. If only the achievers possessed greater self-cultural and historical knowledge, we would also witness even higher self-confidences and developed visions of the future.

Q: *Let's pretend that I am only seven years old and I have a second grade homework assignment to learn about Africa and African American history. If I asked you to help me, what are some things that you would you tell me?*

A: *Well, I think I'd, like, help them on the computer and whatever, and I'll just look up Africa, or I'll just go to my social studies book or something dependin on what exactly they needed. Or I'd go on the computer and whatever, and I'd read this article to them, and if they still didn't understand it, I'd break it down into, like, what's what and answer their questions and stuff.*

Q: *So you've answered my next question of what would we do...but what would you tell me? Just off the top of your head.*

A: *Off the top of my head I would tell...I'd just be like, "Well that's where you came from!" and I would move deeper into it.*

Q: *So what would you tell me about African American history?*

A: *Well, I would say that there were a lot of great African Americans who actually helped the USA a lot or whatever, and they like all, they helped build our country and stuff, so don't underestimate us and stuff like that.*

Q: *Examples. Who are these great African Americans?*

A: *I'd throw out a few people like Thurgood Marshall, and umm, I'd say that, umm, an African, like an African like founded Chicago, and I'd throw in a few things like that.*

Q: *Anything else? Anybody else you could think of?*

A: *Jackie Robinson, Jessie umm...Jessie Owens. Yeah, and a few other people. Just like, off the top of my head, inventors that I knew...*

Q: *You know what I'm very surprised about right now? You didn't say Martin Luther King, Jr.*

A: *Well, he's like the first [person] that comes to mind, but I just didn't bring him up because it's just really tired. I mean, you always, every time you think of, umm, Black History Month, Michael Jackson pops up—I mean not Michael Jackson, but Martin Luther King pops up, and it's like, uhh, aren't we, like, overdoing this just a little bit? I mean he did really great things, and I'm really happy for all he did and whatever, but still like sometimes you haveta think about the other people.*

Q: *That's not all we got.*

A: *Yeah.*

Q: *Anything else you would tell me? You know, maybe you don't know the specifics, but you think it's important for me to know about Africa and African American history.*

A: *I'd have to make sure you knew what part of the globe it's on. Cuz some teachers just be ignorant and don't be wantin to tell you. So...*

Q: Anything else?
A: I mean, we might go to the library, get some books. We might go to, like, older people and ask them...if they knew and whatever.

Assata explicitly connected African Americans to Africa and expressed having a greater sense of confidence to succeed from knowing the achievements and trials triumphed over by the larger African community. Not only did she articulate the importance of knowing your history and heritage, but also of understanding one's geographical and cultural *location*. This is a truly Afrocentric concept relevant to Africans across the Diaspora who have been displaced from their ancestral and cultural origins, voluntarily or involuntarily. Assata explains how her Afrocentric orientation served to influence her goal-setting and determination in this next round of questions.

Q: How does being African American influence you?
A: Well, like, it influences me because our culture is, like, all messed up and whatever. It influences me to like show, like, the White people that...we're not all that bad and whatever. Like you see all these celebrities, like Tiger Woods. We're not all like him, so I'd like to stand out just to like prove them wrong. Like all Black people aren't like this. So...
Q: Okay, interesting. What's really interesting about what you just said is that I know that some time ago, I don't know if he changed his statement, but Tiger Woods said he wasn't African American. He said he wasn't Black.
A: Yeah, I really, I don't even listen to him anymore. Ever since they said he was some kinda sex addict I just stopped listening. So I don't care if he ever was Black or not, because, like, some people still think that he is Black regardless of what he said or not, but I just wanna prove, like, some people wrong, like, "Hey we're not all like him or whatever, so don't just believe what you see on TV."
Q: So what it means to you to be African American, umm, you kinda talked about the history right, our culture...
A: Yeah.
Q: So you think about that in your own identity, in yourself...
A: Mm-hmm.
Q: How does being African American affect what you hope for?
A: Well, I think it makes me want to do better, because... (silence)...(frowning)
Q: That's okay, I think you just said it...
A: Yeah, basically, that's it.

Congruent with the antiracist sentiments so deeply embedded in her identity, succeeding in school and life is as much a testament of Black worth as it is a personal and family need. Assata's success as an African American person, even in adolescence, is important as an act of educating White people of true Black heritage, culture, and abilities. The idea was that true knowledge of history and culture would help to end or weaken racism. Through her achievement, more Black people would know that they are also capable, and Whites would have less fear, dislike or hatred toward the community at large. In addition to the continuing theme of justice, a collectivist orientation is again illustrated here as Assata, a seventh grader, feels responsible for righting the wrongs of an adult African American celebrity for the sake of representing all African people well. These are profound insights and responsibilities taken by a seventh grader.

Overall, Assata's perception of her heritage, from Africa to America, was positive and informed. She understood that the past is important to the present, a simply stated but critical notion still lost on so many. Her strategy for gaining knowledge regarding African and African American history was multimodal and contextually varied, from her schoolbooks to the Internet to the knowledge and understanding of community elders. She sought information regarding her racial-ethnic history beyond the miniscule amount of information taught in school. She raised rarely spoken spirits and names of a proud African and African American history, including Jean Baptiste Pointe du Sable, the Haitian-born businessman and founder of a then prosperous Chicago, Illinois, as well as skilled athletes, intellectuals, artists, and activists such as Jackie Robinson, Jessie Owens, and Thurgood Marshall. The fact is that her self-knowledge afforded her a positive image of herself and her community, including her broken city of Cleveland. It is no wonder that she was as hopeful, successful, and socially secure in school as she was.

Yet, the sad ironies of self-pride and assuredness on one hand, and dejected ethnic origins on the other continued with Assata. Like her peers, her perception of Africa was limited and stereotypical, even negative. Only time will tell what impact the confusion between Western portrayals of Africa and the truth about her history will have on her as she learns more and more about the mis-education and training that she has been rationed.

Q: When you think about Africa what comes to your mind?
A: Dirty.
Q: Okay.
A: I'm sorry, it just comes to mind (Nervous laughter).
Q: You know what, I'm not judging what you say, and you know what? You're not the only person that said that, so that's okay...just say what you think.

> A: Like, dirty, but...we still have, like the people over there still have hopes and dreams and stuff. So, like, I respect them and whatever, but it's still dirty, so...
>
> Q: Anything else comes to...?
>
> A: Like, when I think of Africa I think of the little shape of the continent...And I think of, like...when the boat came over there and just took all those people. I think of that too.
>
> Q: So you think about slavery.
>
> A: Nodded.

Though limited and in many ways negative, Assata's thoughts regarding Africa retained a sense of connectedness, belief in victory, and pride. The only conclusion to be made is that this connectedness, belief, and pride came from self- and community-education, not from school (Assata referenced for instance that some teachers refused to teach about Africa.). From the first question she demonstrated her readiness for using critical thinking with regard to school. Regardless of what she saw or heard, Assata showed that she is culturally centered enough to withstand stereotypes and negative images of her people—as far as she knows the lies from the truths.

More clearly than Talib and Kwame's responses to this question, Assata indicated a lack of awareness of Africa rather than a flawed or self-hating ideological perception. In other words, while she saw Africa as dirty, she understood clearly her connection to Africa as well as African' victimization by the European slave system. She used "we" when she talked about Africans having "hopes and dreams." She sought to locate Africa physically and spiritually. Assata was sure of herself academically, proud of herself racial-ethnically, family oriented, adept at problem-solving and determined to succeed in life. These constitute a profound combination and one that predicts a bright and hopeful future. She was not particularly proud of her school or connected to her teachers though, and her independence from them ironically helped to serve her well.

Research Question Four

Assata's appreciation of Justice Academy was either circumstantial or relative to how the conditions at her school could be worse. Like all three of the boys above, she first and foremost acknowledged learning. Socializing with peers was her second source of school enjoyment.

> Q: What is it like for you to go to your school?
>
> A: It's okay. I mean...it's calmer now, I think, cuz a lot less people are here. And I'm happy with my class size...
>
> Q: Okay, because it's smaller now.
>
> A: Yeah. And it's like, the teacher can pay more attention to me and stuff.

As we learned earlier that she recognized much of her education came from sources outside of school, Assata's focus was on meeting her goals rather than bonding with her teachers or growing as a person with their support. Concordantly, the two positives Assata offered paled in comparison to her list of grievances and sense of disconnectedness. For example, she felt her teachers were often wrong, and she liked pointing it out whenever she could.

Q: What do you like about your school?
A: I like the fact that I get to prove people wrong...like if a teacher messes up on something I like to be the one that catch[es] it, and if I'm not here then it's, like, oh well, I can't catch it now.
Q: Do you argue with teachers? Are you saying arguing or just being smart?
A: (Laughter) Noooo, I don't necessarily argue. They get the impression that I argue, but I don't argue. I just try to prove them wrong—because they are wrong.
Q: Okay, and it sounds like they're not, you don't think they're the most positive teachers...
A: I mean, they alright, there are some positive teachers, but certain teachers are just really just...not very...good.

What should strike readers here is the difference in respect and admiration with which Assata spoke of her teachers versus her family and community members. Connecting this response to her revelation that she and her peers are receiving diluted education regarding African American history and heritage, and her repeated referencing of succeeding in the face of White racism indicates that Assata's attitude toward her teachers is enveloped in a sense of discontentment with their pedagogy and the culture of American society generally. For example, she was discontented with the fact that Martin Luther King, Jr. was made to represent all of Black History Month and that teachers refused to discuss the continent of Africa. To the contrary, where she felt connected to and supported by adults in her family and community, Assata wanted not to prove them wrong, but right.

Assata was "in the know" regarding the multiple layers of African American history, and she was disgruntled about attempts to silence the voice of history; disgruntled, but not dissuaded from her determination to succeed. As a result of her intelligence and cultural consciousness, she seemed to have a sharper sense of her school as a hostile territory.

Q: What do you not like about it?
A: Umm, it's stressful, and boring and lazy and tiresome and it smells funny.

Q: Okay, I think you can stop there! (Laughter) Why stressful?

A: It's stressful because you haveta get up and all that. And then you gotta come and then most of the time you get yelled at about, from some teacher, and for no apparent reason...

Q: A lot of yellin at this school.

A: Yes, a lot of yelling, a lot of yelling.

Q: Okay, we're gonna come back to that. So that's where it's stressful?

A: Yeah.

Q: Boring?

A: Boring...like after a while you get used to the yelling and stuff, and then you're like, uhh, it's kinda boring now because you're all immune to the yelling, like you really don't care if they yell anymore or whatever so it's like oh, it's like the same routine and then it gets boring.

Q: Tiresome?

A: Tiresome because it's like so much work to get up and come here. Like if I was doin something better, you know like goin somewhere fun instead of this place, it would be better...

Q: And it's just the fact that you're getting up to come somewhere that you don't really like to be.

A: No, because then you come and just, it's the teachers and they all look cranky. It's like ugh.

Q: What's lazy about it?

A: Because sometimes, like, it's just like, you'd ask a question and it's just like, oh, you're just gonna sit there at your desk and just not answer? It's like, umm and then they just like yell at you from the desk. And I'm like, yeah umm (smacked lips), if you had got up you wouldn't have to raise your voice so high. And then the next day they come with a sore throat talkin 'bout some, "uhh, I'm losing my voice," and you know, you know just last night they was just out somewhere partyin! You know it, but you don't wanna say anything cuz they're the teacher and that'd be wrong or whatever. But you know it.

Q: How do you know it? (Laughter)

A: Because you can look in their eyes...

Q: Maybe they're just tired from work...

A: They're not, no. It's not the work, it's not the work. I don't know how, I think I just have an eye for things.

Assata described a schooling environment that would make any child's ability to maintain hopefulness extremely difficult. Constant experiences with unmotivated, detached, and hyper-vigilant teachers required a degree of self-confidence in these African American achievers that superseded any assault to their personal sense of worth and ability.

For Ture, Talib, and Kwame, the consequence seemed to be an acquired callus, or immunity as Assata expressed it, to the school environment in general. For Black children not yet hardened, and even for those who are to varying degrees, family and community support are critical to their coping and achievement in school. Assata again articulated what her male counterparts referenced implicitly.

> Q: *How do you keep hope about doing well in school...going to college, all those things, even though you got these teachers who are yelling, who are umm...you know, you've got these teachers who you don't think are very good?*
>
> A: *I'd say that the majority of my hope comes from, like, every now and then when I just feel all bad because the teacher done kicked me out of the classroom for some idiotic reason that was not my fault, I usually just go and I get like, I go to my great granny house and...I go like to the attic and like some of her old photo albums and just look through there. And I look at some of their old little high school and college degrees and stuff, then it's like, hmmm, man, mines is gonna be in this book right next to this person's. And if it's not, it's not gonna be my fault for it.*
>
> Q: *So your great grandmother keeps, like a photo album, with diplomas in it and pictures...[of your] aunts, uncles...*
>
> A: *Yeah.*

Discernment seems to be a skill among these youth, especially Assata and Ture, as they navigate between the divergent worlds of home and school. Racism and cultural dislocation require that Black children be able to decipher which messages and interactions in school are helpful and which are harmful. They must also decide on responses that will assist them in their goal-pursuit rather than delay or derail them. Assata indicated not only the gift of discernment, but also the skill of perspective taking, which she employed to succeed in school and maintain her peace.

> Q: *But what about being in school though? When you're in class...?*
>
> A: *Like when I'm in class, I just think, like, I be there...and I can say like certain classes I treat them like I'm texting. And I know that sounds like really confusing, because I told my mom the same thing...*
>
> Q: *Well explain it to me.*
>
> A: *But, like, when you're texting, like if somebody sends you something...if I text them back I think about how they're gonna read it and what they're gonna think about that because I know this person or whatever. So when I'm in class, and if I think about doing something [then] I think about the people that it may affect, and I think about how they would feel about it.*

> *Q: And when you say the people, do you mean specifically your teachers, your peers...your...who?*
>
> *A: Nah, man, I don't even care about the teachers. Nah.*
>
> *Q: Okay, I got it. So you focus on, more on your family, your own goals and things than the teachers yelling, and the...*
>
> *A: Yeah because, like, as far as I'm concerned, like, they already have their degree so as far as I'm concerned, I'm here to get mine...so they can just be quiet.*
>
> *Q: Okay, got it. But I've seen you around class, so I know you're not disrespectful. I know teachers, you know, like you well enough, and so...but I think I understand what you're saying.*
>
> *A: (Nodded) Yeah.*

It was important to Assata to focus on her peer relationships, not only for enjoyment but also for positive working relationships and moral support against teacher apathy and negativity. It struck me during my interviews with Assata that most if not all of her teachers would be stunned by the degree of indignation that she felt toward them and the entire establishment, she was more than the precocious child they had pegged her to be. Assata was young, Black, bright and impassioned.

It is clear that, despite the significant disconnection with her nearly all-White female teachers, Assata's focus remained on achievement, for which the legacy and strength of her family and community were the biggest inspirations. Though, as she said, she cared less about how her teachers felt about her actions, the reality was that her behavior toward them was usually positive and always respectful. The high grades and positive appraisals that she received from teachers and staff were indicative of her effective relationships with them. Again, I often thought of how surprised her teachers and school administrators would have been had they known how berated and distant she felt at their own hands.

Certainly, Assata's responses regarding experiences with racism from teachers below indicate that she had a keen sense of her position as a student and respect for teachers' positions of authority. Indeed, she tempered her responses when she discerned that something was awry in her teachers' behaviors and appearances. Assata's bark was louder than her bite was painful. That is, she talked tough, but never really acted aggressively or disrespectfully.

When she described her frustrations with her teachers' lack of support and the pain she felt from experiencing racism in school, she sounded, to me, incorrigible at times. Still, she managed to remain high on her teachers' short list of exceptional students. A cursory review of Assata's responses might lead one to interpret her thought processes and behaviors as unruly. She would be quickly labeled oppositional toward school staff. Yet, by asking questions pertinent to her experiences as an

African American girl in a racist, dilapidated Eurocentric school system we learn that her sentiments and corresponding behaviors have merit.

Q: Have you experienced racism?

A: Umm....like, if a teacher, like, gives this White person a good grade and I know, like, if we were in the same group and I did basically what she did and then she gives her a higher grade than me and I ask her why and she, like, if this teacher, like, stumbles over how to explain it or whatever then I know, like, oh, that's just how you feel. Then I really don't care, like alright.

Q: And so that's happened to you?

A: Yeah. Once or twice. But like, I just ignore it because I know that eventually somebody's gonna get them back for that. So it's like, alright.

Q: So when that happened to you, what did you think about it?

A: I thought about it, and I just thought, like, oh, that's wrong...because, like, as far as I'm concerned, I deserved the same grade as her if not better or whatever because I worked hard on it, and I, like, spent my time doing it and you're just gonna give me a lower grade because she's a different color than I am. And it's, like, oh okay, well, if that's how you feel that's how you feel, and I'm like alright. Like, it feels bad for a minute, but then, like, I'll go home and I just, like, write it down on a piece of paper and I write a letter to this person. If I don't feel like [giving it to them]...I just like burn it or whatever. And then I'll be, like, alright, well this person is gonna get what they deserve, so...

Q: Do you think you will experience racism in the future? Why or why not?

A: Ummm, honestly, I think so. And if I do I really just don't care.

Q: Why do you think you will?

A: Because in this day and age, I mean, like, you think it's over, but honestly it's never over.

Already Assata had experienced the hurt and frustration that comes with insults of racism. Rather than an emotional disturbance or oppositional attitude in reaction, Assata demonstrated tempered discontentment and controlled determination. Because she was conscious of the existence of racism and the problems of Eurocentrism, although she may not have known the term, she was able to cope with the issues and continue her striving. Assata made mental notes about the injustices and discrepancies in her educational experiences and stored them for later use toward her personal growth and success. Not only had she managed to channel her frustrations and succeed against all odds, but she also did so largely independently.

> *Q: So my next question was going to be, what did you do about it?*
>
> *A: If I really, really care about it I go home, and like I won't tell anybody because it's like it wasn't that important or whatever so I don't wanna waste their time or whatever, so I just like take a piece of paper and I write it down and I stick it in this notebook, or I'll stick it somewhere and then like, if it ever happens, if like something ever happens again or the person just like apologizes I just like burn the letter or whatever.*
>
> *Q: Do you sometimes give it to them? Or share it with a family member?*
>
> *A: Like, occasionally I will give the letter to a person, but I never actually share it with a family member because that's like not really necessary.*

Certainly with the size and level of family support that she described having Assata could have vented, cried, or problem-solved with her family about hardships at school, and sometimes she did. Typically, however, she opted to carry the burdens without weighing down her family unnecessarily, a choice likely garnered from family lessons and family role models. The developmental lessons that she received at home along with her personal determination helped to shape her autonomy in school, even in sensitive and painful situations involving racism.

Though recognizing that racism may be on the horizon, in part due to a racist school environment, Assata remained resilient and humble in her upward climb.

> *Q: How do you still think positively about yourself even when things like [teachers giving you a lower grade because of your race happens]?*
>
> *A: Like, I look at it, and I examine the work and I think as if I were that teacher. Like look at my previous work in that class and I think ok, this one was as good as this one, or I could've done better on it. Then it's like, well alright, whatever she thinks is what she thinks, so I'm gonna' do better on the next one. If that's your opinion, it's your opinion...*
>
> *Q: So you do some self-evaluation it sounds like.*
>
> *A: (Nodded)*

An observer could discount Assata's perceptions about poor teacher quality, racism in school, impending racism as a social staple in America, and distinct African cultural characteristics from Euro-America, but the fact is that these are her perceptions and that of many other Black students, and one's perceptions are the defining factors of reality and behavior in life.

Chapter 8: Kenya

Achiever 5, Kenya

Kenya was an eighth grade girl who lived alone with her mother in one of the city's infamous "projects." Of the six children, she appeared to be in the direst of straits. She tended to come to school in clothes that were either too small or ragged. Many of her shirts were not big enough for her to wear without an undershirt to cover her midriff should she raise her arms or bend her waist even slightly. On some shirts she had removed the bottom seams in order to give them more length. Her shirts and pants often had holes or stains on them. Kenya was darker skinned than most of her peers, and her hair was shorter, usually brushed and pulled into a ponytail at the top of her head. In a society so heavily focused on race, Eurocentrism, and class, Kenya's position was a volatile one.

While her grades tended to be average her teachers expressed to me their certainty that she could do much better on her schoolwork and tests if she had more belief in school, and maybe even herself. Kenya's attitude was so often anti-school, anti-American dream, oppositional, and "ghetto" that other school staff had pegged her as a doomed failure and a "loss of potential." Unlike Assata, for example, whom teachers often referred to more lightly as goofy or smart-alecky, much of the staff saw Kenya as un-resilient and hopeless. Still, she attended school regularly and completed her schoolwork consistently enough that she passed the OAT and progressed through grades. Several of her teachers saw enough of a spark in her to support her participation in this study.

Kenya's responses during much of the interview were curt. Her brevity is distinguishable from Kwame's short responses, however, in that her replies were also delivered with a hint of indignation. In many ways, Kenya progressed in school amidst stress and hopelessness that the other five students did not know or feel (remembering that hopefulness does not require strife like the notion of resilience does). Not only was her family income lower, but also there was more intergenerational distress. Kenya's determination and school behaviors had been shaped by life experiences more familiar to youth in the poorest and most destitute segments of our society. Her story seems to have created a sense of anger and resentment that the other participants did not have. Yet, we also observe that Kenya operated from a similar determination and worldview as her relatively more advantaged peers (e.g., those with two active parents, more involved extended family networks, living quarters outside of the projects, etc.). By Ohio state achievement standards and local norms, and with respect to the uneven playing field upon which she functioned, Kenya too is a high achieving student. What are the qualities of her personality?

Research Question One

Kenya believed that to do well in school, students simply needed to study. She spoke only of academics, not about classroom behavior or teacher relationships in relation to grades. While this attitude of school being a means to an end or "necessary evil" was not immediately evident amongst the other achievers, Kenya's feelings on this point held no nuances. Her sole reason for working hard in school was to make good grades "to impress [her] momma." Similar to Assata, Kenya was first focused on her mother's pride in her, and this attachment defined her biggest source of motivation.

Like her peers, Kenya envisioned herself going to college and making enough money to support herself and her family after school. Laughing nervously, Kenya said success meant "havin money in her pocket." Again, her idea of what "havin money" meant was shaped by her cultural values and experiences.

Q: *What makes someone's life a success story?*
A: *Them not havin kids until they're older… uhh, them goin to college, them doin something with they life…that's it.*
Q: *Why is it important to wait until you have kids? Give me an age. What's older?*
A: *25.*
Q: *Why do you think 25's a good age?*
A: *Cuz I'll be outta college, then I won't have nothing to do even though I still gotta work.*

Clearly, Kenya understood the obstacles presented by early pregnancies and a modest or subpar education. Her experiences taught her that children should come after career success because unprepared parenthood might prevent you from attending college and attaining economic stability—and making your momma proud. Within her response is yet another message from African American student achievers that being able to take care of their families is instrumental to them.

It is comprehensible then that she disassociated herself with the idea of hope, despite working hard and setting college and career goals. For even as she expressed having goals and working toward them, her first response to what she hoped for was, "Me? I don't hope for nothing." The degrees of hope and hopelessness seemed to have been divided by a much thicker, harder to cross line to Kenya. It is notable that Kenya's reaction to this question deviated from the other five achievers', and this begs further the question of what values, philosophies, and actions these African American children have in common that they all manage to perform above expectations. She did not articulate hopefulness, but she practiced it in much the same ways.

Caught in a seemingly perpetual state of social contradiction, Kenya nonetheless believed that "[she] can do whatever [she] put[s] [her] mind to," thus continuing the themes of great self-confidence and determination. The only real bump in the road to excelling consistently in school for Kenya seemed to be that she did not believe in the promise of school, or the American dream, which for her seemed more of a pipe dream than an apparent reality. To her credit, living with daily reminders that the odds are stacked against your will and agency would make anyone indignant, at least some of the time.

Research Question Two

Kenya wanted to be a lawyer when she grows up. A continuing theme among the achievers, she chose her career path based on what she perceived her natural talents and enjoyment to be: which included arguing her point and being "in front of a crowd." Becoming a lawyer seemed to be a natural goal, regardless of her current level of income or pedigree, or recurrent pessimism.

Having selected a profession, Kenya then considered the educational requirements to reach her goal: "go to high school" and "get at least a four year degree, or more...[and] study law." In this academic planning, she understood that skill development and academic resilience were needed to reach her goal of "havin money in her pocket." This wisdom and foresight is familiar among her high achieving peers.

Family connectedness also held prominence with Kenya. Her mapped out plan and determination to improve her life did little to soften the blow from the realization that by doing so she would have to leave her people physically and in some ways spiritually.

Q: What are some things that might stand in your way?
A: Uhh, leavin my friends and...my lil' cousins.
Q: Why would that be an obstacle?
A: Cuz I'd wanna stay with them.
Q: So friends are important to you, too.
A: Some of them.
Q: Sounds like family is important to you. Why?
A: Cuz if I ain't got them I ain't got nobody.

Often the phrase "my people" is used within the Black community to indicate the sentiment that all those within the extended family network, including friends and the entire Black community, are our only true allies. These are the people closest to you, no matter how extended in bloodline, no matter how often you see or speak to them. No matter their education or success level, they are the people who understand you best and care the most about you as a human being, such that Kenya could feel "if I ain't got them then I ain't got nobody."

Kenya's desire to leave and go to college in order to attain greater life success had been fueled *by* her people and reinforced with every hard life lesson received with them. From an Afrocentric perspective, we can detect her disenchantment (so to speak) with her school, her desire to impress her mother, and her heartache about leaving family and friends in the projects—her people, as aspects of the cumulative state of inequality and dislocation that African children experience in many sections of the Diaspora.

Kenya's remedy for the pain of branching off from her friends and family was to have a parting celebration and "take a whole buncha pictures wit 'em before [she] leave[s]" for college. Obviously her friends, family, and elders within her extended family network were people she cherished and from whom she received support.

> *Q: Do you get support from someone or someplace to reach your goals?*
> *A: My momma, my momma boyfriend, my grandma, my auntie, and my auntie friend.*
> *Q: How do they support you?*
> *A: By tellin me I can do it.*
> *Q: Is that all it takes?*
> *A: Yeah.*
> *Q: Tell you that you can do it, and that motivates you?*
> *A: And if I do it, then I get something.*
> *Q: What do you get?*
> *A: A lot of stuff: Mp3 players, a mp4 player, computers, cameras...*
> *Q: Anyone else, friends, or place that supports you?*
> *A: No.*

Kenya was the only student to mention material reinforcements for academic achievement. This was interesting given her impoverished living conditions in the projects. Her first response, however, presumably the most relevant one to her experience, was that she was motivated by her family's praise and encouragement, which is congruent with her peers in this study. The connections between her resentment toward the school system, living under some of the most oppressive inner city conditions, and receiving material incentives and rewards is worthy of discussion, but falls outside the purview of the present study. Kenya was doing well in school, and the primary purpose here is to identify the mechanisms of her success rather than focus on family thinking and behavior. For meaningful discussion about the problem of material fixation and living outside of one's means in the Black community, it would be useful to read *The Mis-Education of the Negro* (Woodson, 1933/2000). Kenya's extended family network's belief in her ability and encouragement to succeed was as critical to her as it was to her peers:

> *Q: Do you have any role models, people you look up to?*
> *A: My grandma.*
> *Q: Why?*
> *A: Because she went to college and all that stuff, and if I look up to her then Imma do the same thing.*
> *Q: Any other people you look up to?*
> *A: No.*

A self-identifiable role model again surfaces. Kenya's family had no connection to her school, opting, as usual, to contain support of her school activity to reinforcement at home.

Her role model was related and self-identifiable, but the influence of Black culture and history on Kenya's hopefulness (or hopelessness) was unclear, lost in confusion caused by poorly developed self-cultural awareness. On the other hand, being a girl who was capable of becoming pregnant had taught more clearly pronounced lessons.

> *Q: Do you think you have a different type or amount of hope to reach your goals because you are a girl?*
> *A: Yeah.*
> *Q: Why?*
> *A: Cuz some girls, they don't do nothin with theyself, but then have babies... I ain't havin no kids.*
> *Q: You're not havin any kids ever?*
> *A: No, Imma adopt kids. Ain't no kids comin outta me.*

Her life experiences with being subjected to teenage pregnancy, poverty, and limited mobility is made even more lucid here. Whether Kenya's interest in having kids will change as she matures and progresses through school is likely, but unknown. She has learned early that responsibility for parenting rests most heavily on mothers. Understandably then, for Kenya, being a successful girl turned successful woman required advancing through school and prolonging motherhood. Further, she is Black and from the hood, these are heavy odds, requiring an amazingly strong mind to put toward "doing whatever she wants to do" in life.

Research Question Three
Being African American meant being Black to Kenya, and being Black meant being subjected to a high level of oppression both forced and self-inflicted to the point of not being able to "do nothin." Digging deeper, when queried further about how she was influenced by her racial-ethnic identity, she moved beyond the conditions brought about by racism to her own values. Woe the dirt and grime that Black children must remove from their lens to see and learn beyond the anti-African scene.

Q: *How does being African American influence you?*
A: *Cuz it's a lotta African American heroes.*
Q: *Before you just said when you think about being Black you think about the fact that...a lot of African Americans don't do anything with their lives, but then you're influenced by the fact that there are also a lot of African American heroes...*
A: *Yeah.*
Q: *Can you give some example of heroes?*
A: *Like Martin Luther King and 'em. And the rest of 'em.*
Q: *Alright. Can you name any of 'em?*
A: *(Laughter, looking away)*
Q: *Any other people come to your mind?*
A: *Rosa Parks, Coretta Scott King, Malcolm X... and all the rest of 'em.*
Q: *Out of all the ones you just named, is there one that you think is a bigger hero than the others?*
A: *Martin Luther King.*
Q: *Because what?*
A: *I don't know.*
Q: *You don't know?*
A: *No, I just like 'em.*
Q: *Okay, you just like 'em. Who do you hear the most about?*
A: *(Laughter) Martin Luther King.*

Using what little information she had regarding her race and heritage, Kenya made the simple but poignant statement that African American heroes exist and they influence her. What is most important in interpreting Kenya's expression of racial-ethnic identity is that she has an unarticulated pride in being Black. Unspoken because she lacks the words to express her racial-ethnic pride, rather than lacking in desire. In reflection, when I asked Assata this series of questions she expressed frustration regarding African American history in schools being so often reduced to the work of Martin Luther King, Jr. Kenya's responses only solidified Assata's point. And for not knowing much more than him, Kenya was shamed.

With each interview, the problematic themes of limited intracultural knowledge, stereotypical views of Africa, and poorly developed racial-ethnic identities were more and more evident, although less true for some of the youth. Paradoxically, each student said they found inspiration and motivation through their self-knowledge of historical contributions and perseverance, but knew very little about African and African American history to speak of. Kenya's depth of knowledge about her racial-ethnic history directly connected to what she believed about her own possibilities in a critical way.

She attempted to speak about her belief in the existence of many African American heroes, but could only point to one or two with any level of detail or fact, and she was embarrassed about her lack of knowledge. The self-identifiable role models that could fill her mental ocean of possibilities had been drowned at the shores of America. Unfortunately for Kenya, the motivation "to do whatever she put her mind to" was yet again assaulted by the erroneous idea that Blacks had contributed little to the world. As a result, her ability to develop a balanced and healthy identity was constrained. Also, she was under the mistaken impression that even as she strived to achieve in school she hoped for, or perhaps *could* hope for, nothing.

She laughed and lowered her gaze, thus avoiding eye contact when she described her image of Africa. After I reassured her that there were no wrong answers in telling me what she thought or knew, she said that her only understanding was "that they poor" in Africa. If she were to teach a younger child about Africa and African American history, she would say that in Africa "they don't wear a lot of clothes [and] they carry stuff on they head." Regarding African Americans, she would add that "a lot of people did a lot of stuff for us" to be integrated with White people. On the one hand, Kenya was conscious of the disparities that existed between Africans and others (most times "others" meant "White people"). On the other hand, she had little awareness of what Black people had done themselves to reduce the inequalities she knew existed, or even better, whether or not the disparities have always existed. Is being who she is, being African American, really something to be proud of or not?

Like several of her achieving peers, Kenya's current level of understanding of her racial-ethnic identity included phenotype, genealogy, and race. However, ethnicity was missing from her self-definition. The achievers generally understand very little about how race impacts, but heritage creates culture, and this lack of important knowledge affected their thinking, goal-setting, achievement, and perceptions of success. I ached to console and educate them regarding their rich history and abilities during our discussions, as they each clearly yearned to know more about the historical and cultural ground on which they stood. For the cultural knowledge that they did have, each of these young achievers was proud and motivated toward college and a life of peace and stability for themselves and their people.

Research Question Four

Akin to responses from Assata and Kwame, Kenya described her school experiences as boring and hostile. She, a kid who cited several mediums for learning about Africa and African American history, including research on a computer, books from a library, and visits to museums, was bored by classroom instruction and school fieldtrips. Like Ture, she coped by applying analytical relativism to the situation.

Specifically, having just spoken of field trips, she appreciated "the activities…and that [they even] *get* field trips" at her school. By showing a simultaneous appreciation for extracurricular activities including participation in mediation and dances, but disengagement from school, Kenya once again demonstrated that she enjoys learning and enrichment as functions of personal development, but school was another story. Like her peers, she was connected to education, but not to school.

Q: *What do you not like about [going to your school]?*
A: *The teachers.*
Q: *What's wrong with the teachers?*
A: *They annoyin.*
Q: *In what way?*
A: *Cuz they be makin you do stuff you don't wanna do.*
Q: *Like?*
A: *When my stomach be hurtin they make me do my work anyway, then I get mad… other than one of 'em.*
Q: *Which one?*
A: *Ms. Jackson. She'a tell me to go put my head down or something.*
Q: *Anything else?*
A: *Some of these people at this school (inaudible, something about kids).*
Q: *Students, okay. What don't you like about them?*
A: *They attitudes.*
Q: *Example?*
A: *Cussin in front of the teachers and stuff.*
Q: *Okay, anything else?*
A: *I don't like them yellin when, instead of the teacher, when the teacher bout to yell at us they yell…*
Q: *What do the teachers do when the kids are cussin in front of them or yellin?*
A: *Nothin!*
Q: *Nothin?!*
A: *Nothing. They just sit in front of the class…lookin dumb.*

I observed these same dynamics between students and teachers that the girls described. Assata and Kenya were both significantly displeased with the constant conflict between teachers and students, and they perceived limited support from teachers for their academic and behavioral progress overall. The boys also perceived limited support from teachers, but seemed to expect less and therefore accepted the dissonance as simply the way it was. To the contrary, the girls were unlikely to silently accept "annoying" teachers who "don't do nothin," or uncaring teachers who "yell a lot" and never reference Africa or "African American heroes."

> Q: *How do you keep hope about doing well in school and reaching your goals even when the teachers tell you to keep working when you're sick, and the teachers and kids are yelling?*
> A: *Don't listen to 'em. Think about something else, anything else. And even when the teachers tell us, tell me to do something, I don't do it.*
> Q: *Example.*
> A: *If they tell me to, if they said I cain't go to the bathroom, I still go cuz my momma said if I gotta go to the bathroom go.*
> Q: *So when bad things are happening you don't listen to it...if you need to go to the bathroom—*
> A: *I go anyway.*
> Q: *—or you need something else—*
> A: *I go get it.*
> Q: *—even though the teacher said no. Hmm, okay. That kinda sounds like then...you just focus on what you need to do to do well. Or if you have to go to the bathroom or you're not feeling well, something that's blocking you from focusing on your work, you go take care of that.*
> A: *Yes.*

Like the previous four students, Kenya learned to tailor her actions and concentration toward meeting *her* goals rather than focus on the teachers' or school's agenda. Her primal desire was to show respect to her teachers whether or not she liked them, but she was also willing to defy them when conflict arose and her goals were infringed upon. At once Kenya, much like Assata, was rebellious and agreeable, or effectively oppositional. The data has clearly indicated a general feeling of disconnect with school, resulting in distal relationships. A student displaying defiance or oppositionality in such a context could not justifiably be marked as defiant or oppositional without attaching a positive hyphenation or preposition, especially if the student is succeeding toward her goals.

For example, we see that Kenya did not like it when students spoke out of turn in spite of teachers, used profanity in front of them, or made teachers' jobs of managing the classroom more difficult. However, we also see that when she needed to, she would take a stand against the teachers if she felt she was being treated uncaringly. In the book of a schoolteacher and administrator, Kenya's behavior would be characterized as problematic and leading to failure, but in her family's eyes, she was a warrior winning the fight over the right to hope.

Obviously the students felt that they were on their own in school rather than under the tutelage and guidance of their teachers. Under these conditions it becomes permissible for a student, with approval even from her family, to choose plans of action that benefit them and further their goal-pursuit, versus falling victim to a teacher or system that care less about the student's well being or success. Numerous studies and discussions have ensued in education from the point of view of teachers, however, they are only one side of a two-sided, or actually poly-sided, educational exchange, and they are meaningless in and of themselves. Kenya's truth was that surviving the hardships of unsupportive, negative, teachers sometimes means being defiant toward them. Hugely contradictory to African cultural values, Kenya knew that she was expected to respect adults, but like Assata, she found herself in a situation of dislocation such that she needed to discount bad authority and hold firm to her determination to achieve in life.

Through Kenya's narrative we see again that school for her and a great many of her peers is not a positive place or refuge from the ills of the world. Kenya experienced racism in school when a White female peer called her "Black" in a derogatory tone. Kenya did not seek support from her teacher, which makes sense given the negativity characterizing the teacher-student relationships. She felt she had to cope with a hurtful racist event on her own. Yet a child, Kenya's response was reflexively emotional and aggressive. She admitted to having pushed the offending student into a desk, although she was not particularly proud of her reaction.

She had no words for how she felt during this experience of racial hostility. In hindsight she understood that she was apparently angry and "ain't think about it, [she] just reacted to it…in a bad way." In unison with her peers above, Kenya perceived racism to be imminent in her future, "because some people don't like how other people look." Through it all, Kenya tried to think positively about herself and disregard racist epithets by reminding herself that "if this [is] how [she] look, then this [is] how God meant for [her] to look." During any future confrontations of racism, she intends to walk away and remain steadfast in her spiritual resolve and determination to be successful.

Chapter 9: Aisha

Achiever 6, Aisha (pronounced i-ee-sha)

The sixth and final scholar in this study, Aisha, was a seventh grade girl who lived in a single parent household close to Kenya. She was often observed working quietly and independently. She tended to set herself apart from the in-crowd or social cliques more so even than Ture, socializing with everyone equally and minimally. Her disposition and behaviors were best described as independent rather than antisocial, however, as when she did interact with her peers and staff she did so easily and appropriately.

Like Ture, Aisha was clearly focused. In both attire and attitude, she always appeared neat and ready to work. She seemed not to waste words or time. Like Ture and Assata, she wore glasses daily. Most of her teachers reported that she was a good student and a "respectful" girl toward everyone. One teacher, however, said that Aisha sometimes "caught an attitude with her." It is important to note that the other girls in this study (and much of the general student body) had frequent conflict with this teacher. Analysis of Aisha's narrative indicates a fiercely resilient spirit similar to Assata and Kenya's.

Research Question One

Aisha advised, between lip smacking, kids to "make sure they come to school prepared...and ready to listen to what the teacher ha[s] to say." Through ostentatious expressiveness that many might coin attitudinal, Aisha nonetheless provided specific instructions for acting studiously. Not only should kids come to school prepared with "a sharpened pencil, pen, notebook and paper," and focused attention on their teachers, but they should also "do all the[ir] work and participate in class." Aisha added a psychological component to the idea of studious actions set forth by her peers above. According to her, doing well in school involved both a set of actions and a mindset of preparedness.

Aisha believed in doing well in school specifically "because...it's important to get the education you need to so that you can go on to [high] school and college and get a good job [to] make a life for yourself." Once again we learn that school to Black student achievers represents a means to the end of learning and providing for themselves and their extended family networks. As for the meaning of success, Aisha had the following to say.

Q: What does a successful life look like?
A: Having a good job that make, that...where you make a decent amount of money, and you have your own house and car and stuff.
Q: When you see yourself in 10 years, or you know 15 years, and you're grown, what do you see for yourself?
A: Going to school and bein a nurse or...start as a nurse then become a doctor.

Aisha looked forward to independent and stable living in much the same way as her peers above. She also valued education in much the same way, looking forward to working her way up to being a great doctor and all of the intellectual rigor that it would require.

> *Q: What makes someone's life a success story?*
> *A: Umm....I'm not sure.*
> *Q: You're not sure? Think about it...thinking about people who are successful. When you think about successful people—*
> *A: Umm, when they do something....hmmm, when they do something at they job that makes a person say that...they're like the best doctor...and want, they wanna um...want them to treat them or something.*

Success itself means surviving in peace and comfort from having achieved professional excellence. Getting their means being and doing your best. Aisha was not focused on getting something for nothing; she wanted only to receive the fruits of her labor. Like her peers, she aimed to work hard and live harmoniously. Aisha hoped to use her hard earned academic success toward personal life satisfaction and contribution to others, especially her family: Taken together, she espouses an Afrocentric orientation indeed.

> *Q: What do you hope for in life?*
> *A: I hope to...help myself out as well as my family, and then.... stay...stay on the right track and don't get in any trouble.*
> *Q: When you say help yourself out and your family out, what do you mean? In what way, help by...*
> *A: Like when they need...money or something, or need a place to stay.*

Overall, hope to these young achievers is a spiritual, psychological, and behavioral composite or toolbox that they bring with them to school consistently. Sometimes their hopefulness was strengthened by a determination to combat the odds, but always it was braced by a spirit of connectedness to family and community and with these an adherence to African values and beliefs systems. The hardships that Aisha and her peers experienced in school and society were but fuel to the fire of their spirits of determination and consciousnesses of victory.

Based on her narrative, Aisha navigated every day with a preparedness that was stabilized by the knowledge that meeting her goals to complete college, gain a career, and provide for her family required academic resilience and professional stamina. So deep was this understanding that she envisioned herself starting out as a nurse prior to becoming a doctor so that she would "be prepared for what's going to happen" when she becomes a doctor. Like her peers, she had a capacity for delayed gratification and endurance that came naturally from their pride and determination. The shared philosophies and experiences of these youth are important factors in their having patient assurance of their success to come.

Aisha was not only interested in getting the job and getting paid, she was intent on *mastering* her trade. She understood that success is a long-term process worth working for, and the stability of her finances would be based on having a trade and successful career, not banking on quick-fix money schemes or so-called pyramid organizations (i.e., businesses which require amassing memberships to make money). Having reached an understanding of the important role that school plays in economics, housing, physical health, peace, and general sustainability, Aisha was dedicated to improving quality of life for herself and her family—her greatest valuable.

> Q: *What are the values and beliefs that you live your life by?*
> A: *To care for family members and help 'em out when they need it.*
> Q: *Sounds like you value family...you said, it's important to help family out. Is there anything else that you think is important for a person to think or to believe...to do?*
> A: *To...make them think that you won't turn your back on them when they need help.*

Like Kenya, it was important to Aisha that her family knew the strength of her love and connection to them, no matter where she moved to or how much of a success she became. These achieving Black students were clear: success wasn't about class, it was about family and community.

Research Question Two

All of the young scholars in this study indicated that they value family connectedness and pride, but only Aisha and Kenya expressed a feeling of impending guilt or concern for family members feeling abandoned as they reached success. What these two students share in common is gender and, at least then, living in the most impoverished conditions of the participants. Both girls lived in single parent households in one of the poorest communities in Cleveland. For them, their life goals included another level of pressure—making sure that the family and friends who supported and encouraged hope in them from the beginning knew that they would remain dear to them. Added pressure and all, the girls moved forward toward their goals, armed with the pride and the values that their families and community instilled in them. Their SigHT saw beyond fear and pushed past anxiety.

Like her peers, Aisha expressed being "very" confident in her ability to achieve her goals. Her studiousness and goal planning were only a part of her confidence for meeting her goals however. As we have seen with the first five students, Aisha was primarily supported and influenced by her family.

> Q: *What makes you confident?*
> A: *Because...because...like, my mom and 'nem didn't finish high school so I wanna...umm show them that I can do it.*
> Q: *Do you get support from someone or someplace to reach your goals?*
> A: *Yeah, my mom.*

While Ture, Kenya, and Talib's resolve to achieve stemmed in part from a desire to continue their family legacies, a part of Aisha's tenacity, like Kenya and Kwame, came from wanting to begin a new and more successful family legacy. All the same is that all six considered strongly their heritage. In proving to her elder family members that she, their blood kin, could complete high school and college she would be, in many ways, redeeming their shortcomings or righting the wrongs of a broken system that has dealt with them harshly. The depth by which Aisha and Kenya's success held meaning for their families speaks to their connectedness and sense of collectivism: their families would share in the pride of their high school diplomas, college degrees, and successful careers because they represent the whole, and vice versa.

Though they would be considered ignorant or "low-class" by the standards of many academics and teachers, Aisha's mother and grandmother apparently had the wit to support her success by encouraging scholastic prowess. The same may be said for the first five achievers. The ways in which Aisha's family offered her support are almost identical to the other students.

> Q: *How does your mom support you?*
> A: *By lookin at my homework and stuff when I go home, askin me do I got homework and stuff and helpin me with projects.*
> Q: *Any other place or person that supports you?*
> A: *My grandmother.*
> Q: *Your grandma, how does she support you?*
> A: *Doin the same thing. She come to my school and see what I'm doin.*
> Q: *Do your family and school influence each other or come together anytime?*
> A: *No.*
> Q: *Well you said your grandmother comes to school...*
> A: *Oh yeah (laughter).*
> Q: *Your grandma comes to school (laughter). Okay, how often does she do that?*
> A: *Not often, when I ask her to come up.*

Aisha's family encouraged and monitored her school achievement and that was enough for her, just like it was for Ture, Kwame, Assata and Kenya (Talib seemed to need a bit more help). These youth hung onto their family and community's encouragement and watchful eyes during their daily trek through school. They were convicted about managing their success and contributing to the well being of their families and community. Formidable was their determination and resolute was their self-confidence. Aisha, in seventh grade, living with her mother, African American, and from the hood of Cleveland, Ohio, could not "think of anything" that might stand in her way of becoming a doctor.

Q: *Can't think of anything that can stand in your way?*
A: *(Shook head).*
Q: *Do you think you're invincible?*
A: *(Shook head).*
Q: *(Laughter) No, okay, what do you think makes you, umm, so confident then that nothing can stand in your way?*
A: *(Silence, inquisitive facial expression).*
Q: *Is it just the, what you said, the power...how much you wanna show your parents—*
A: *Yeah...*
Q: *—and your family that you can do it?*
A: *Yeah, it's....something can only stand in yo way if you let it.*

Almost entirely motivated by the adoration and respect that she had for her family, especially her mother and grandmother, it was somewhat surprising that she did not perceive herself as being significantly influenced by them or the larger African American community. She felt that she had no role models, for example. Perhaps, like Kwame, Aisha's idea of success—a college degree and good enough job to be free from financial strain—prevented her from seeing her mother and grandmother as role models. Their personal resilience in providing for her, and helping her with her schoolwork despite not having high school diplomas or college degrees precluded them from being labeled as successful to her at her current psychological development. Aisha seems only to have looked at what her mother and grandmother did not have versus what they had lived through and given her.

Similarly, she did not recognize her race-ethnicity as having any impact on her goals. As a result, Aisha had not seen the connection between being Black and experiencing life in a 100% Black neighborhood in the inner city and her resolve to succeed—at least not yet. Similarly, in spite of being raised in what sounded like a female-prominent family struggling to make it, Aisha felt no concern for the experiences of females in the social and political domains—she felt that males and females were on equal ground to hope and expect equal returns. Yet, her family's difficult social and financial experiences inspired her to reach further. It can only be concluded that her social understanding of success and race were continuing to evolve.

Although she had a strong sense of family togetherness and ambition, the building blocks of Aisha's goal orientation were unclear to her. Her goal orientation was devoid of any social or cultural consciousness outside of the goals themselves. All else was subconscious. Heading into the third and fourth research questions there is serious concern that Aisha is shortsighted on the social and cultural components affecting her hopefulness and likelihood for success.

Research Question Three
The disease of racism established prominence in the identity development of Aisha as much as her peers above.

> *Q: What does it mean to you to be African American?*
> *A: It means…I'm a person, that I have the same amount of rights that everybody else have.*

Here we have a statement of racial-ethnic identity that is simple, too simple, and externally defined. Is it not assumed today that every American has equal rights? Is it not yet unquestioned that every human being is a person? And is it not understood today that African Americans have a history and culture of their own that asserts on their own the birth rights granted to them? Apparently these things are not known among all school-aged children of African descent. As self-confident and supported by her family as she was, Aisha still defined her existence as one on the periphery of others'. Clearly, her ethnicity and culture were not discussed at home as much as her homework and future medical degree, or race for that matter.

On the one hand, Aisha's self-definition consisted of rejecting marginalization, which is good, but on the other hand, her Blackness meant reliance on social affirmation as a person. Neither of these equate to freedom or agency. Sadly, they both show that Aisha's mind is not liberated, her heart is strained against a history limited to oppression and controlled by others. Her very self-concept "as a person" is reactionary against racism and still striving for liberation, leaving less space to focus on self-development, peace and life achievement.

Case in point, Aisha spoke about her realization, and mortification, that schools and larger corporations (which schools more and more often are) often commoditize African American abilities, such as athleticism.

> *Q: How does being African American influence you?*
> *A: It gives me a chance to do something that other people cain't do.*
> *Q: Explain that to me so I can understand better.*
> *A: Like…umm…..I don't know like sports or going out of the country.*
> *Q: So you said it gives you the opportunity to do things that other people can't do…so African Americans…can…have more opportunity to play sports?*
> *A: (Silence)*
> *Q: Is that what you're saying? Or not exactly?*
> *A: (Laughter)*
> *Q: Or do you think African Americans do it in a different way, or maybe they…what do you mean?*
> *A: (Silence, looked away)*

Uncomfortable with discussing the subject any further, Aisha seemed to have considered in that very moment the disenfranchisement underlying African American experiences in a society that is more likely to support their physical agility over their intellectual abilities. It is telling that her greatest association with her racial-ethnic community was with sports rather than the myriad of other fields available—such as the medical field that she herself hoped to enter.

Aisha explained later that she felt influenced by the fact that African Americans do (at least) have full citizenship rights to travel abroad and re-enter the country without breaking the law. With this, she demonstrated some attunement to social policy and the realities of other marginalized groups, such as "illegal immigrants" who hope for their own success. Also, for what it's worth, Aisha's response to how her race-ethnicity influenced her was first positive, with a "we can" statement. She compared being African American to being able to engage in certain activities versus *not* being able to do them as a non-African American person. After discussing mobility through citizenship, which must have been a more neutral topical area for her, Aisha was ready to confront the issue of sports in the African American community a bit more, and even offer a third influence on her race-ethnicity.

> Q: *Okay, and about sports...when you think about, are talking about professional sports...or high school....or.......?*
> A: *(Nodded).*
> Q: *All of them. Okay, anything else?*
> A: *It gives me a chance to learn where my people came from.*

Aisha's hesitancy to discuss African Americans in sports indicates that this is a reality that she was not entirely proud of or comfortable with. Pushing past unpleasant confrontation of social and professional inequality, she continued the standing theme of Black pride and desire for greater self-cultural awareness by stating that she values "chance[s] to learn where [her] people came from." Knowing that Black people now "have equal rights" Aisha has determination to actualize her potential to excel in more areas than simply sports, and with this learn more about where she can go and what she can do as an African American person. As Ture said, *We came through a lot so...[I] just wanna be successful cuz we came through it. Now we can...so what's the point of not takin a opportunity to become successful?* From Assata, being African American means *that you've suffered. African Americans have suffered so much that you should try to be better just because.* From, Kenya, *it's a lotta African American heroes,* and knowing of them motivates African American children to perform higher. And Kwame, it is critical to understand the influences of history because even today *a lot of African Americans don't get good jobs.* Aisha is right: As an African American child she should know where her people came from reaching as far back as the earliest of time, before the enslavement and demoralization of their people's culture, mind, body and soul. Their knowledge should start with Kemet by way of Kush.

Up to this point, Aisha had successfully channeled her discontentment with her family and community's current conditions into conscious hopefulness, but she had not yet come to full awareness of the influences that her race, family, and culture had on her in order to then act optimally. This did not mean that she was color-blind or naïve to racism. In fact, she was disgruntled, as much as her peers were, to the point of positive action about the calamitous conditions faced by her family and community. What she lacked was the self-cultural awareness necessary to understand the internal frustrations and determination that she felt and the racial contradictions and disparities that she saw. Along with her social awareness, it seems likely that her racial-ethnic identity was simply growing, not yet set but rather budding as her knowledge of self builds. It is likely that her participation in this study was the first time that she had even discussed the topic of her identity (Talib had endorsed this as true for himself). And that is unfortunate.

Q: *When you think about Africa what comes to your mind?*
A: *I don't know about Africa (laughter).*
Q: *What do you think? What comes to your mind when you think about Africa?*
A: *(Laughter) Umm....people....umm, workin hard.*
Q: *People workin hard, okay.*
A: *For...things that they need to survive.*
Q: *Anything else?*
A: *(Shook head)*
Q: *No, okay. And when you say to survive do you mean to have a Mercedes Bens?*
A: *Like water and stuff.*
Q: *Let's pretend that I am only seven years old and I have a second grade homework assignment to learn about Africa and African American history. If I asked you to help me, what are some things that you would tell me?*
A: *Umm....that.....there's parts where people are poor...and don't have anything, like the people here. Umm...that they have lots of animals....and they carry baskets on they heads and stuff.*
Q: *Anything else?*
A: *(Silence)*
Q: *You can tell me anything. I'm seven. I'm just depending on you.*
A: *Umm.....they don't wear shoes?*
Q: *Okay, what about African American history? What would you tell me? What do you think I should know?*
A: *That people did, Black people did a lot for their country...and they were slaves and stuff (looking at the floor). A lot of people died for they freedom.*

Like her peers, Aisha saw Africa as poverty- and grief stricken first, and exotic second. However, Aisha also connected the image of a destitute Africa to the impoverished conditions of her own community. Considering that the human subjects of our discussions were Black people and she was raised in a predominately Black section of Cleveland, OH, her reference to Africans on the continent bearing an economic resemblance to "parts where people are poor and don't have anything like the people here" in the United States is taken to mean Black people. Aside from the stereotypical portrayals of Africa regurgitated by Aisha from Western training, she harbored within herself a positive perception of African people generally. Her family and teachers' jobs are to help her develop that positive perception of "her people."

Her vision of Black people both in the U.S. and on the continent was that they "work hard." In Aisha's eyes, Africans are survivors and proponents of victory, and so is she. She spoke of Black people having done "a lot for their country" and even dying for freedom and democracy. Surely, her image of Africans on the continent being hard working "for things that they need to survive" is relatable to her circumstance of working hard in school to eventually provide for her family—African people everywhere plow through much of the same meadows as she does.

Continuously indicating a deeper Black consciousness as the discussion went on, Aisha extended the learning experience of African and African American history to actually visiting Africa. To Aisha and her peers above, African and African American history represents information worthy of homage and continuation.

Q: *What would we do [and] where would we go?*
A: *Umm, go on the computer and look stuff up...We can travel to Africa.*
Q: *(Laughter) We could travel to Africa?! Anywhere else?*
A: *We could go to museums.*
Q: *What if I said, you know what, so what, that's in the past, that happened a long time ago. Would you say you're right, that's done? Or would you want me to know something else about what that means, what the history means?*
A: *Uhh, I would want you to know something else.*
Q: *What's that?*
A: *That...if....umm, the stuff...that didn't happen a long time ago, you wouldn't be here.*

Research Question Four
Aisha did not have a lot to say about, nor did she have an affinity for, school. She was deliberate in her answer about what her school experience was like: "It's...good because I'm learning a lot." Her concise and specific response informs us that she has a positive perception toward education and learning, but little connection to school. When one asks a

child about how school is going, especially an achiever, she expects to hear about class projects that have the child's attention captured, or about a favorite teacher, upcoming exam or field trip.

By now we know that Aisha had a vested interest in channeling her school achievement into life success. It is unsurprising then that she did appreciate when her teachers provided assistance when asked, thereby "helping her learn" and progress toward her goals. She was otherwise uninterested them and disconnected from the school generally. Her focus in school was on forward movement toward her goals of caring for her family and restoring the self-knowledge that contemporary schools have mostly devastated.

Bored also by the monotony of the dress code as Kwame expressed feeling, she stated that she would find possibility for creative engagement in the aesthetics of the "cool designs" on her and her peers' clothing if they were allowed to wear them. Both Aisha and Kwame expressed that their personalities were being stifled by the school's dress code policy, which only added to the dissatisfaction that they felt in the classroom generally.

Q: *How do you keep motivated about going to school and achieving your goals, even though you have to wear a uniform?*
A: *(Sighing) Cuz you don't wanna have to do the same thing over again.*
Q: *You mean like make-up work?*
A: *And getting the same grade. You learn it the first time so you don't have to learn it over.*

Aisha had a sense of urgency toward "making it," but she was willing also to patiently endure the time and effort required to attain stability. Like the youth above, she demonstrated a motivated work ethic that was in constant motion toward success. Inspired by school or not, they went in on a mission to meet high expectations and greet success when it was all said and done.

Aisha said she never experienced racism but expected that she might in the future. Not only do Black people tend to have limited opportunities, except for in sports, but also Black people "can just bump into somebody in the street [today] and they might not [be treated right because of] what color [they] are." Watching her family members struggle and perceiving the limited opportunities given to Black people in general were enough to keep her motivated in school and alert toward racism everywhere. This was one social issue that she understood existed, and because of her awareness she was determined to succeed that much more. As it was for her peers above, in the dual between racism and her success, and her feeling worth-less and knowing better, she was like Muhammad Ali in the ring with Floyd Patterson demanding that her name be called and her history acknowledged according to the legacy of pantheons from which she hails.

Chapter 10: Follow-Up Questions

Q: Do you listen to music?
A: Yeah!
Q: Ok (laughter). How often would you say, every free chance
you get, every day, [just] whenever someone else plays it?
A: I was listening to it this morning, everyday.
Q: Ok, so every day, multiple times a day.
A: Yeah.
Q: What kind of music do you listen to, what's your favorite type
of music?
A: Hip hop and R&B...[really] hip hop. –Kenya, 8ᵗʰ grade

Each of the African American achievers showcased here discovered a winning strategy for their school success that could be summed up as follows:

1.   Keep family and community primary.
2.   Go to school to secure a life for yourself.
3.   Have faith in your personal agency and God.
4.   Focus on your future not aggravations or distractions. Even if you're dealing with racism or poverty, focus on winning. Note that a change of focus on winning does not mean that social, school, family, etc. problems should be ignored or dismissed.
5.   And, if you really want to excel, know yourself, meaning your ethnic history and heritage well.

Their follow-up responses served to support and in some ways extend these key philosophies and activities. By the time the six primary interviews and classroom observations were completed, Talib was withdrawn from the school because his family had moved outside of the school district. During follow-up interviews, I enjoyed asking the five remaining achievers more pointed questions about their personalities and views on race, their relationships with teachers, the Black community, and the first Black President of the United States, Barack Obama. In addition to learning more about them, I wanted to know how witnessing the historical event of President Obama's victory had impacted (or not) their personal capacity for hope as African American children, from their mouths rather than the opinions of theorists talking *about* them. The strength of follow-up questions is that concern of respondents framing their responses according to politeness or pleasing the interviewer is significantly reduced because the nuts and bolts of their opinions and experiences, whether positive or negative, have already been revealed. Here is a summary of what Ture, Advanced in reading and Accelerated in mathematics, Kwame, Advanced in mathematics, Assata, Kenya and Aisha, all meeting state achievement standards had to say in response to the follow-up interview questions asked of them.

Hobbies and Interests

Young Black achievers tend to be centered on who they are racial-ethnically and socially, as I found out with greater confidence through the follow-up interviews with the five standing students. Though race is a social construct, most people do not recognize it as such, and therefore treat the idea as a stamp of genealogy and culture. What I mean by socially centered in this section is that the achievers in this study, although chosen because they stood out from their peers academically, did not stand apart from their peers in their social interests and behaviors.

Their hobbies were normal for their age and culture. Ture often played sports (basketball and football) in the school gym and reflected on the metamorphoses of the Black community while sitting silently on his front porch. Kwame played video games, while Assata often made cards for family and friends—"better than Hallmark," between playing pranks on her cousins. Assata said her cards were better than Hallmark because she takes longer to make them, meaning that she puts great care into what she creates for her family and friends. Kenya liked to watch movies at the community center and visit her grandmother and cousins at her grandmother's house, where she would laugh a lot and do things on her grandmother's computer. Aisha also frequented the community center, where she enjoyed listening to music, dancing, watching movies, acting, singing, playing sports, and using the computer. Above all for each of them, there was music.

All of the achievers said that they listened to hip hop and/or rhythm and blues music on a daily basis. Ture and Kenya expressly listed listening to hip hop music as their number one hobby. Ture, the highest achieving student in the sample and one of the top achievers at Justice Academy, said he regularly listens to hip hop music that would be considered explicit—such as that released by Drake, Lil' Wayne, and Ludacris, who were his top three favorite artists. Creative in its form though it may be, Ture's brand of music, I suspect, would not make most educators' or parents' "appropriate" list.

He attributed his affinity for music lacking in scholarship and consciousness to the fact that affirming hip hop tunes were given limited rotation on radio and television. For example, he stated that Lil' Wayne is "basically in every kinda song so it's impossible not to like him." For Ture and other Black kids like him, it is possible to separate the entertainment from the despondent messages heard in the shallower hip hop, and these from his thinking and behavior. It is a good thing that he is himself conscious and secure enough in his identity and social awareness to achieve his goals without being "dumbed down" (Fiasco,

2007). Ture is wise enough to understand that the music played on Cleveland's radio stations and national TV is antithetical to him and his goals.

Ture was not alone in his identifying with the above named music personas. Kwame and Kenya also listened to Drake and Lil' Wayne frequently. Interestingly, Kwame looked away and smiled, one of his typical looks of shame or embarrassment, before finally working up the nerve to share that he listened to Lil' Wayne. True to her personality, Kenya stated that she listened to the same music *before and* after school with unabashed honesty. While Assata was also strongly connected to the music, she said she played it less often than she liked, about "every other day," because she was adamant on the point of listening to music that she believes is quality and truer to the artists' experiences. She felt that music created by female rap artist Eve is "the truth."

Perhaps with the exception of Kenya, these young Black achievers were wise to extend to their social interests the same innovation and discernment that they used to parse through school issues. Just as they engaged school with a clear purpose, they listened to music with clarity— to further develop their minds and replenish their energy and spirits. When quality music was not possible, then they were clear on the point of treating music played on the radio or TV as mere entertainment, not their way of life or road to success. Again, Kenya, project born and bred, may have walked a fine line between treating foodless entertainment as a way of life in the voids that she sometimes felt in her existence.

Ture and Assata especially agreed that their entertainment choices were limited. What began as a basic discussion of interests with young African American achievers confirmed the valuing of music in the African American youth community, and revealed the importance of the larger community's vigilance about feeding the children substance and monitoring their exposure to mainstream influences. Just as there is a harmful mainstream culture in schools, there are popular tools used to train rather than educate African youth in the music industry and general media. School and hip hop, two important areas in the lives of so many Black youth, have neglected opportunities to expose them to information important to African and African American success.

Black Student Achievers and Their Peers: It's Cool

Indicative of education and camaraderie being values in the African American community is the fact that none of the students in this study were attacked, harassed, or socially isolated for their academic achievement or rapport with teachers neither in school or their neighborhoods. Each said that their peers, most of whom were not school achievers, were aware of the fact that they always completed their homework and made good grades. Yet, they experienced no insults or accusations of "acting White." There was no sense of the achievers thinking that they were somehow better than their peers or community members because they were reaching for the stars in school. To the contrary of Ogbu's (1993) theory of oppressed group members demonstrating opposition toward in-group members who appear to "cross cultural boundaries" (p. 492), none of the participants in this study experienced any maltreatment or rejection from their poor, underachieving, inner city peers. Actually, these students expressed having many friends in school, despite differences in attitudes and behaviors toward school achievement. Congruent with their responses, I observed each of them mingling and working well with their peers.

By the same token, the participants did not require that their friends excel in school. They did, however, require that their peers be fun to hang around and act as good friends to them by accepting who they are and treating them fairly. Assata expressed this best: "If you're, like, cool and whatever, and you're funny and stuff then I'll hang out with you." Drawing the line between friend and caregiver she explained, "I don't care what your grades are. That doesn't concern me. That's between you and your parents and teachers and whatever." The achievers of this study viewed themselves as equal to their peers, and their peers saw them the same way. They were, in fact, all accepted members of the same community.

The only evident division between them was that the excelling students had learned to navigate their school world while still maintaining their community and cultural identities. What seems to make their paradoxical realities work (e.g., majority African American school, all Black neighborhood, but nearly all Euro-American school staff and curriculum, etc.) is their senses of racial-ethnic and family identities, which are in many ways one in the same. In spite of differences with school staff and culture, they maintained the important senses of Kujichagulia (Self-Determination in defining and dignifying themselves) and Umoja (Unity as an ethnic and social community) (Karenga, 1988). Theories and studies that observed conflict between achieving and underperforming African students (e.g., see Ogbu, 2004) may have missed the important step of closely examining the students' level of racial-ethnic identity and cultural centeredness. These have proven to be key to the continued success of the achievers in *SigHT*.

The Role of Consciousness and Community
The follow-up questions connected to research questions two and three erase any question of a collectivist orientation imbedded in the responses in Chapters 4 through 9 above. All but Kenya said President Obama's victory in the 2008 election was symbolic of the full potential of all Black people. As Kwame said, President Obama made him feel even more hopeful "because if one Black person can become President, then I think everybody can." Not easily fooled into complacency, however,

several of them made sure to express that President Obama's presence was a reinforcement, but not a testament of guaranteed social progress and opportunity for the whole community in a still racist world. Cognizant of continued racism in national systems and daily activity, they were not gullible as to think that conditions for the Black community had been miraculously improved. African American President or not, they still need to work hard, indeed harder than most, to succeed. Assata and Aisha expressed this sentiment with the following words:

Q: What does Barack Obama represent to you?
A: Umm, growth. Because, if you think about it, there was a time where like it was impossible for us to even vote, and now there's like a President there and stuff so, that's cool.
Q: Does knowing about President Obama make you feel differently about your own life?
A: Umm, I would say that knowing that we have a Black President makes me think like, this way I can spend time working, if I work as hard as he did or whatever, I could end up being President...I don't wanna be President, but I could end up being something big and stuff. –Assata

Q: What does Barack Obama represent to you?
A: Ummm....what he represents? Black people.
Q: Ok. So do you think that his becoming Presidents means something to Black people?
A: (Nodded) Ummm,....like, that, not only...it means that, that African Americans can become President as well as Caucasians.
Q: Does knowing about President Obama make you feel differently about your own life?
A: (Silence)
Q: Do you feel more hopeful, or about the same?
A: No, about the same. –Aisha

They were all surprised at the inauguration of an African President in 2008. Except for Assata, they did not think that they would witness there being a Black President during their lifetime. Living in one of the poorest areas in Cleveland, Kenya was the most fervent in her reflections on institutional racism, which she knew was represented by the U.S. government as a whole. To her, President Obama did not represent "nothin at all but the President," just like the rest "of them Presidents." When I asked her if she had anything in common with President Obama, she, rather dramatically, shook her head. Her dejection was directed at President Obama not as an elder in the African collective, but as a representative of the highest office in an unjust system, perhaps the one place most capable of preventing the racism that she knew all too well.

All of the achievers believed that Black people are a special collective and should act as a unified group. Kenya exclaimed, "We [are] the same race!" Sadly though, they all felt that the Black community today is often "chaotic," as Ture put it. Aisha said that Black people should become more unified "because if we [are] in a group, then [we] can help each other when...something's not going right or [someone] get let go from their job or something." Each of them, including Kenya, expressed a belief that nothing comes easy to Black people in this (Eurocentric) world and that Black people would best serve themselves by working hard and supporting one another based on shared lineage and experiences.

Ture, Assata, and Kwame explicitly connected the Black community's shared lineage and experiences to their personal hope and success. In their view, they were to be role models and sources of motivation for all Black people in their future positions as architect, chef, and doctor. In their path could be seen contributions to the African (American) legacy and welfare of their people, such as by "gettin homeless people off the streets" (spoken by Kwame). The students felt that the unity that once embraced the community ended with Emancipation and desegregation.

Each of them believed the Black community has become increasingly fragmented. When asked what she thought happened that reduced the strong unity that once characterized the Black community Kenya stated, for example, "They used to fight a lot...them and us." Said another way by Assata, when "we got free...once we escaped [slavery]...and after we got past all that segregation and all that stuff we were just like, 'Well I'm free now so forget you guys.'" Unity in the African world has eroded with the confusion brought on by divide-and-hide tactics used colonize Africa and conceal racist agendas. The reality of racism and discrimination in its contemporary covert forms seem lost on many Black people today. Lacking in consciousness has resulted in less and less unity. Asante (1980/2003) said it best: "Consciousness precedes unity" (p. 35). As these bright young achievers see it, Black people have lost sight of the need to remain unified in an individualized and pro-European society that still marginalizes them not individually, but collectively.

The pervading theme among them is that African descended people are a collective primarily because ancestry and heritage say so, and secondarily because contemporary social problems require a sense of community. With hopefulness in her voice, Assata articulated that much of the Black community remains unified today in our own way—"nobody's completely separate." Similarly, Ture expressed that, "Black people are a kinda hectic community…kinda chaotic in some ways, but…I still feel like we do what we need to do…even though we don't do it in the right way all the time." The "right way" for Africans to interact with and support one another resembles pre-desegregation African America, or even better, pre-colonial Africa. These perceptions are critical to the youth's achievement in hostile school environments and against other odds. Achieving Black students believe in the unity of their community and responsibility of each member to contribute to the collective legacy. Their role models fueled their ambitions, and with this they desired to see the same hope that they manifested in school in the adults around them.

> *It's just like, for a while like you know, back in the Martin Luther King days—[they] was like all together. Now all of a sudden, seems like they just spread apart. It's like they don't try to help each other all like that anymore, unless they come from a certain generation. It's like now, it's like kinda hard because people do ignorant stuff just for no reason. –Ture*

Culminating *Njia*
The remaining follow-up questions focused on the achievers' daily and weekly routines regarding school. These questions were important to ask because standing research regarding goal achievement asserts definitive, or mechanistic processes that are in many ways counterintuitive to the spiritual or emotional nature of African cultures, and the social experiences of Africans across the Diaspora (e.g., Klein et al., 1999; Snyder, 2002). With the richness of spirit and fluidity characteristic of African communities comes a flexibility and freedom in the achievement process that the majority European academics are not used to recognizing or appreciating.

On the point of social counterintuitiveness, typical education research fail to consider that African American youth, for example, often have limited access to family and community members who have completed the professional courses that they may be striving toward under recent desegregation, post-Apartheid, etc. eras. Many European American children on the other hand, being the recipients of centuries of African "cotton money," "sugar cane money," "coffee bean money," "gold money," etc. are also provided with nepotism and trust funds from the very beginning of their goal-setting, role-modeling, college choice, and career entry. African American students having not this nepotistic foothold means a scarcity of detailed goal plans, even while achievement is occurring.

True indeed, while they did not have rigid schedules or daily planners for school (which I have seen be required materials in some suburban, White schools), they did have determination, unwavering expectations and visions of short- and long-term goals that guided them fluidly through their days, weeks, and years in school. Homework was prioritized, but not really completed at the same time or in the same space everyday. Assata sometimes completed homework during lunch. Homework just "got done" at some point before the next school day.

For many of them, the first step after getting off the school bus in the afternoon was to going to their grandmother or aunt's homes to spend time with elders and cousins. Then there might be music on the radio or television. Ture often sat on his porch after school, taking in the neighborhood happenings. For Assata, Kenya and Kwame who vocalized feeling injustice and negativity in school, taking a break at their grandmother and aunties' homes to exhale and regroup before preparing for the next school day was probably essential. The hobbies that the students referenced in the beginning of the follow-up interview, from listening to music to playing ball, dancing or watching movies at the community center, making cards for friends and family to reflecting on the conditions of the Black community, supported their equilibrium as Black student achievers. Even for Talib, whose racial-ethnic identity and self-cultural awareness was the least developed of all, strong family values and connectedness kept him on course, seemingly filling in the gaps in consciousness that he evidenced.

Ture, Kwame, Assata, Kenya, and Aisha have begun to figure out the complexities of their racial-ethnic community, and with this they have figured out how to go about school the right way for them. No doubt they will improve their achievement process even more as their personal social and cultural understanding rises. Their actions reflect those of young, intelligent people who have established goals and commitment to reach them. They are not young and ignorant, as Ture described some Africans in the younger generations, aimless in their actions, without focus or self-understanding. The achievers stated with clarity that their goals and commitment to success came mostly from lessons rendered by family and African Ancestors. In addition to the words of their family and history, they put thought into their observations of struggle and triumph in the Black community.

They will not make the same mistakes that their elders did, but rather build from their elders' successes. They will also not participate in their peers' or younger elders' idleness and destruction of the community and nation. They understand *Njia*—the path has been laid out for them through the values, wisdom, and experiences from Africa down through the Middle Passage to the experiences of their grandmothers, grandfathers, parents, aunts and uncles today (Asante, 1980/2003). Clear vision for them means that race and culture inform their goals as family and community envelop them in love and support for motivation to reach them. No rigid and mundane rules of order necessary.

Part 3: Putting SigHT to Work

Chapter 11: Messages to the Grown-Ups: What the Student Narratives Mean

[T]he minorities who are doing relatively well are, in fact, those closest to their ancestral cultural practice in socialization and social orientation, not those closest to the Western model. For example, immigrant blacks from Africa and the Caribbean are more likely to be doing better than African Americans in the United States, and Mexican immigrants are more likely to be doing better than Mexican Americans or Chicanos. (Ogbu 1993, p. 483–484)

In-depth case analyses of six African American junior high school achievers demonstrated that certain philosophies, attitudes, and behaviors lead to their academic achievement. The results of the first major study focused on understanding hopefulness in a Black student community corroborated Ogbu's (1993) statement made nearly 20 years ago, that close proximity to self-cultural values and practices are critical for self-development and optimal performance in school. The degree to which proximal self-cultural values and practices can be achieved, however, is inevitably contingent upon one's awareness of the contemporary relevance of their cultural lineage and history. As a primary extension of one's culture, awareness of family values and expectations is perhaps the first indicator of self-cultural health, especially for young people. In other words, and as Talib's narrative showed, family connectedness can be a doorway to the cultural balance necessary for contemporary Black student achievement. For those Black students whose families have suffered most profoundly from oppressive forces that have fostered educational poverty, material poverty, substance abuse, imprisonment and family separation, etc., it will be imperative that they rely even more so on history and the community for extended family networks in order for kinship and original cultural value sets to be reestablished.

Hope Unveiled

Three main points inform my conceptualization of hope in the Black community, and the narratives of the six achievers above support my theorization. When we are hopeful we are (1) actively moving toward our goals with (2) personal and (3) social awareness. What exactly should Black children's personal and social awareness consist of you ask? Based on the results of this study, SigHT in the African world must include at minimum:

1. Family and community
2. Secure racial-ethnic identity

3. Spiritual grounding
4. A sense of determination
5. Expectations of excellence

In practical terms, hope for all African peoples must include a secure and positive identity, social consciousness, and action toward constructive goals for self and the community. I believe that this is what Ogbu's work was tapping into. In both African continental and Diasporic locations hope must mean unadulterated knowledge and love of self in order to have belief in self, and a clear understanding of social factors that help or harm progress toward goal attainment. Again, this is why I refer to hope as "SigHT". We can have 20/20 vision and still be blind to the conditions that shape our realities. Blindfolded, we leave ourselves dependent on, and disposable to others. Hope is the ability to achieve goals envisioned according to a person's history, culture, and present conditions. One cannot be conscientious, dignified, or understanding without having clear vision—SigHT—of oneself and others.

In order to effectively navigate the complexities of Eurocentrism and discrimination, African people must engage in hopeful thinking and acting while also considering their cultural dislocation and cross cultural interactions. According to the African traditions of wholism and universal harmony, intention and behavior work together for communal *djed* (stability) (Asante, 2000). The youth in this study backed up their goals with consistent and productive behaviors that reflected their confidence and family/ethnic pride. In other words, their thoughts and feelings were culturally centered and they acted based on that position in a cyclical nature with fluidity and success. This is how they were able to be successful even while surrounded by chaos and contradiction.

The five factors above were in the direct line of vision among successful African American youth. Other factors discussed were peripheral. Whereas hope for all requires goal-driven action based on personal/interpersonal and social consciousness in our modern, multicultural world, the "must include" components will depend on the historical, cultural, and contemporary contexts pertinent to particular racial-ethnic groups (see Figure 2 below). To this end, Allen and Boykin's (1992) assertions of African cultural characteristics and educational needs (discussed in Chapter 2) ring true and have important meaning for hope of African Diasporic students' school achievement today. That they found communalism, harmony, vitalistic spirituality, affect and expressive individualism to be important to African American student achievement in 1992 and these line up next to the five points listed above for this study completed in 2010 is yet another indication of the timelessness and continuity of culture.

128

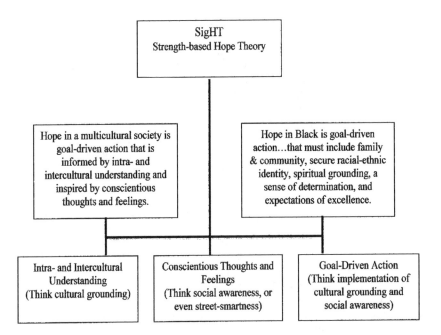

The boys and girls who lent their thoughts, feelings and experiences to this inquiry into the ingredients of Black student achievement in a 21st century that continues to be warped by failing schools and low expectations have established that self-cultural and family pride serve as the backbone for their achievement. Some had stronger racial-ethnic identities and self-cultural awareness than others, however, cultural and historical knowledge was nevertheless pronounced in their stories of hope. What some may have assumed are now parts of ancient African American history, such as collectivist orientations, strong spiritual beliefs (versus religion in the Arabic and Western senses; Ani 1980/1997), adoration and use of music and creativity to cope, and appreciation of education in fact remain customary in the families and philosophies of the young, Black, and hopeful.

At times it was necessary to make sense of the discomfort that the youth demonstrated at what they did *not* know intraculturally versus what they expressed knowing. When they could not communicate their valuing of self-cultural knowledge in explicit terms, they sent the message through nonverbal cues, such as with nervous laughter, averted eyes, or Talib's throat clearing at revealing that they knew little. The unspoken message was that they were uncomfortable, or in some way displeased about their lack of knowledge about something important. How could they call themselves achievers and representatives of their race and

129

families, which they all wanted to be, and at the same time know so little about their heritage? Just how far could they claim to succeed in the future without knowing how much their racial-ethnic community had excelled before them? The majority of them proclaimed the importance of "African American heroes," but several could name only Martin Luther King, Jr., Rosa Parks, or Malcolm X.

With remarkable transparency, the students with higher levels of self-knowledge in African and African American history and contributions had the greatest combination of academic excellence, family pride, and secure racial-ethnic identity. They also had the strongest articulation skills. Without a doubt, personal identity, that matrix of biological, cultural and social influences, is the central most important determinant for the choices that we make in life. Personal values, choice of friends, respect for authority, and goals are all determined by identity. Self-definition impacts self-belief, and self-belief determines whether goals such as graduating from high school and college will even be set.

The fabric of Ture, Talib, Kwame, Assata, Kenya and Aisha's cognitive and conative processes toward school were found to be of the same material. Correspondingly, the patterns of their behaviors in and toward school were methodically similar. These six notable students have given us standards that educators, school psychologists, parents, and other vested parties can use to help their students of African ancestry and heritage progress in school and life. As with any sample of people from a larger population, generalizations of findings should be made carefully. However, much can be taken from the strength of the similarities found in the responses of Ture, Talib, Kwame, Assata, Kenya and Aisha.

In order to make the best sense and use of the mountain of data gathered from more than 210 responses, each item was coagulated into 38 meaning units or codes representing the essence of all six narratives. These were three more codes than anticipated for each of the 35 primary interview questions. From these codes, 13 Principles (or themes in academic terms) were drawn. The themes found represent the essential "take-home," and in this case also "take to school" and "take to policy" messages from the study. They are presented in ascending order, meaning the higher number Principles signify greater value. Principles 11, 12 and 13 are foundational to 1 through 10. All are of course important, and we must begin where we are before attempting to reach the heights. Recommendations according to the Principles are provided to educators, parents, and policymakers in Chapter 12. Here are the 13 Principles that describe how they embodied hope through feeling, thought and action in their school strivings.

Principle 1. Expect Excellence

High expectations beget hopeful thinking and spur hopeful actions. Students should enter their school building knowing that they will succeed in class. They will make good grades. They will turn in all homework. They will excel on all tests. This may seem obvious, but many children do not enter class believing these things possible for them, often, especially amongst African American children quite the opposite is true. The achievers here were confident in their ability to succeed, and they had their parents, extended families, communities, and awareness of Black culture and history to thank for their confidence, this last even if in limited amounts. Indeed, making their families and community proud was too important for low expectations. Despite the majority of the achievers having parents and other family members who had not completed high school or college, they set and worked toward career goals befitting to their peers in distant, more privileged neighborhoods and school districts.

Without question, researchers have found that a healthy dose of self-confidence correlates positively to good performance (e.g., Bandura, 1977, Gaudreau & Blondin, 2004). Excellent expectations seem to be the skin of the achievers' hopefulness, the sensory or protective shell of their positive attitudes and behaviors. However, what creates the expectations that make the self-confidence and effective actions possible must be understood in order to help more Black children make the seemingly impossible possible.

Principle 2. Code of Conduct: Play Your Part

In the African tradition there are finite roles played by elders and children. There are certain responsibilities held by each, and to treat children as elders or forget that every elder is a role model and teacher to children is to seriously break custom and bring shame to the family and community. One is to know at all times where they stand in relation to other people and things, and pay respect or credit where they are due. This belief in the roles and boundaries, or the code of conduct, between children and adults has been held in African cultures at home and abroad, although many are beginning to lose remembrance (this tradition is also discussed in Principle 11, "Bridge Divergent Worlds").

Generally speaking, Black children know that they are to have decorum according to the location or context that they are in. The achievers were clear about their role as students, and they respected their teachers. Where their teachers failed to meet their obligations as educators and role models, the achievers continued to hold themselves apart and in many ways beneath their teachers out of reverence for their adulthood and role. They could not change their teachers, but they had learned how to adjust their own behavior in ways that extended their goals and upheld their family's honor. They played their part as children and as scholars, generally withholding their arguments or disobedience even when it was warranted, and always completing their assignments. They treated school as a place to work. They came to school prepared and studied for tests

131

even in classes that they disliked. The code of conduct they described included both proactive and reactionary behaviors, however, proaction through self-determination tipped the scale. These students exercised *agency* based predominately on the notion that they, their families and personal community were the main *subject* of their success (Asante, 1980/ 2003; 1998).

Principle 3. Be Academically Resilient

One of the aspects that I find interesting and humbling about the achievers in this study is that they were not all qualifiers for Gifted and Talented school programs in the traditional sense of mathematical or linguistic genius, but they were, however, all diligent and resilient in their determination to achieve. Being a Black student achiever requires academic resilience. Black students must be academically resilient on at least two levels. First, they must get up, dust themselves off and meet adversity with greater determination and firm confidence should they get an "ugly" grade or face a school challenge. Second, they must remain on their course of ultimate success in achieving life stability, health and prosperity, even if they find themselves having to change their intermediate goals, career choices, etc. They must keep their eyes on the prize and remember Njia. They should expect nothing to come easily or for free. Our world is one of reciprocity and balance in which you receive what you give.

Rather than exhaust all possibilities by placing their entire focus on a single target, or by putting all of their eggs in one basket as the American adage goes, Black student achievers consider multiple avenues to success. Just in case football does not work out for Talib, then he is ready to set his SigHT on another career option. Aisha had a staggered career plan, wherein she will first master the skills of nursing en route to being a great doctor. An enduring characteristic of academic resilience is important for Black students because they are so often bombarded with false images of prosperity and probability (e.g., every African American boy can be a professional athlete or rapper). In reality, Assata is right, becoming an architect, lawyer, doctor or chef is significantly more sensible than striving for sports or music industry stardom from statistical standpoints alone. And as Ture explained, as long as he has a bright mind, no amount of life challenges can ever truly defeat him. It is critical that Black students, place a premium on academic resilience. Very telling, resilience was the factor present in each of the role models selected by the achievers above. Go hard or go home was the motto here.

Principle 4. Be Determined

How can one be academically resilient without also being determined? Neither racist teachers nor family histories of school dropouts deterred these achievers. What the children expressed being determined toward might be said to be the very crux of their hopes, the gold at the end of the rainbow for them. In reflection, they were determined toward several final destinations that centered on two things; living happy and free lives (e.g., free from debt, free from fear of property loss, free from racism, free from stress, etc.) and extending the legacies of their families and ethnic community. The source of their determination came primarily from family connectedness, a spirit of ethnic collectiveness, and spirituality. We might say then, than spiritual belief and communal relationships are the driving forces of hope for Black children—or the determination to have hope.

Failing was not an option for the achievers as long they knew where they came from—created by "God" and lead by "African American heroes"—and that their families and community supported their efforts. Whereas social scientists following the mainstream school of thought would claim that concrete plans or quantifiable methods are what drive hope, the greatest motivators for Black children are immeasurable in the anti-spirit, scientific sense. This is not to say that the achievers here did not respect the power of a plan, or that they did not have markers for which to track their actions, but that they all believed they could do whatever they put their minds to and relied on mental and emotional gauges relating to their families and community just as much or more.

Principle 5. Focus on Quality-of-Life

M.K. Asante, Jr. (2008) captured the essence of the post-hip hop generation's mindset with regard to art and life. He concluded that African youth who are positively engaged in life understand that their goals and actions are bigger than anything that their eyes can see, hands can touch, and ears can hear. More than their physical appearance being hot, having the latest car, or hearing the tightest beats laid over the message in a song, what the "Black stars" in his book cared most about was their history, life purpose, and contribution to humanity (Black Star, 1998). The prolific hip hop group Dead Prez asserted the same in their 2000 song *It's Bigger Than Hip Hop*. Ture, Kwame, Talib, Assata, Kenya and Aisha revealed this as truth again here in *SigHT*.

Although there is ostensible value in "being rich", as we all want to live in comfort, Black students must avow the importance of all things invaluable as reward for their labor in school. Their contributions to their families and ethnic community are far more important than fame, which can be fleeting, or personal gain, which can be isolating. Their mentality must not be one of, "cash rules everything around me, cream, get the money" (Wu Tang, 1994). It is this perception of happiness and merit being important in life that helps to explain the achievers' choosing enjoyable and meaningful career fields. None of them selected careers based solely on their belief in the financial return of the position, but

133

instead focused on professions that connected to their natural skills and personalities under the premise that they would be happy doing the perspective job long-term, and others would benefit from their work. While big homes, sometimes more than one, and nice cars were desired bonuses among these achievers, they were decidedly bonuses, not payment for their hard work in school. They understood clearly that a successful life is one enriched by things that money cannot buy, like freedom, family togetherness, peace of mind, health, and heritage. The most important things come from learning and understanding order, for which school success can be a door or gateway. Rich to them meant financially stable and happy. Quality-of-life, not quantity in it, reigns.

Princiiple 6. Value Education and School Too

The achievers evidenced understanding that education is the door to illumination and riches that are life sustaining. On top of this, unlike many of their peers, the achievers believed in the power of school to help deliver what they needed and desired. In the Introduction we established understanding that education differs from school today. As much as the achievers and their families recognized the difference (observed in their treatment of school being only a means to an end), they also believed in the returns that would come from succeeding in school enough to work hard. The achievers were in business to be happy and to improve their family and community's conditions for the long-term.

Without their belief in the viability of education (i.e., school is a great route to take for me to acquire a solid career and life of stability), their efforts in school would have been lesser and their achievement cut down. Appreciating knowledge and believing in school, the young achievers were willing to make the investments of completing their schoolwork, minding their business in class, and showing respect to their teachers for future profit. The fact is that belief in the power of school *supersedes* the first six Principles. It must be present for expectations of excellence, playing the part of student, and being academically resilient to exist. It also undergirds student determination and focus on quality in life. Ture, Talib, Kwame, Assata, Kenya and Aisha agreed that college training would greatly increase their chances for stability and contribution, and going to college begins with taking school seriously today.

Principle 7. Seek Harmony and Justice

Values of harmony and justice surfaced across several items, but most strikingly during discussions of identity and history. Not only are the virtues of harmony and justice longstanding African ethical beliefs found throughout Maat in Kemet (Asante, 2000; Karenga, 2002), but also post-colonial experiences shared by Black people have reinforced these values. Black student achievers appreciated harmony and justice so much that they tended to *define* themselves by them. In some instances, such as with Assata, harmony and justice were basic personality factors, in others, the values were summoned to the fore by racism and teacher mistreatment. Because so much of their experiences were full of *dis*harmony and *in*justice, they were that much more intent on harmonizing and equalizing their and their family's lives.

Some of them had already experienced racism directly as adolescents. Those who were conscious of the injustices they had experienced, especially in school, smartly stored the incidences away into the banks of their memories, and used the weight of them to assist in propelling them forward toward victory. Each of them knew enough of their history to understand something of the depth that racism has taken to treat them and their community unfairly, and each understood that they might very well have to face maltreatment in the future. Armed with values of peace and reciprocity, or harmony and justice, these achievers are better prepared for any disorder or inequality thrown at them now or in the future.

Principle 8. Collectivism

After half a millennia in the West, African Americans continue to be collectivist in their family and community orientation. In spite of years of American graduate school training asserting otherwise, I knew this to be true as an African American woman coming into the SigHT study. Alas, however, direct questions to the point were needed to confirm my what I already knew in spirit for Western scientists, teachers, and the like to listen and treat African American children and families accordingly. Indeed, the Black student achievers in this study, representing some of the youngest and brightest of our community, demonstrated that their strivings have as much to do with their families and community as it does with their individual pursuits. Each of these students felt that they have a responsibility to support not only their personal material and emotional needs, but also that of their family members. Further, most of them extended this care to the development and image of the Black community at large.

For Ture, Assata and Aisha, kinship extended the entire length of the Black community's umbilical cord back to Africa. Interestingly, the collectivist orientation of the SigHT participants mirrors that of a study done with African Diasporic college students who almost entirely chose graduate programs and career fields based on the likelihood of their being able to support the needs of the Black community (Chandler, 2011). However underdeveloped their racial-ethnic identities might have been, and however shallow their understanding of social influences on their aspirations, each of the achievers addressed a "we" factor ascribed to family connectedness, the conditions facing Africa and African America, and pride in African heroes and heroines. This is a profound finding as it relates the very ethos and behaviors of successful African American students to their family and ethnic community.

Principle 9. Be Spiritually Grounded

Most of the students subscribed to a guiding belief system versus a religious affiliation with any of the popular world religions. This was somewhat surprising given the strong role that modern religion, especially Christianity, has played in the African American community since the 17th and 18th centuries (Lincoln & Mamiya, 1990). Ture referenced his grandmother's "extreme belief in Jesus Christ," but otherwise the students spoke of belief in God generally. Kenya believed that God had created her ebony complexioned for good reason. Kwame believed that "as long has you have faith in God, all things are possible." None of them named a religion when asked about their beliefs and values. Instead they listed many common values and beliefs that they lived their lives by, including being close to family, supporting family and community, and appreciating education, harmony, reciprocity, justice, and strong work ethics.

Rather than claim religious doctrine or affiliation, what the majority of the students subscribed to as their guiding belief system were ethics that work together to form a spiritual grounding. They recognized a supreme force overseeing their human experience, and this played an important role in their hopeful thinking and acting. Nobles (2006) and Akbar (2003) have connected African peoples' spirituality to their musical emphasis and collectivist orientation. All three of these, spirituality, collectivism and music, were pronounced in the narratives of the African American achievers above. Therefore, the significant relationship between Black students' spirits, morals and music should be supported as one by their families and communities. If achievement is of interest, then their consciousness and musical intake should be encouraging a spirit of success and positivity.

Principle 10. Have Clarity in Racial-Ethnic Identity

Collectivism and clear racial-ethnic identity are a pair, the former coming out of the latter.

Asante (2001), for example, explained that "if you confuse the issue of racial identity or seek to explode it, you minimize the possibility of collective action," and further, "[o]ne does not see other ethnic or racial communities clamoring to explode [or absolve of] their racial identity" (p. 50). All of the Civil Rights advancements and general progress in African communities everywhere were begotten from Black people acting as a collective against spiritual, psychological, and physical threats. Yet, some Africans in America have been gravely affected by what Asante (2001) has called the "post-Martin Luther King, Jr. phenomenon," which has involved Black men and women putting forth concerted effort to shed their racial-ethnic identity and disassociate with other Black people on the basis of mainstream patriotism (p. 50). Now there is a growing post-Mandela phenomenon occurring among Africans in South Africa (Sesanti, 2012). Families of African children must consider seriously that every one of the student achievers here perceived that racism was imminent for them, that they would inevitably face harsh discrimination in some form in the future. On what grounds will they contest it?

Gloria Ladson-Billings (2008) realizes that education and other everyday activities in the U.S. are so embroiled with racism that "it looks ordinary and natural to people in [U.S. society]" (p. 11). The same is true in Africa, Europe and the UK. Racial-ethnic identity must be developed and embraced rather than shunned or ignored as the precursor to full self-understanding, pride and determination. Without clear personal identities, Black families will experience the chaos referenced by Ture in his narrative and follow-up response. In order to succeed, one must understand both his cultural and social position or else he will lack understanding of his role(s) in family and society. Lacking in effective social understanding, he will not have the clarity of knowing who or what his friends and foes are in relation to his peace and goal achievement.

The only way to develop healthy racial-ethnic identity is through self-historical and cultural knowledge. We learned from the narratives above that where knowledge in personal history and culture were lacking, racial-ethnic identity was complicated and uncomfortable, such as in the cases of Aisha and Talib. Even as they espoused connections to their families and Black community, they stood on shaky identity ground, unsure of whether to endorse being Black and proud or plead the U.S. Constitutional 5th so as not to incriminate themselves. While Talib was very clear on what his family values were and where he stood in his home, his family identity did little to help him make sense of complex social issues such as those created by racism and male chauvinism. His improvisational history lesson to a younger Black student started and stopped with desegregation in the 1950's and 60s. Naturally then, he did not know how to feel, what to think or what to do when he encountered racism in school. Racial-ethnic identity, not only family, gender or professional identities, matters greatly to Black student achievement.

Principle 11. Bridge Divergent Worlds

The interesting thing about working with children and understanding the essential meaning behind their thoughts and behaviors is that they often know what they don't know, and other times show what they don't know whether they know that they don't know or not. As mentally discombobulating this may be, it is a good description of what the student achievers above indicated in their responses regarding their identity and school relationships. For example, the youth expressed determination to succeed in life through school knowing that what separated their community from those at Case Western Reserve University and Cleveland State University just a few miles from their school was a college education and "good job," but they sensed at the same time that school was not the place for their culture or personal development. While not expressly stating or understanding this sense, they *felt* the detachment between themselves and their school.

I have heard many times White teachers, and sometimes Black teachers decry the lack of caring that Black parents show for their children's education. The reality, however, is that people interface with schools according to their cultural beliefs and social experiences. This is why clarity in racial-ethnic identity is key. The achievers' families showed great investment in the children's education by monitoring their grades, praising them for high marks, disciplining them for poor performance and frequently encouraging them to continue toward success. The families' expectation was that the children knew what was expected of them and they would act accordingly, regardless of the mistreatment or lack of support they felt from the school system. The same expectation was held for teachers. On the cultural level, the notion behind Black achievers serving as bridges between the divergent worlds of their home and school points to the African philosophy of the village in developing children. Within the "village," every person and organization has a role to play, and all are expected to play their part to such effectiveness that the other members of the society, organization, community, etc. are not obligated to check up on others' status or effectiveness, for they are busy doing their part in their position. If in the African value system everyone has a role, then teachers must teach, students must learn, and parents must govern *at home.*

The effectiveness in the families' approach lies in the fact that the children knew their family values and felt their families' care and support. As a result, they were motivated to perform well. When every man, woman, and child fills the obligations of their role with a spirit of excellence then the society runs smoothly and no time is wasted on breaching organizational lines of duty. The achievers took it upon themselves to bridge the gap that exists between their Eurocentric school and African homes, in which caring and education do not always exist in the void but learning and achievement are still expected. Black students must understand that an important part of their role involves mending their school experiences where breaks in culture and support exist. Black student achievers bring school home by completing their homework and telling their families when they are needed on location, and they bring home to school by always remembering and acting on their family values and goals. Independence and responsibility must be fostered in them, preferably early, for school achievement. This should be the rule even in predominately Black schools, but especially if they are attending mainstream schools. In doing so, Black student achievers learn to play their part of "being the bridge", as Ture so aptly put it, between their divergent home and school worlds. As unfair as this may be to them, it is necessary.

Principle 12. Be Proud of the African in African American

Closer to the foundation of all the 13 Principles leading to Black student achievement is the very meaning of their ethnic and cultural heritage. For many of the students in this study, Africa represented a missing link. African people and activities were represented as parodies of a distorted European history rather than agents in an African reality. Continental Africans were viewed as victimized, dumb, dirty, and poor. Correspondingly, African Americans were at best wise to fight against slavery and segregation from European Americans. Only to then imitate European Americans, since African Americans' origins and cultural depths were foreign. This view of Africa and African people is an unfair one to both Black and White people, sure to have negative impacts on the *intra*cultural health of Black people, and the *inter*cultural relations between the two groups.

Where Europeans are perceived as the omnipotent destroyers of history and executioners of anything positive that Africans could have been responsible for, they are also positioned as the gatekeepers of Black people's hopes and dreams. Black people then have little chance of being victorious as long as White people are around. As sure as White supremacy has been a historical curse and many continue to fight for White privilege, this is still a half-sighted view of African history and agency that leads only to resentment, hostility, and/or fear in Black and White interactions. Remember that many schools today have a majority White staff. The "poor Africa, evil Europe" perspective fosters a dependency state and robs Black children of the wealth of information in African, not European history.

Considering the importance of this principle, "Being Proud of the African in African American," it becomes clear how so many of the children were confused in their racial-ethnic identity. That Africans were enslaved in America and became African Americans was consciously accepted as fact in all but two of the students' minds, but what to do with Africa, what to think of their and their community's longer pre-Columbian beginning was a mystery for almost all of them. Reflecting on Africa was the most uncomfortable and frustrating part of their long and varied

139

discussions with me. They knew that they didn't know what they had rights to and for this the gap between them and school will only grow wider as the children recognize that they could know if their teachers would only teach them as they should. One day they might have access to the books, museums, and airplanes they expressed needing to learn about and visit Africa but for now they struggle to fathom that African American history and achievements actually exist within *African* history. This was because they had little idea of the many contributions and civilizations that they could recite about Africa. No middle schooler I know would want to be associated with a "poor, dumb and dirty continent that only gets robbed by White people." Using the predominate identifiers given to Africa by the young achievers in this study, they could be called Dumb American or Dirty American, instead of African American.

Yet, they are African American and they maintain hope in school largely because of the existence of African American heroes, and, for Ture and Assata, the "dream" place that Africa once was. They care about who they are and all of what made them. We must imagine their confidence and motivation if they knew more. Exposing Black children to their history just makes good sense. They are eager to learn about themselves and waiting to turn their self-knowledge into higher achievement.

Principle 13. Have Family Bonds

Family connectedness was without question the bedrock of the students' school success, followed closely by community adoration and pride. As an African American woman who has committed my life's work to remaining attuned to the developments of African communities everywhere and the African American community of which I was born especially, I have observed corrosion in the African family as neocolonialism and philosophical distancing from indigenous cultural norms progress. I was therefore surprised by the strength and explicitness with which the students expressed being influenced by their families. For the boys, the ability to take care of their spouse and children in adulthood was very important. Certain African cultural elements such as collectivism and expectations of excellence in education were prominent and expected, however, the placement of family at the center of focus was a profound finding. The achievers' statements of how much their families meant to them were simply touching:

> *"I work hard in school—to impress my momma."*
> *"I want to have a secure career—to help take care of my family so they won't be poor."*
> *"I hope to show my family who dropped out of school—that we can do it."*

Several of the achievers even based their career goals on advice they had received from parents or grandparents, where according to mainstream psychology adolescents would opt for alternative careers to assert their autonomy or power *away* from family. Amongst these achievers, direct family members often took the position of role models. The omnipresence of family in the achievers' narratives is significant. When asking the children about the values and beliefs that they live their lives by, what they aspire to become and why, and how confident they are in achieving their goals, we learned first of the influences that their parents and extended family networks had on them. Further, rarely did the achievers limit their family to their mothers, fathers and siblings. Family included all of the friends, distant relatives and community members who offered their encouragement, advice and belief in their abilities to achieve in school and reach their goals, no matter how lofty their vision may have seemed in comparison to where they lived. When scolded, the children appreciated the discipline their families enforced when they failed to meet goals. It must be said, however, that while the students' families served them well in some ways, they assisted them poorly in other important areas.

Whereas the families had done well with instilling in the achievers self-esteem and high expectations, they nearly failed at ensuring that the children were clear on their *cultural-esteem* and identity. With this, many of their families neglected to ensure that the teens and pre-teens knew how to think and what courses to take if confronted with racism or questions of community history and contribution. Tatum (1999) explained the following:

Viewing the Black child as embedded in the social system of the Black family, the Black family embedded in the social system of the Black community, and the Black community embedded in the larger White society [in America]...the Black community forms a protective buffer zone for the family, and subsequently the child. This is especially true if both the family and the community share a sense of peoplehood or collective pride...Certainly the family's protective function is tested as the child enters a more heterogeneous environment. (p. 15-16)

What Tatum endorses here is the criticalness of racial-ethnic identity in the growing of healthy and successful Black children. More than 10 years after the publication of her words, the present study continues this lesson with evidence from the mouths of the children themselves: In order for Black youth to be raised to their highest abilities, they must know who they are as individuals within family and community collectives. Black parents and extended family members can no longer abdicate their responsibilities of laying the foundation for our children's success any more than teachers can abscond their role as pedagogical leaders, or politicians, principals and superintendents as educational overseers. Parents, friends, distant relatives, and community members must continue to offer encouragement and advice to Black youth, even when it seems they are not listening. Do not be fooled by "the cool" of Black youth, they are observing and listening. The family and community together continue to be the nucleus for which all else magnetize or repels.

Chapter 12: A Hope Epidemic: How Your Black Students Can Do It Too

How Your Black Students Can Do It Too

In order for Black students to have vision and see their goals into fruition, they must have SigHT. Otherwise, without personal and social awareness to act effectively from, they will be but wishful thinkers or dreamers who never match their actions to their potential. It turns out that the ultimate vision of six African American middle school achievers was to evoke pride from and extend the legacies of their families and larger Black community. This then must be considered firstly in any discourse or program designed to increase Black student achievement.

For educators, this means changes in your pedagogy, except in the rare occasion that culturally responsive instruction is already being included in your classroom or school's planning for Black children. Restorative changes do not have to mean a complete overhaul of your class curriculum, for it is understood that some things lie outside of your authority to change, but rather strategic refocusing in your professional convictions, language, and teaching style. We live in a pluralistic society and it is time that our pedagogy reflects our collective reality.

For parents this means never allowing your remembrance of cultural and family values to drift into indolence. It also means never allowing awareness of Black history from Africa to the Diaspora to be devalued. In other words, speak about and enforce family values actively with your children, and require self-knowledge as fun activities and traditions in your home. As Black youth strive to achieve in spite of cultural dislocation and repression, their senses of ethnic pride, self-confidence and expectations for excellence must be instilled and strengthened at home base. They must have as much cultural-esteem as self-esteem. As your students' first and forever teachers, you must establish home spaces that encourage personal dignity, determination, and academic excellence in them.

Having said this, one of the most significant findings in the study for both parents and educators to note was that home and school represented divergent worlds. It is evident that there exists many differences in cultural orientation between African and European peoples generally (Akbar, 2003, Diop, 1987), and these distinctions naturally create inconsistencies in values and behavioral norms. Cultural differences are good things unto themselves, as distinctions contribute to diversity and enrich life. However, in situations where one group imposes assimilation and rejects personal development of others, cultural distinctions are problematic and create conflict and distancing. Rather than encourage a forced alliance between homes and schools that are disparate, I suggest that the predominately White teaching force (including principals, counselors, etc.), in spite of preconceived notions or perceived ineptitude, treat every Black student as a member of a family full of hope, that is as having expectations of excellence, aspirations of achieving a life of peace and stability, and pride in or desires for greater knowledge about their history and culture.

Parents and families of Black children who are nurturing hopefulness in their students should continue to encourage them and monitor their school activity, *as well as* consider ways to communicate their expectations to their children's teachers and counselors. Do this with a note or phone call in the beginning of the year for instance, not necessarily with the intention of building half-hearted relationships that may end negatively, but to voice your family's strength and dedication to school achievement. I know that many African American parents experience the frustration of their children's teachers demonstrating lower expectations for them. Especially for African American boys, a "C" is all too often enough to evoke a, "He's doing just fine!" from teachers. I have been called in many times by family members and coworkers to mediate conflicts of cultural difference and unequal expectations between school staff and Black families. To make matters worse, often the realization of incongruent expectations does not become evident until the middle or end of the school year, so important time is wasted for the children.

What happens in the context of Eurocentric schools serving African families to create conflict is that the village community is rendered ineffective, as the shared expectations, interests, and behaviors assumed by parents to exist are actually nonexistent. In the village everyone works for the success of the community out of caring and responsibility. Children are prized, monitored and taught by all naturally. As "mainstream" schools exist outside of the community model, those outside of the village often care less and teach through contract. Working under-contract-to-care, focus is placed on the terms and conditions of the agreement between the staff and the system rather than the children and the community. Especially in the case of teaching "other" people's children (Ballenger, 1998), contracts are easily broken, expectations lowered, rigor in teaching diminished, interest in *educating* decreased.

Many Black parents and extended families do not realize that they have in fact maintained a village-type philosophy and that their children's schools exist outside the tradition. Black families entrust far too much care to teachers and staff who are under-contract-to-care but may not—because they do not operate within the context of the same traditions and they have not shared in the community's experiences. Unconscious of this fact, the common result is that Black families hold unrealistic (outside of reality) expectations for teachers and staff who do not fully understand their children and community, and who therefore do not care for their children and community as they do.

Because the cultural locations of African and European people are different, both groups can only serve African students by approaching school through a combined intra- and intercultural lens: As in "I am aware of where I stand on the issue of education, and I can see how to approach schooling effectively based on how the school system views education," and "I am aware of where I stand on the issue of education, and I can see how to approach schooling effectively based on how my student's family views education." Instead of taking a truly multicultural stance, however, school staff have continually perceived that Black parents and families do not value education or care about their children's success, and Black parents and families have accused school staff of simply being racist or picking on their child. In this scheme, both sides force Black children to bridge the two warring worlds, and thus put perhaps too much adult responsibility on their young shoulders.

Buckling under the pressure, many Black children wind up disengaging in the schooling process all together. While racism does in fact exist in contemporary schools, some of the time the issue is more simply a not-knowing and/or a negating of personal culture and cross-cultures, increasing the possibility for Eurocentrism to turn into racism (understand that Eurocentrism is a touting of European history whether true or stolen, that may breed racism but mostly intends to massage European ego and insecurity) (e.g., see Asante, 1998). Just as the achievers presented here understood their positions and played their roles well, Black families and school staff must learn how to play theirs. The outcome of parents and teachers "Playing Their Parts" (Principle 2) along with Black student achievers would very likely be improved school outcomes.

Certainly there is a part to play by others. School psychologists and community mental health workers who work with Black children must discard their deficit models of assessment and intervention for a positive, life affirming approach that respects the inherent strengths within African cultures and among African people. Academicians in colleges and universities must train educators and mental health workers toward understanding the populations they are privileged to serve. Policymakers must find ways to uphold some civic honor and create spaces and opportunities for educators to educate all children, and for all children to learn and be inspired to trust in the system to work. We all have important roles in supporting hope and achievement among our children. The following thoughts and strategies are offered to help African families, teachers, service providers, and legislators transform their thinking and policies. These strategies represent a beginning to launching a hope epidemic. There is yet work to be done.

Teachers

Educational interventions, in the form of compensatory education (to compensate for the deprivation and disadvantage assumed to be inherent in African American homes and communities), often were based on a view of African American children as deficient white children…One reason is a stubborn refusal in American education to recognize African Americans as a distinct cultural group. While it is recognized that African Americans make up a distinct racial group, the acknowledgement that this racial group has a distinct culture is still not recognized. It is presumed that African American children are exactly like white children but just need a little extra help. (Ladson-Billings, 1994, p. 8–9)

Although I am not a teacher by trade, I have experienced standing before a classroom full of children and teenagers with energetic bodies and inquisitive minds. I have also taught college students. I understand the complexities involved in managing the personalities and sustaining the interest of 20 to 30 young, diverse people.

I know without a doubt that students respond best to lessons that are relatable and multimodal. Students of African descent especially appreciate curriculum that teaches them how to better understand themselves and the people around them. Honest instruction that extends their knowledge of how to manipulate the world and manifest their particular hope is key. They want and need to know more about themselves as freethinking and immensely capable people.

Black students appreciate teachers and staff who "keep it real" about their personal limitations and expectations. For example, if you genuinely want your Black students to learn, then recognize the limits of your knowledge on Black history and contemporary news rather than simply omit the presence of Black people in your pedagogy. Similarly, Black students want and need teachers who will let them know when they are succeeding or falling short of meeting expectations. Great teachers of Black students challenge them to learn self-critical information and raise questions. *Allow your Black students room for self-exploration and self-assertion.* As a required or extra credit assignment, your students can share their answers or research findings with the entire class.

The point here is that teachers are not expected to be expert historians or sociologists for every ethnic group they teach. Instead, learn what you can because you care about your students and incite them (and their families) to work with you. Awaken them to themselves. The more you understand them and the better they know themselves, the greater your classroom experience will be. The approach of teaching in terms of co-developing high achieving Black students—working with your students—is an enduring one relevant to early career or veteran teachers. Keeping them engaged requires lessons and activities that project their realities and future success.

Consider the fact that many Black children live in communities that are nearly (or exactly) 100% Black, but their schools are nearly (or exactly) 100% White in staff and administration. At Justice Academy, there was only one African American teacher of science in the entire school. Black students, even if subliminally aware, know racism continues in the favor of others, and at very young ages (e.g., Quintana, 2007). They know that there is no such thing as a closet racist or colorblind school. As Assata said, the children always feel it.

The motivation of the participants in this study was linked to their perception of family and community happiness. In the Black community, direct representation of family and ethnic community is not viewed as an unwanted obligation. It is a natural function of philosophical orientation that Black people across the world have maintained from African cultural beliefs and value systems (or at least in Kenya, Nigeria, Kemet/Egypt, Puerto Rico, London, the Continental United States, Jamaica, Bahamas and several other regions that I have worked in or made contact with). Family and community connectedness is where you can begin to build greater success within the Black students in your classroom. As the second most frequent contact for Black children after home/community, there are ways that you can improve the hopefulness of Black students (and their families).

Teachers: What to Do
1. Teachers and Black students often meet in schools from different locations only to find themselves in complicated and disconnected shared spaces. In order to frame the schooling experience in ways that speak to Black students, and no matter the content area, the outcomes of their actions should always be viewed as family and community-based, not only individually relevant. Place the responsibility that Black youth have of representing their family and community members well directly in their laps. Reminders, sometimes subtle ones and other times long-winded and continuous ones, that their mother, father, grandparent, aunt or uncles would be very disappointed in their behavior have worked with great effectiveness in my work with Black youth. Give it a try, and the more specificity that you can gather about (a) the people closest to your student(s), and (b) the ways in which the student desires to please those family members the better.

2. If one or more of your Black students are failing to execute the Code of Conduct referenced in Chapter 11, Principle 2, then do your best to figure out why they are refusing to act on the intelligence and strengths that they have been endowed with from the beginning of time. This does not have to include a referral for testing or staff problem solving meeting. Instead, use your authority and the rapport that you have established with the student in question to establish the basics with him or her:

a. What are their values?
b. What do they want for themselves and their families?
c. Do they see school as a viable option for them to succeed in life? Or rather, do they recognize the qualitative and quantitative benefits that they can receive as a result of school achievement?

Very often the case is that Black children, and for that matter many other children, have not thought carefully about what their and their family or community values are, and they therefore have not connected those values to their everyday behavior at school: They have not been *conscientious in their thoughts and feelings*, beliefs or goals as they make their trek through school. Both they and you their teacher suffer as a result. Establishing the basics with Black youth can be easily done with paper and pencil, and honest discussions of "who are you," "who do you represent," and "where are you going kid." With this, ensure that your Black students are aware of multiple career options to set their sights on and focus their behavior. It is quite simply a matter of providing direction.

3. Prerequisite to engaging in a meaningful teaching relationship with Black children is recognizing that they are not, as Ladson-Billings (1994) said it, White children in costume. Realize that African Americans represent a distinct cultural group as well as a racial group. Where schools readily treat students transferring in from the West Indies or Africa as ethnic, they do not extend any cultural rites whatsoever to African American children although they represent yet another African ethnic group. Once this realization is made teachers will begin to teach all Black children more effectively, and the children's hope and achievement will soar as they learn more about their connections to Africa and the African Diaspora, all African contributions, and their responsibility for success as descendants of the continent and/or Diaspora.

4. Recognizing African American students and families as members of a larger African collective not only in physical appearance but also in cultural orientation will help teachers with dealing effectively with the important reality of dissonance between Black families and schools. Multiple consciousnesses, or at least, nonjudgmental poses are critical. In considering the important theme of divergent worlds, for example, many teachers have fallen into the trap of mistaking different for wrong, and mistrust for uncaring. Not only does the theme stem from incongruent village versus single-dwelling orientations (so to speak), but also

from discontentment for the predominantly Eurocentric curriculum and culture of most contemporary schools. The irrelevancy with which the African world is treated in mainstream schooling experiences intuitively eliminates special interest or relationship building among many Black students and families with schools. Before rendering a verdict about your Black students' hopefulness or the care of their family, judge the multicultural quality of your pedagogy and school culture. Are the people in question present? Plug in the gaps where you can through multicultural innovation and partnering with your students and/or families. Even if you can only find time for one or two specialized assignments a quarter or semester, make your Black students' school experience count. And please, move beyond the comfortable Martin Luther King, Jr. "we shall overcome" routine. Imhotep, Ramses II, Amentutankh (Tutankhamen), Malcolm X, Mbuya Nehanda, and Shirley Chisholm had dreams too.

Parents and Families

My study participants were not much different from their peers who did not qualify for participation. They had essentially the same taste in music, hobbies, styles of dress, sense of humor, and manner of speaking as other Black children. Their desires of receiving praise from their families and becoming successful doctors, lawyers, and athletes were also very similar to what I have observed of Black children from the continent to the United States and Bahamas. They were different from many of their peers, however, in that they had figured out what's up with school in relation to their values and community. While many Black middle and upper class parents suffer from cases of restless leg syndrome, where they find themselves "racing to leave the race" (Asante, 2001), the truth is that Black is Black no matter where you live or how professionally successful you are. It behooves us all to raise children who are culturally centered and socially conscious for lifetime success.

The narratives of these achievers tells us that the Black youth far too often concern themselves with the negative in being Black due to racism and a lack of self-knowledge. Interestingly, this very point confirms the importance of our children understanding that they are more than just Black, or Be-lack as in you are lacking as Heru Se Ptah would say. Instead of defining themselves in relation to racism, they should be focused on knowing that Black is intelligent, Black is beautiful, Black is full of history, Black is creative, and more because Black is African. Instead, the children found themselves being anti-African in the same way that the very racists they opposed are. There must be clarity in their values and personal identities without shame or hesitation in connecting who they are and what they do to where they come from and where they are going. Theirs must be a resolve strong enough to withstand any racism, sexism, classism, or other neocolonialism that they may find themselves up against.

We should be comforted by the fact that each of the African American achievers expressed appreciation for their community's heritage of resilience at least from slavery up to the Civil Rights Movement in the United States. Although too few, about half of the students indicated positive awareness of the African American connection to Africa as homeland. In doing so, the latter youth demonstrated awareness of a life for Black people before slavery. This is a very good result. In the same way that we want teachers, principals, psychologists, etc. to view our children as more than little sambos and picanninies, Black children must also know that there is far more to them and their people than colonialism, slavery and integration into White history and culture. It is critical that African families, Diasporic especially, know enough to dispel the stereotypical images of Africa that we constantly receive from the media, and sadly even most mainstream textbooks and programs.

Not only is there an extremely rich history of Africa to know, but also contemporary beauty and innovation thrives. Most Black families are unaware, for example, that Africa is a strong model for shared leadership between males and females. Maat was built on the very idea that women and men are equal and complimentary beings critical throughout life, as the ankh shows. There are more female members of parliament in Rwanda and Tanzania alone than there are in all of the United Kingdom (Pitcher et al., 2007). Even through all of the devastation that the continent has experienced at the hands of the European Union, Middle East and United States, Africa "is home to five out of the 10 fastest-growing economies in the world" today (Chandler, 2008; Pitcher et al, 2007). People from around the world, Whites most especially, travel to Africa annually to experience the spirit and beauty of the place that Black people come from. They go to see for example amazing African-made monuments in Kemet and Zimbabwe, and natural wonders like Musi wa Tunya, the Red Sea Reefs, Sahara Desert, Tsingy de Bemaraha, and Ngorongoro Crater, also referred to as Africa's "Garden of Eden" (The Seven Natural Wonders, 2008). Natural beauty and natural resources remain more plentiful in Africa than in all of the rest of the known world. What happens to Africa's people and resources, or whether Africa will continue to be exploited for its wealth will depend on people's awareness of the exploitation, and Black people especially.

Begin building your family's hope today for achievement tomorrow. No longer should Black youth have to wait until young adulthood and entrance into Historically Black Colleges or Universities (HBCUs) to learn more about Black history and contemporary topics than slavery, racial discrimination and integration. By compiling a small portion of writings, documentaries, movies, music and even recorded speeches on the Internet you can grow your and your children's self-cultural knowledgebase. A good way to find quality material is by a simple internet search of "Black classic books," or "African novels," etc. In virtually every city with a 15% or higher Black population in the U.S. there is an African American museum or historical center. This means that most of us can quickly locate a meaningful museum, as we tend to live close together. And don't forget about the "Egyptian" exhibits in mainstream museums. This is the history of your child's first and most important birth rite. Start where you need to based on your means or time. The bottom line is that you can no longer expect your children's teachers, the media controllers, or even churches to inform your family of all that you need to know about your heritage and possibilities for achievement. To be sure, neither the school system, church, mosque nor temple have prevented the mass incarceration of African American men, raping of African resources and women, or failure of half of our school-aged children.

As American schools improve their attitudes toward education, families must begin to supplement the Eurocentric schooling provided to their children with independent scholarship relevant to their lineage and heritage. Their knowledge and appreciation of self will surely translate to the classroom and from the classroom beyond to impact your family and the world through their contributions. As Tatum (1999) so rightly explained in Chapter 11, Principle 13, Black children learn best how to think, what to do, and what to become through their families and community. Black boys and young men should be especially focused with the following strategies:

Parents and Families: What to Do

1. Ensure that you have established clear values and expectations with your children. Do not run the risk of assuming that your children know your family values, or that they "know exactly how to act" when they are at school. You may attend church service every Sunday, fuss when they do act up, or even attend school events, but I assure you that nothing beats frank and serious dialogue between parent and child, aunt and niece, uncle and nephew, and so on. Family values and expectations encircle everything that contributes to our children's hope (just take another look back at the 13 SigHT principles and you will see this point). Are they supposed to look out for their family members or not? Should they value school as a legitimate way to access a career and future stability, or do they attend school simply because they have to? The truth may be that *you* need to reflect on your family values. If this is true, then do just that and make sure that you translate your conclusions to your children soon after. Teach your children the power of hope by demonstrating it and progressing with them.

2. Commit to reading one book or article focusing on African or African Diasporic (e.g., Kemetic/Egyptian, African American, Jamaican, Haitian, Brazilian, etc.) history with your child every quarter, which is to be exact every three months. Add to that one documentary or movie a month. The books that you choose may occasionally be fiction, although restricting your family to purely creative works will weaken your learning of the true history and achievements of Black people. In the summers, visit local African American museums and historic locations. The idea here is to make conscientious efforts to engage your children and entire family in self-cultural knowledge and activities. When we allow ourselves to become "too busy" with work and other social or professional agendas to even perceive and develop ourselves, what we are actually doing is giving our children and our families up to the wolves—i.e., the prisons, corporate exploiters of the music industry, movie companies and TV stations, etc. Enjoy self-development with your family, even when the history is grim. To make it really fun, you might throw in some geography and travel to nearby cities or states to learn of how Black folks live and have achieved there. Passports are 21st century must-haves. Use your passports to visit Africa and African Diasporic regions and see our connections for yourself.

3. Remember that your children must learn how to operate successfully in school in much the same way that we adults often have to figure out ways to "code switch" for job interviews and daily work. Too often we lose sight of the fact that our children are attending, with the exception of some Afrocentric schools, another White corporate and political institution, designed with the same communication styles, energy, attitudes and customs as the places that we tend to avoid until we have to intersect with them (Ani, 2012). Think about that, and then think about how difficult it must be for our young people to attend schools where they are uncomfortable and uninspired. Principle two, "Code of Conduct: Play Your Part", speaks a great deal to this recommendation, however, considered in isolation from Principles 10 and 13 on having a secure identity and family will result in only temporary or shallow achievement. Code switching too well or without consciousness can mean we lost one (shout out to Lauryn Hill, 1998). Proper care must be taken. As you make your way through recommendations two and three, be sure to discuss how your children's experiences in school relate to or differ from your family values, history, and goals. What do they need to continue doing, start or stop in order to succeed in school as Black children? Be specific with them about their role and responsibilities at home and in the community first, and in school second.

4. Just as teachers and school counselors should ensure that Black children are aware of multiple career options, you must also enlighten your children on this point at home. If your son or daughter is a star athlete and you support them in their sportsmanship, then that is fantastic, however, you must also support them in being able to think practically about their goals if your ultimate desire is for them to have a stable and happy life for the rest of their lives. Based on sheer proportion sizes of aspiring athletes versus available positions, it is unrealistic to have a singular ambition in sports, or entertainment for that matter. Factor in the possibility of physical injury (but pray not), and your son or daughter is placed at a great disadvantage if their only hope is to play ball, act, rap or sing. Indeed, there are more Denzel Washingtons, Kobe Bryants, Jay-Zs, and Mary J. Bliges to come from us, but we will have far more great intellectuals, CEOs, teachers, doctors, lawyers, scientists and other professionals. Sadly, they just aren't shown as much on television or in textbooks.

Academics, Practitioners and Policymakers

Psychologists often opine about the problems of research-to-practice gaps. Increasingly, teachers are complaining about problematic policy-to-teaching gaps. It is certainly important for the sake of children and state of nations that there be consistent messages and practices between researchers and practitioners, and policymakers and teachers. Taking a note from Ture and his fellow achievers, I have organized the recommendations to academics, professionals and policymakers in "three-part harmony" with the hope of bridging the gaps. The first of each, (A), are written for academics, while the second, (B), are offered to professionals, including psychologists, social workers, counselors, etc., and the third, (C), to policymakers as well as funding associations in education. It is recommended that each of these three groups also review the brief section for teachers above. As a final note, while the United States is prominent as the target locale for these recommendations, this is primarily a matter of terminology. As other nations face many of the same issues, readers outside of the U.S. can easily amend the phrasing for their physical location.

Academics, Practitioners and Policymakers: What To Do

1. (A) School must have meaning to Black children and families if they are going to participate in or collaborate with it. Academic research is instrumental to understanding how Black children and families view the school system. Terrell and Terrell's (1981) notion of cultural mistrust has made significant waves in the counseling psychology subfield, however, too few social scientists connect to their theories and interventions the very

real possibility of Black youth and families having little confidence in the school system. Lack of interest shown by schools increases lack of trust in them and subtracts from the number of Black students and families who believe in the power of school to help meet their goals. Researchers must consider questions of cultural mistrust and interracial dissonance more often in discourses of Black student achievement (Ani, 2012).

(**B**) To begin assessing Black youth's belief in school achievement, professionals should consider utilizing the Cultural Mistrust Inventory (CMI; Terrell & Terrell, 1981). If possible, their parent or primary custodian should also complete the CMI. Understanding the level of trust that Black students and families feel toward American systems will also inform practitioners about their values—whatever students and families feel they are not getting from school and causes them to disengage are the very things that they value. While the CMI has not (to my knowledge) been utilized in research among students at the K-12 level, its reliability amongst Black college students has been tested (e.g., Bell & Tracey, 2006; Nickerson, Helms &, Terrell, 1994; Phelps et al., 2001). Though dated, its reliability has been continuously demonstrated. It could be used among youth to offer important qualitative information. Once an understanding of the student's faith in school is attained, the next step is in helping to increase or maintain their belief. Critical among strategies for helping Black students see the viability of school are (a) identifying their values, natural strengths, and interests to then set and work toward their goals; (b) providing them with a list of career options; (c) providing them with a monthly breakdown of salaries for each career option; and (d) informing them of the benefits of college—from meeting lifelong friends to studying abroad and living in dorms. Certainly, professionals hoping to help Black youth see the importance of school had better be prepared to answer some tough questions.

(**C**) In saying that researchers and professionals should seek understanding of, and strategies for increasing Black student's (and family's) belief in school means that there must indeed be a pot of gold at the end of the rainbow for them. The role of Congress then is to ensure that options are plentiful and employment rates are equal. In 2012, over 50 years following the desertion of the north from industrial and manufacturing corporations, many cities with predominately African American populations continue to be destitute, abandoned by the local and national government for which they are expected to hold allegiance (The Economist, 2009; Friedman, 2003). Of particular note are Detroit and Saginaw, MI, Indianapolis, IN, and Cleveland, OH, where SigHT was conducted. To make matters worse, during the past two decades, affirmative action policies intended to ensure racially equitable representation across businesses and schools in America have come under attack (Chandler, 2010; Vasquez & Jones, 2006). It is essential to Black student engagement and achievement that Congress, and for that matter the Supreme Court maintain an honest and democratic eye toward affirmative action legislation (O'Shaughnessy, 2012). Such legislative mandates continue to be necessary in America, perhaps for the next several generations, as the nation continues to grapple with its racially contentious past and present. The Black community is filled with intellect and innovation, as the Obamas have demonstrated on a grand stage. Black children and families, however, are justifiably uninspired by the thought of school participation only to face racial discrimination in the business sectors. It is the job of policymakers to ensure that their talents do not go to waste and their efforts in school are not justifiably dissuaded.

2. **(A)** In light of the extensive literature review examining Snyder's (1989; 2002) hope theory in the beginning of this book, researchers must see the need to extend the revelation that cultural distinctions result in value, interest and even skill differences. Once the previous hope theory was contextualized to Black philosophies and experiences it became clear that hope has various shades, not a singular, nationalist shade of White. In research and in training, it will be imperative that the values and interests of the Black community be understood in order that we may begin to understand the values, interests and behaviors of Black children. What this will mean in the academy is greater attention to the social and political events happening in the Black community, as well as re-viewing of the community from an African, not (only) American standpoint. Why else should we refer to ourselves as *African* Americans? We place African in front of American for good reason.

(B) Practitioners can tap into the values, interests, and goals of Black youth more frequently than academicians because of the context their jobs. As a professional, you encounter young people regularly. Use your time with students to ask them about their values and hopes for the future. Even better, you will have the support of quality research offered by academics conducting culturally centered and contemporaneously relevant work if researchers are playing their parts. Templates for identifying Black children's natural talents and interests based on their personal ethics and values are offered as Appendices A and B. Use them to help your students set short- and long-term goals.

(C) After school programs and 501c3 organizations are federally grant funded with target goals of improving student achievement. For Black youth focus should be placed on promotion of values and ethics as two of the most critical deciding factors of goal-setting and attainment. Given that the types of goals that children set are tied to what they value in life and what they believe their conduct should be, then helping them to realize what they believe in and value in relation to their academic and life goals must be preliminary for underserved or so-called "disadvantaged" youth. Require that organizations or programs vying for funding to support Black student achievement indicate in their proposals that they understand and plan to respond to cultural relevance and goal development.

3. (A) As ethics and values are the basis of goals, culture is the root of ethics and values. Greater understanding of the continuities between African and African Diasporan peoples can significantly ease the process of researchers' making sense of Black people's interests and social experiences. Without acquiring an additional degree in Black Studies, academics can learn a great deal in a short period of time by considering the work of scholars who *do* have degrees in Black Studies and/or engage in Afrocentric scholarship. Especially if you are an academic engaging in Black racial identity research, you cannot discount the importance of historical and cultural exploration for Black people, especially Diasporic (as Cross, 1971, and Sellers et al., 1997 demonstrate in their Black racial identity research). Key strategies to implement for academics interested in Black racial identity, student achievement or family structure include subscriptions to high-quality social science journals that support agency in the Black community, such as the Journal of Black Studies, the Journal of Pan African Studies, and the historic Journal of Negro Education (hence its dated name). Also, consultation with Afrocentric contemporaries on your course of research pertaining to or involving Black people is encouraged. Most every researcher is available by phone or e-mail, if not by guest lecture. Our children, schools and nation have no space for lazy or apathetic researchers or trainers. Act for truth and equity in research. Play your part.

(B) En route to their goals of graduating from high school, attending college and achieving a career Black children must also be encouraged to strengthen their identity. In my practice, when African American children have been accused of "acting disruptively" or being oppositional, the truth of the matter the vast majority of the time was that they were only acting from their own cultural norms in communication and energy, or expressing frustration from cultural dislocation and lack of caring by the adults around them. The more they understand about their own culture, the better equipped they will be to manage their irritations and stay the course of their goals. In therapy settings, cultural infusion can take the form of introducing adolescents and young adults to Cross's (e.g., 2001) Nigrescence theory, reviewing and discussing major events in Black history, and discussing relevant film clips. I have also assigned therapeutic homework readings or discussion of community events for Black youth and families. Youtube.com is a great resource for immediate lectures or presentations today. Connect these exercises to the life experiences, personality factors, beliefs, values and goals of the youth and families that you work for.

(C) It is imperative that Black children receive greater attention in the curriculum and instruction of the nation's public schools. Where legislatures have become obsessed with standards and school accountability for student achievement, African children (and Latino and Indigenous American children) have been left further and further behind. That the curriculum should even be standardized for student achievement is flawed logic in a society so racial-ethnically diverse. While education remains Constitutionally up to the prerogative of the states, it is a well-known fact that the federal government provides incentives for certain practices. The African American community being such an instrumental group in the making and continuing progression of the United States is due a course or other specialized programming in schools. There is a college professor, student or community member in virtually every city in the United States who would be willing to teach Black students as a part of their course requirements in K-12 schooling. Black community organizations, such as fraternities and sororities are apt to respond positively to any district, state or federal invitation to implement a program designed to increase the hope and achievement of Black students in their area. Facing deplorable rates of Black student achievement across the country, our government and school leaders should be willing to meet the community partway.

4. (A) Full understanding of the results in *SigHT* requires understanding of qualitative research. The power of sheer determination and personal consciousness are outside the bounds of quantitative projectiles, such as IQ test scores. The message to social scientists is that sometimes a sense is enough to

encourage positive thinking and behaviors. Consciousness and spirit must be reunited with psychology and education for Black children's achievement. This does not mean that numbers have no place in science, but that figures do not define or describe people or their abilities (unless you are adept in numerology, which few academics are). African psychologists understand this and their research demonstrates their intelligence on this point (Helms, 2006; Hilliard, 1996; Nobles, 2006).

(B) Another concrete and efficient way for school psychologists and other professionals to improve the rates of Black student achievement is to guide Black children through the goal-setting and goal-attainment processes. As the result of centuries old systematic repression of resources and opportunities for Africans in America, many Black children have the determination to succeed in school and life, but not the access to adults who have experienced the school and professional success that they are striving toward. Whereas many of their European American peers have had the benefits of nepotism and social privilege, most African American youth do not have the benefits of learning specifically what to set their sights on, how to set short- and long-term goals, or how to plan to meet their goals with fewer resources. In my practice with Black youth, I have utilized Conzemius and O'Neill's (2001) S.M.A.R.T. Goals template. With outlined guideposts for future success that are more clearly envisioned, Black students begin to see school more clarity as a viable option for supporting their individual and family needs. In addition to the S.M.A.R.T. goals sheet I have employed the templates provided in Appendix C and D. The "Life Goals" sheets are personalizeable and encouraging to Black youth by maintaining an expectation of excellence—failure is not an option.

(C) The role of policymakers in improving goal-setting and pursuit among Black youth lies again in supporting effective curricular and extra curricular programming. Until state and federal Congress see fit to educate Black children effectively, academics and professionals will be required to work harder. Rather than being in the position of having to find ways to establish Black students' engagement in school, or instruct them on how school can serve their life goals, teachers and staff could be enjoying the challenge of moving the country beyond the basics. The 21st century goals of Congress must include developing the strengths of its children to meet their goals and advance world stability in the next age.

Chapter 13: Hoping for the Best in Black Students

Q: Do other kids in school make fun of you for doing well in school?

A: No.

Q: They don't call you a nerd, or... say it in a way that's like, 'school is stupid, why are you workin? Don't, who cares if you make good grades in school?

A: No...they don't do that. Cuz they care about school too, in their own little way...yeah.

Q: What do you mean by that, in their own little way?

A: Umm, like everybody's different, and some people have their own techniques so in their own little way they do that.

Q: Sure, they may not go about school the way you do, but they appreciate it.

A: Yeah. –Assata, 7ᵗʰ grade

Whether you prefer to speak of the achievement gap or the achievement debt (Ladson-Billings, 2008), the bottom line is that unless we begin to listen to the voices of successful children about what their values and needs are we will continue to talk about the wrong things. Successful African American students demonstrated through personal narratives that young people who lack strong racial-ethnic identity and family connectedness tend to be rudderless in the sea of life, and highly dependent on others to motivate them. They go whichever way the wind blows. This makes them highly vulnerable to negative peer pressure and institutional neglect, even when they actually value education and appreciate school—in their own way.

Now one decade into the century, we can say with certainty that effective education for Black children still requires heeding to the words of Du Bois in 1903, for Africans "to be a co-worker in the kingdom of culture, to escape both death and isolation, to husband and use [their] best powers and latent genius," we all must know and keep alive African history (2003, p. 9); Woodson in 1933, honest reflections on the African experience together with the experiences of all other races must be "given as a corrective for methods which have not produced satisfactory results" (p. XV); Asante in 1998, echoing Fanon, "always, the protestor must use symbols, myths, and sounds that are different from those of the established order...The oppressed must gain attention and control by introducing another language, another sound" (p. 127); Mazama in 2001, "Afrocentricity contends that our main problem as African people is our usually unconscious adoption of the Western worldview and perspective and their attendant conceptual frameworks" and therefore, "The challenge is monumental: Our liberation and Afrocentricity contends and rests upon our ability to systematically displace European ways of thinking, being, feeling, and so forth and consciously replace them with ways that are germane to our own African cultural experience" (p. 387-288); and Kunjufu in 2006, "True integration requires that changes be made to the curriculum. You can't say you have an integrated school if you have a Eurocentric curriculum" (p 101).

I have attempted to highlight in this book as many insights and recommendations as possible in a single text. Profoundly, six African American student achievers found significant motivation in their history and modern day community heroes, she-roes, and families. They were not too hip or too young for old wisdom. These young people found refuge and courage in knowing that their hopes and school achievement made perfect sense for them because history had positive messages for them too. Their SigHT, Afrocentric as it was, refused to be blurred because, if nothing else, they were proud of being African American and aware of their family values and culture.

History offers corrective lessons for modern problems, and culture prevents the identity confusion that enables Eurocentrism and school failure for African children. The problem of underachievement amongst Black children becomes a nonproblem once we begin to embrace our individual and cultural truths. As much as people around the world celebrate the work of W.E.B. Du Bois in *The Souls of Black Folks,* for his embracing of dual nationality, of African and American at once, very few people know that in the years following his youthful idealism he renounced his American citizenship, became a citizen of Ghana, and cursed the American system of capitalism. Eldridge Cleaver (1968/ 1991) called Du Bois' actions "three symbolic gestures as a final legacy to his people" (p. 111). I see it as Du Bois' awakening to the truth of a national culture that has built its image and wealth on the backs of Black and Brown people (Du Bois, 1940). Collectively, we have come to a place of resting on our shoddy assumptions, and Black youth, their families, and now the nation, are feeling the pain at almost every turn.

In concluding this work I cannot escape the irony in the American adage, "the riddle of the Sphinx" which is used to describe a thought or phenomenon that boggles the mind. How did the Horemakhet, the Sphinx, of Kemet come about? Who conceived it and how was it built?

Years of human energy, money, and research have been dedicated to solving the actual "riddle" when the answer is clear (Asante & Mazama, 2002): Africans built the Sphinx at the command of their Neteru and King. Too often the abilities of Black people are questioned. Black culture is treated too often as either a relic of ancient history or a figment of ridicule. President Obama raised the issue of mockery against his African name several times during his 2008 campaign, and while the President attempted to make light of being referred to as "the guy with the funny name," we must recognize that cultural ridicule is a serious matter on the road toward racial stereotyping and contempt. To be made a joke of simply for being who you are and representing your culture is a serious problem, especially for children. Someone's "funny name" is but a stone's throw from the same person's "silly clothing," "nappy hair," "behavioral abnormality," or "cognitive deficiency."

The intolerable situation of integrated schools with Eurocentric pedagogy is akin to modern day sharecropping plantations; they still serve the interests of White people over others while the less fortunate are held in educational and material debt for their toil. The disparities in health, employment, home ownership, and formal education rates between racial-ethnic groups demonstrate the degree to which we have continued to live under the lie of full citizenship in the United States. Nations take care of their citizens because the people are considered integral to the interests of the nation. Black people, however, continue to be treated like disconnected limbs of the American body, not members of the whole, and this is so because Black history and intelligence beyond 1619 have been dismissed rather than embraced in our school buildings and legislative offices. Teachers, academicians and policymakers are often too focused on defending their character and that of their fore parents against historical transgressions to actually see and deal fairly with Black people.

As I write the final chapter of this book on hope and achievement for Black children, sympathizers, especially in the Black community, mourn the senseless and cruel murder of Trayvon Martin, who was shot to death while walking home alone from a convenience store on February 26, 2012. He was carrying an iced tea and a bag of Skittles. He was a college-bound 17-year-old. His crime was being born Black and looking the part in Sanford, Florida—a city named after Henry Sanford, whose work of "civilizing African natives" and transporting African Americans back to Africa in the 1800s for the purpose of colonization has been honored by historical societies and newspapers (e.g., the Sanford Historical Society and The Sanford Herald).

"Mainstream" America has wallowed in the false rhetoric of Eurocentrism and racism, reminding us constantly of how little Black youth are valued and how negatively Black people are regarded (Zirin, 2012). Should we pack up and leave the country for Africa as Du Bois and so many other Black intellectuals and activists did in the 1960s? Short of a mass exodus back to Africa, which is unlikely, the only answer to the problems imposed on Africans across the Diaspora is recognition. We must re-think who we are and who we will become, Africans and Europeans alike.

That African Americans have no culture distinct from White America to speak of is a lie, and this fallacy has failed African American children and their teachers in schools. Further, African American cultural values, traditions, and philosophies are more than hip hop, soul food, and the Black church. That African American children have no desire to succeed in school for the sake of appearing to "act White" has also been proven to be a lie. Education started in Africa and continues to thrive on the continent today wherever Africans are free (or freer) from neocolonialism (Browder, 1992; James, 2009). All of the lies that warp education today began either as racist propaganda or ignore-rance of African culture(s) in Eurocentric locations. Like a cancer, they have metastasized over the light of African Americans, Jamaicans, Puerto Ricans, Brazilians, South Africans, and other members of the African collective, and like Trayvon, Black children by the millions become the sacrificial offerings to status quo idolatry.

SigHT does not espouse a single Black truth pertaining to African cultures or African people, except that we are many bound by a common ancestral beginning and a common social plague. Black youth today, just as the Black youth of decades and centuries prior, share in the spiritedness and capabilities of our rich beginnings in the same way that Asian children, Indian youth, European and all others do in their respective cultures. This is the meaning of heritage. The task before those of us interested in the development and achievement of all children is much more simple when placed in the perspective of history and culture instead of convenience.

All hope is not lost and never will be as long as those of us willing to teach, write, and talk for the good in people do so wherever we are. I hope that *SigHT: Unveiling Black Student Achievement and the Meaning of Hope* contributes to the beauty of diversity and the perpetuation of truth, justice, harmony, balance, order, reciprocity, and propriety in Black students and the world (Karenga, 2006). In the 21st century and beyond, we shall refocus our energies on what works rather than what fails. May the SigHT of Black children everywhere be clear and capable of seeing far into their past and future. And may you see the Black children around you more clearly, not as hopeless and helpless, but as infinitely capable youth who will help shape the world.

Appendix A

Basic Template for Identifying Beliefs and Values

Stand for something or fall for anything!

Be honest! There are no right or wrong answers. Nothing will be considered unimportant or silly. As you answer these questions, reflect on what is important to you.

1. What do you believe in? What are your personal ethics?

2. What do you value in life?

3. Do your goals make sense in relation to your personal ethics and values? If you have not yet decided what you want to do in life and who you want to be, then set your goals and then come back and check them against your ethics and values. If your goals do not match or make sense next to your ethics and values, then reconceptualize them.

Appendix B

Basic Template for Tapping into Strengths and Interests

Ture's Wonderful Strengths

1. I really enjoy

_____

2. I am really good at

_____

3. I am proud of

_____

**These are things about me that I think are good. Even when
life gets tough, I can think positively and build on these things.**

Appendix C

Basic Template for Goal-setting

Assata's Life Goals

The first thing a young woman must realize is that life is about choices.

Life = Choices

What goals are you choosing for yourself?

1. _____

2. _____

3. _____

Appendix D

Basic Template for Goal-achievement

Resource Check for Assata's Goals

1. (Write or Type Goal 1 Here)
    a) How will you achieve this goal (relating to long-term goals or actions)?
    b) What can you do (relating to short-term goals or actions taken to achieve goal)?
    c) Who can help you (relating to external support or affirmations of ability)?

I will achieve my goal of _____ by _____

_____

I can _____

to teach my goal step by step. _____

_____

can help me by _____

2. (Write or Type Goal 2 Here)
    a) How will you achieve this goal (relating to long-term goals or actions)?
    b) What can you do (relating to short-term goals or actions taken to achieve goal)?
    c) And who can help you (relating to external support or affirmations of ability)?

I will achieve my goal of _____ by _____

_____

I can _____

to teach my goal step by step. _____

_____

can help me by _____

3. (Write or Type Goal 3 Here)
   a) How will you achieve this goal (relating to long-term goals or actions)?
   b) What can you do (relating to short-term goals or actions taken to achieve goal)?
   c) And who can help you (relating to external support or affirmations of ability)?

I will achieve my goal of _____ by _____

_____

I can _____

to teach my goal step by step. _____

_____

can help me by _____

Failure to reach your goals is not an option.
You have the power, skills, and support to do everything.

References

AAM Dallas. (2011). Permanent collection.

A&E Television Network (2009). *Celebrate Black history*. Retrieved on March 1, 2009 from http://www.biography.com/blackhistory/ .

Abelev, M.S. (2009). Advancing out of poverty: Social class worldview and its relation to resilience. *Journal of Adolescent Research, 24,* 114–141.

Akbar, N. (2003). *Papers in African psychology.* Tallahassee, FL: Mind Productions & Associates, Inc.

Allen, R.L. (2004). Whiteness and critical pedagogy. *Educational Philosophy and Theory, 36,* 121–136.

Allen, B.A., & Boykin, A.W. (1992). African-American children and the educational process: Alleviating cultural discontinuity through prescriptive pedagogy. *School Psychology Review, 21,* 586–597.

Allport, G.W. (1979). *The nature of prejudice.* NY: Perseus Books Publishing, L.L.C. (Original work published 1954).

Ani, A. (2012). Crackas and coons: Interracial dissonance and hope for the future. *Journal of Pan African Studies, 5,* 66-84.

Ani, M. (1997*). Let the circle be unbroken: The implications of African spirituality in the Diaspora.* Trenton, NJ: Red Sea Press. (Original work published 1980).

Asante, M.K. (1990). *Kemet, Afrocentricity, and knowledge.* Trenton, NJ: Africa World Press, Inc.

Asante, M.K. (1998). *The Afrocentric idea: Revised and expanded edition.* Philadelphia, PA: Temple University Press.

Asante, M.K. (2000). *The Egyptian philosophers: Ancient African voices from Imhotep to Akhenaten.* Chicago, IL: African American Images.

Asante, M.K. (2001). Racing to leave the race: Black postmodernists off-track. *The Black Scholar, 23,* 50–51.

Asante, M.K. (2003). *Afrocentricity: The theory of social change.* Chicago, IL: African American Images. (Original work published 1980).

Asante, M.K. (2005). *Race, rhetoric,& identity: The architecton of soul.* NY: Humanity Books.

Asante, M.K. (2007). *The history of Africa: The quest for eternal harmony.* NY: Routledge.

Asante, M.K. (2008). *Afrocentricity.* In V.N. Parrillo's *Encyclopedia of social problems, Vol. 1.* Thousand Oaks, CA: Sage Publications, Inc.

Asante, M.K. (2011a). *As I run toward Africa: A memoir.* Boulder, CO: Paradigm Publishers.

Asante, M.K. (2011b). *The spirit of freedom.* Keynote address given at the Ujima Enterprises 12th Annual Juneteenth Celebration. Retrieved on November 3, 2011 from http://www.youtube.com/watch?v=n_Nix WivzI8&feature=related.

Asante, M.K., & Abarry, A.S. (Eds.) (1996). *African intellectual heritage: A book of sources.* Philadelphia, PA: Temple University Press.

Asante, M.K., & Hall, R.E. (2011). *Rooming in the master's house: Power & privilege in the rise of Black conservatism.* Boulder, CO: Paradigm Publishers.

Asante, M.K., & Mazama, A. (Eds.) (2002). Egypt vs. Greece and the academy: The debate over *the birth of civilization.* Chicago, IL: African American Images.

Asante, Jr., M.K. (2008). *It's bigger than hip hop: The rise of the post-hip-hop generation.* NY: St. Martin's Press.

Badu, E. (2008). The healer. On *New Amerykah, Part I.* [CD]. CA: Motown.

Ballenger, C. (1998). *Teaching other people's children: Literacy and learning in a bilingual classroom.* NY: Teachers College Press.

Bandura, A. (1977). Self-efficacy: Toward a unifying theory of behavior change. *Psychological Review, 84,* 191–215

Banfield, W. (2004). Black artistic invisibility: A composer talking 'bout taking care of the souls of Black folk while losing ground fast. *Journal of Black Studies, 35,* 195–209.

Bass, C.K., & Hardin, C.K. (1997). Enhancing the cultural identity of early adolescent male African Americans. *Professional School Counseling, 1,* 48–51.

Bauval, R., & Brophy, T. (2011). *Black genesis: The prehistoric origins of ancient Egypt.* Rochester, VT: Bear & Company.

Bell, T.J., & Tracey, T.J. (2006). The relation of cultural mistrust and psychological health. *Journal of Multicultural Counseling and Development, 34,* 2–14.

Black Star. (1998). Thieves in the night. On *Black Star* [CD]. New York: Rawkus.

Blanchett, W.J., Mumford, V., & Beachum, F. (2005). Urban school failure and disproportionality in a post-*Brown* era. *Remedial and Special Education, 26,* 70-81.

Blumenson, E., & Nilsen, E.S. (2003). One strike and you're out? Constitutional constraints on zero tolerance in public education. *Washington University Law Quarterly, 81,* 65–117.

Boser, U. (2011). Teacher diversity matters: A state-by-state analysis of teachers of color. *Center For American Progress.* Retrieved on February 20, 2012 from http://www.americanprogress.org/issues/2011/11/teacher_diversity.html .

Browder, A.T. (1992). *Nile Valley contributions to civilization.* D.C.: The Institute of Karmic Guidance.

Caracciolo, D. (2008) Addressing anti-Indianism in the mainstream curriculum: A partnership model. *Multicultural Perspectives, 10,* 224-228.

References

Cartwright, P., Lassiter, V., Lynn, M., Nlandu, T., Sanko, H., Seaton, S. et al. (2012). *Harlem Renaissance : Multimedia Resource.* Retrieved on February 25, 2012 from http://www.jcu.edu/harlem/Development Team/ Page 1.htm .

Chandler, D.R. (2008). Examining the impact of hope on childhood academic performance: *Focusing normative development research on a minority population.* Unpublished master's thesis). University of Wisconsin-Madison, Madison, WI.

Chandler, D.R. (2008). Republic of Djibouti, Africa report. Unpublished paper.

Chandler, D. R. (2010). The underutilization of health services in the Black community: An examination of causes and effects. *Journal of Black Studies, 40,* 915–931.

Chandler, D.R. (2011) Proactively addressing the shortage of Blacks in psychology: Highlighting the school psychology subfield. *Journal of Black Psychology, 37,* 99–127.

Chavous, T.M., Bernat, D.H., Schmeelk-Cone, K., Caldwell, C.H., Kohn-Wood, L., & Zimmerman, M.A. (2003). Racial identity and academic attainment among African American adolescents. *Child Development, 74,* 1076–1090.

Cheavens, J.S., Feldman, D.B., Gum, A., Michael, S.Y., & Snyder, C.R. (2006). Hope therapy in a community sample: A pilot investigation. *Social Indicators Research, 77,* 61–78.

Children's Defense Fund (2007). *America's cradle to prison pipeline.* Washington, DC: Author.

Cho, S., Hudley, C., Lee, S., Barry, L., & Kelly, M. (2008). Roles of gender, race, and SES in the college choice process among first-generation and nonfirst-generation students. *Journal* of *Diversity in Higher Education, 1,* 95–107.

Churchill, W., & Wall, J.V. (2002). *The COINTELPRO Papers: Documents from the FBI's secret wars against dissent in the United States.* Cambridge, MA: South End Press.

Clark, W.A.V. (2009). Changing residential preferences across income, education, and age: Findings from the multi-city study of urban inequality. *Urban Affairs Review, 44,* 334–355.

Clay, A. (2006). "All I need is one mic": Mobilizing youth for social change in the post- civil rights era. *Social Justice, 33,* 105–121.

Cleaver, E. (1991). *Soul on ice.* NY: Dell Publishing. (Original in 1968).

Cleveland Live Census (2009). Data central: Cleveland Ohio statistics, demographics & census. Retrieved on March 15, 2009 from http://www.cleveland.com/datacentral/index.ssf/census and other demographic d/ .

CMSD (2008, September). 2007-08 report on academic achievement and 2008-09 continuous *improvement plan.* Report presented to the board of education.

CMSD (2009). *CMSD facts.* Retrieved on March 15, 2009 from http://www.cmsdnet.net/en/AboutCMSD/Facts.aspx .

Cokley, K.O., & Chapman, C. (2008). The roles of ethnic identity, anti-white attitudes, and academic self-concept in African American student achievement. *Social Psychology of Education, 11,* 349–365.

Collins, W.J., & Smith, F.H. (2007). A neighborhood-level view of riots, property values, and population loss: Cleveland 1950-1980. *Explorations in Economic History, 44,* 365–386.

Considine, N.S., Sabag-Cohen, S., & Krivoshekova, Y.S. (2007). Ethnic, gender, and socioeconomic differences in young adults' self-disclosure: Who discloses what and to whom? *Cultural Diversity and Ethnic Minority Psychology, 13,* 254–263.

Conzemius, A., & O'Neill, J. (2001). *The power of SMART goals: Using goals to improve student learning.* Bloomington, IN: Solution Tree Press.

Cormier, S., & Nurius, S. (2003). *Interviewing and change strategies for helpers: Fundamental skills and cognitive behavioral interventions* (5th Ed.). Pacific Grove, CA, Thomson Books/Cole.

Cose, E. (1997). Memories in blood. *Newsweek, 130,* 68.

Cross, W. E., Jr. (1971). The Negro-to-Black conversion experience. *Black World, 20,* 13–27.

Curriculum Review (2005). What the numbers say. *Curriculum Review, 44,* 3-3.

Dead Prez. (2000). It's bigger than hip hop. On *Let's Get Free* [CD]. New York: Loud Records.

Dei, G.J.S. (2006). Black-focused schools: A call for re-visioning. *Education Canada, 46,* 27–31.

Demby, G. (2012, June 1). Black unemployment ticks upward during rocky month for jobs. *The Huffington Post.* Retrieved on July 3, 2012 from http://www.huffingtonpost.com/2012/06/01/black-unemployment-ticks-upward_n_1563948.html .

Diop, C.A. (1991). *Civilization or barbarism: An authentic anthropology.* NY: Lawrence Hill Books. (Original work published in 1981).

Du Bois, W.E.B. (2003). *The souls of Black folk.* NY: Barnes & Noble Classics. (Original work published 1903).

Du Bois, W.E.B. (1940). *Dusk of dawn: An essay toward an autobiography of a race concept.* NY: Harcourt Brace.

Du Bois, W.E.B. (2003). *The souls of Black folk.* NY: Barnes & Noble Classics. (Original work published 1903).

The Economist. (2009). *Detroit's emptiness: The art of abandonment: Some weird and wonderful things are rising from the ashes of the Motor City.* Retrieved on March 4, 2012, from http://www.economist.com/node/15108683 .

Edwards, L.M., Ong, A.D., & Lopez, S.J. (2007). Hope measurement in Mexican American youth. *Hispanic Journal of Behavioral Sciences, 29,* 225–241.

Elliott, T.R., & Sherwin, E.D. (1997). Developing hope in the social context: Alternative perspectives of motive, meaning, and identity. *Group Dynamics: Theory, Research, and Practice, 1,* 119–123.

Ellison, C.M., Boykin, A.W., Tyler, K.M., & Dillihunt, M.L. (2005). Examining classroom learning preferences among elementary school students. *Social Behavior and Personality, 33,* 699–708.

Este, D.C (2004). The Black church as a social welfare institution: Union United Church and the development of Montreal's Black community, 1907-1940. *Journal of Black* Studies, 35, 3–22.

Fagan, T.K., & Wise, P.S. (2000). Historical development of school psychology. In T.K. Fagan and P.S. Wise (Ed.), *School psychology: Past, present, and future, Second Ed.* (23–68). Bethesda, MD: NASP.

Feldman, R.S. (2003). *Development across the life span.* Upper Saddle River, NJ: Prentice Hall.

Fiasco, L. (2007). Dumb it down. On *The Cool* [CD]. New York: Atlantic/Wea.

Fiasco, L. (2007). The coolest. On *The Cool* [CD]. New York: Atlantic/Wea.

Ford, D. (2011, October 13). Rushing to label Black boys. *The New York Times.* Retrieved on July 14, 2012 from http://www.nytimes.com/roomfordebate/2011/10/12/are-americans-more-prone-to-adhd/racism-and-sexism-in-diagnosing-adhd .

Friedman, E. (2003). *Vacant properties in Baltimore: Strategies for reuse.* Archives of the Abell Foundation, Baltimore, MD.

Gable, S.L., & Haidt, J. (2005). What (and why) is positive psychology. *Review of General Psychology, 9,* 103–110.

Gamst, G., Dana, R.H., Der-Karabetian, A., & Kramer, T. (2004). Ethnic match and treatment outcomes for child and adolescent mental health center clients. *Journal of Counseling & Government, 82,* 457–465.

Gaudreau, P. and Blondin, J.P. (2004). Differential associations of dispositional optimism and pessimism with coping, goal attainment, and emotional adjustment during sport competition. *International Journal of Stress Management, 11,* 245–269.

Goffe, L. (2012, May). Don't call me African-American. *New African,* 86-89.

Gottschild, B.D. (2002). Crossroads, continuities, and contradictions. In S. Sloat (Ed.) *Caribbean dance from Abakua to Zouk: How movement shapes identity* (3–10). Gainesville, FL: University Press of Florida.

Gould, S.J. (1996). *The mismeasure of man: The definitive refutation to the argument of The Bell Curve.* NY: W.W. Norton & Company, Inc.

Griffith Corp. (Producer), & Griffith, D.W. (Director). (1915). *Birth of a nation* [Motion Picture]. U.S.A.

Hagen, K.A., Myers, B.J., & Mackintosh, V.H. (2005). Hope, social support, and behavioral problems in at-risk children. *American Journal of Orthopsychiatry, 75,* 211–219.

Harley, S., & Middleton, S. (1994). Voices in African American history: Civil Rights. Cleveland, OH: Modern Curriculum Press.

Heckman, J.J., & LaFontaine, P.A. (2007, December). *The American high school graduation rate: Trends and levels.* Paper presented at the meeting of Institute for the Study of Labor, Germany.

Helms, J.E. (2006, November). Fairness is not validity or cultural bias in racial-group assessment: A quantitative perspective. *American Psychologist,* 845-859.

The Heritage Foundation (2009). *Let me rise: The struggle to save school choice in the nation's capital.* Retrieved on January 2, 2012 from http://www.heritage.org/multimedia/video/2009/10/let-me-rise .

Herodotus (440, BC). *The history of Herodotus.* Retrieved on February 10, 2009 from http://classics.mit.edu/Herodotus/history.html.

Hill, L. (1998). Lost ones. On *The Miseducation of Lauryn Hill* [CD]. NY: Columbia.

Hilliard, A.G. (1996). Either a paradigm shift or no mental measurement: The nonscience and the nonsense of the bell curve. *Cultural Diversity and Mental Health, 2,* 1-20.

Hines, A.M., Merdinger, J., & Wyatt, P. (2005). Former foster youth attending college: Resilience and the transition to young adulthood. *American Journal of Orthopsychiatry, 75,* 381–394.

Hinton-Nelson, M.D., Roberts, M.C., & Snyder, C.R. (1996). Early adolescents exposed to violence: Hope and vulnerability to victimization. *American Journal of Orthopsychiatry, 66,* 346–353.

Hockenbury, D.H., & Hockenbury, S.E. (2000). *Psychology* (2nd ed.). NY: Worth Publishers.

Homer (800a, BC). *The illiad.* Retrieved on February 10, 2009 from http://classics.mit.edu/Homer/iliad.html .

Homer (800b, BC). *The odyssey.* Retrieved on February 10, 2009 from http://classics.mit.edu/Homer/odyssey.1.i.html .

Hughes, D., & Chen, L. (1997). When and what parents tell children about race: An examination of race-related socialization among African American families. *Applied Developmental Science, 1,* 200–214.

Hughes, D., Hagelskamp, C., Way, N., & Foust, M.D. (2009). The role of mothers' and adolescents' perceptions of ethnic-racial socialization in shaping ethnic-racial identity among early adolescent boys and girls. *Journal of Youth & Adolescence, 38,* 605–626.

References

Hurley, E.A., Boykin, A.W., Allen, B.A. (2005). Communal versus individual learning of a math-estimation task: African American children and the culture of learning contexts. *The Journal of Psychology, 139,* 513–527.

Jackson, C. (2008). Harlem Renaissance: Pivotal period in the development of Afro-American *culture. Retrieved on March 11, 2008 from* http://www.yale.edu/ynhti/curriculum/units/1978/2/78.02.03.x.html .

James, G.G.M. (2009). *Stolen legacy.* NY: Classiic House Press.

JBHE. (2011). Black student college graduation rates inch higher but a large racial gap persists. *Features.* Retrieved on August 2, 2012 from http://www.jbhe.com/preview/winter07preview.html .

Johnson, M. (2011). Ohio mom goes to jail for lying to school district to get kids into better school. *Playground Dad & Playground Network, LLC.* Retrieved on January 2, 2012 from http://playgrounddad.com/2011/01/26/ohio-mom-goes-to-jail-for-lying-to-school-district-to-get-kids-into-better-school/ .

Jordan, K.A. (2005). Discourses of difference and the overrepresentation of Black students in special education. *The Journal of African American History, 90,* 128–149.

Kaplan, A., & Maehr, M.L. (2007). The contributions and prospects of goal orientation theory. *Educational Psychology Review, 19,* 141–184.

Karenga, M. (1988). *The African American holiday of Kwanzaa: A celebration of family, community, & culture.* CA: University of Sankore Press.

Karenga, M. (2002). 9/11, Liberation struggles and international relations: Sharing the burden and the possibilities of the crisis. *The Black Scholar, 32,* 12–15.

Karenga, M. (2006). *Maat, the moral ideal in ancient Egypt: A study in classical African ethics.* CA: University of Sankore Press.

Kaylor, M., & Flores, M.M. (2007). Increasing academic motivation in culturally and linguistically diverse students from low socioeconomic backgrounds. *Journal of Advanced Academics, 19,* 66–89.

Klein, H.J., Wesson, M.J., Hollenbeck, J.R., & Alge, B.J. (1999). Goal commitment and the goal-setting process: Conceptual clarification and empirical synthesis. *Journal of Applied Psychology, 84,* 885–896.

Kliewer, W., & Lewis, H. (1995). Family influences on coping processes in children and adolescents with sickle cell disease. *Journal of Pediatric Psychology, 20,* 511–525.

Kozol, J. (2005). *The shame of the nation: The restoration of Apartheid schooling in America.* NY: Crown Publishers.

Kubrin, C.E. (2005). Gangstas, thugs, and hustlas: Identity and the code of the street in rap music. *Social Problems, 52,* 360–378.

Kunjufu, J. (1995). *Countering the conspiracy to destroy Black boys: Series.* Chicago, IL: African American Images.

Kunjufu, J. (2005). *Countering the conspiracy to destroy Black boys: Series*. Chicago, IL: African American Images.

Kunjufu, J. (2006). *An African centered response to Ruby Payne's poverty theory*. Chicago, IL: African American Images.

Kunjufu, J. (2011a, November 23). National education consultant cautions, 'Keep Black boys out of special education!' *InsightNews.com*. Retrieved on July 14, 2012 from http://insightnews.com/education/8211-national-education-consultant-cautions-keep-black-boys-out-of-special-education .

Kunjufu, J. (2011b). *Understanding Black male learning styles*. Chicago, IL: African American Images.

Ladson-Billings, G. (1996). Silences as weapons: Challenge of a Black professor teaching White students. *Theory into Practice, 35,* 80-85.

Ladson-Billings, G. (2008). Pushing past the achievement gap: An essay on the language of deficit. *The Journal of Negro Education, 76,* 316–323.

Ladson-Billings, G., & Henry, A. (1990). Blurring the borders: Voices of African liberatory pedagogy in the United States and Canada. *Journal of Education, 172,* 72–88.

Lagana, M.T. (2004). Protective factors for inner-city adolescents at risk of school dropout, Family factors and social support. *Children & Schools, 26,* 211–220.

Li, S.T., Nussbaum, K.M., & Richards, M.H. (2007). Risk and protective factors for urban African-American youth. *American Journal of Community Psychology, 39,* 21–35.

Lincoln, C.E, & Mamiya, L.H. (1990). *The Black church in the African American experience*. Durham, NC: Duke University Press.

Loewen, J.W. (2007). *Lies my teacher told me: Everything your American history textbook got wrong*. NY: Simon & Schuster.

Lugard, L. (1997). *A tropical dependency: An outline of the ancient history of the Western Sudan with an account of the modern settlement of Northern Nigeria*. Baltimore, MD: Black Classic Press. (Original work published 1906).

Magaletta, P.R., & Oliver, J.M. (1999). The hope construct, will, and ways: Their relations with self-efficacy, optimism, and general well-being. *Journal of Clinical Psychology, 55,* 539–551.

Majors, R., & Billson, J.M. (1992). *Cool pose: The dilemmas of Black manhood in America*. NY: Lexington Books.

Maluccio, A.N. (2002). Book Review Essay: Resilience: a many-splendid construct? *American Journal of Orthopsychiatry, 72,* 596–599.

Masten, A. S. (2001). Ordinary magic: Resilience processes in development. *American Psychologist, 56,* 227–238.

Mazama, A. (2001). The Afrocentric paradigm: Contours and definitions. *Journal of Black Studies, 31,* 387–405.

References

Mazama, A. (2007). *Africa in the 21st century: Toward a new future.* NY: Taylor & Francis Group, LLC.

McCabe, K., & Barnett, D. (2000). First comes work, then comes marriage: Future orientation among African American young adolescents. *Family Relations, 49,* 63–70.

Mcdougal, III, S. (2011). The future of research methods in Africana studies graduate curriculum. *Journal of African American Studies, 15,* 279-289.

Merrell, K.W. (2003). *Behavioral, social, and emotional assessment of children and adolescents.* Mahwah, NJ: Lawrence Erlbaum Associates, Inc.

Merry, M.S., & New, W. (2008). Constructing an authentic self: The challenges and promise of African-centered pedagogy. *American Journal of Education, 115,* 35–64.

Michney, T.M. (2006). Race, violence, and urban territoriality: Cleveland's Little Italy and the 1966 Hough uprising. Journal of Urban History, 32, 404–428.

National Collaborative on Diversity in the Teaching Force. (2004). *Assessment of Diversity in America's Teaching Force: A Call to Action.* D.C.: Author.

National Research Council (2002). *Minority students in special and gifted education.* Washington, DC: National Academy Press.

NPS. (2004). A history of Black Americans in California. *On-line book: Five Views: An Ethnic Historic Site Survey for California.* Retrieved on February 25, 2012 from http://www.cr.nps.gov/history/online_books/5views/5views2.htm .

Newark Advocate (2009, February). More Ohio school districts struggling with budgets. Retrieved on March 15, 2009 from http://www.newarkadvocate.com/apps/pbcs.dll/article?AID=2009902020310 .

Newman, R. (2005). APA's resilience initiative. *Professional Psychology: Research and Practice, 36,* 227–229.

Nickerson, K.J., Helms, J.E., & Terrell, F. (1994). Cultural mistrust, opinions about mental illness, and Black students' attitudes toward seeking psychological help from White counselors. *Journal of Counseling Psychology, 41,* 378–385.

Nobles, W.W. (2006). *Seeking the Sakhu: Foundational writings for an African psychology.* IL: Third World Press.

O'Donohue, W., & Fryling, M. (2007). How has applied behavior analysis and behavior therapy changed? An historical analysis of journals. *The Behavior Analyst Today, 8,* 52–62.

O'Shaughnessy, L. (2012, February 21). Supreme court may halt college affirmative action. *CBS News.* http://www.cbsnews.com/8301-505146_162-57381768/supreme-court-may-halt-college-affirmative-action/ .

Obama, B. (1995). *Dreams from my father: A story of race and inheritance.* NY: Crown Publishers.

Ogbu, J.U. (1989). The individual in collective adaptation: A framework for focusing on academic under performance and dropping out among involuntary minorities. In L. Weis, E. Farrar, & H. Petrie's (Eds), *Dropouts from school: Issues, dilemmas, and solutions.* NY: State University of New York Press, p. 181–204.

Ogbu, J.U. (1993). Differences in cultural frame of reference. *International Journal of Behavioral Development, 16,* 483-506.

Ogbu, J.U. (2004). Collective identity ad the burden of "acting White" in Black history, community, and education. *The Urban Review, 36,* 1–35.

Oppenheimer, D.B. (2008). Why France needs to collect data on racial identity…in a French way. *Hastings International & Company Law Review, 31,* 735-752.

Orfield, G. (2001). *Schools more separate: Consequences of a decade of resegregation* (Harvard Civil Rights Project Rep. ED 459 217). MA: Harvard University.

Ott, T. (2008, July 27). Cleveland schools CEO Eugene Sanders thrives amid challenges. *The Plain Dealer.* Retrieved on March 15, 2009 from http://blog.cleveland.com/metro/2008/07/cleveland_schools_ceo_eugene_s.html .

Parajes, F. (2001). Toward a positive psychology of academic motivation. *The Journal of Educational Research, 95,* 27–35.

Payne, R.K. (2005). *A framework for understanding poverty.* Highlands, TX: aha! Process, Inc. (Original work published 1996).

Pedrotti, J.T., Edwards, L.M., & Lopez, S.J. (2008). Promoting hope: Suggestions for school counselors. *Professional School Counseling, 12,* 100–107.

Penang Conference. (2011, June). *Decolonising our universities: Another world is desireable.* Conference held at Universiti Sains Malaysia. Retrieved on August 12, 2012 from http://globalhighered.wordpress.com/2011/07/22/decolonising-our-universities-another-world-is-desirable/ .

Phelps, R.E., Taylor, J.D., & Gerard, P.A. (2001). Cultural mistrust, ethnic identity, racial identity, and self-esteem among ethnically diverse Black university students. *Journal of Counseling & Development, 79,* 209–216.

Pilgrim, D. (2000). The picaninny caricature. *Jim Crow: Museum of racist memorabilia.* Retrieved on January 9, 2012 from http://www.ferris.edu/jimcrow/picaninny/ .

Pitcher, G., Andrew, D., Armstrong, K., Bainbridge, J., Bewer, T., Carillet, J., et al. (2007). *Africa.* CA: Lonely Planet.

Quintana, S.M. (2007). Racial and ethnic identity: Developmental perspectives and research. *Journal of Counseling Psychology, 54,* 259–270.

References

Quintana, S.M., Castañeda-English, P., & Ybarra, V.C. (1999). Role of perspective-taking abilities and ethnic socialization in development of adolescent ethnic identity. *Journal of Research on Adolescence, 9,* 161–184.

The Relocation Professionals (2009). *Welcome to Cleveland, Ohio.* Retrieved on March 15, 2009 from http://www.cleveland-ohio-living.com/government/.

Rennie, D.L. (1994). Clients' deference in psychotherapy. *Journal of Counseling Psychology, 41,* 427–437.

Rios, D., Stewart, A.J., & Winter, D.G. (2010). "Thinking she could be the next president": Why identifying with the curriculum matters. *Psychology of Women Quarterly, 34,* 328–338.

Rivas-Drake, D., Hughes, D., & Way, N. (2009). A preliminary analysis of associations among ethnic-racial socialization, ethnic discrimination, and ethnic identity among urban sixth graders. *Journal of Research on Adolescence, 19,* 558–584.

The Roots. (2004). Stay cool. On *The Tipping Point.* [CD]. California: Geffen Records.

Rosenthal, D.J. (2006). 'Hoods and the woods: Rap music as environmental literature. *The Journal of Popular Culture, 39,* 661–676.

Ruef, M., & Fletcher, B. (2003). Legacies of American slavery: Status attainment among Southern Blacks after emancipation. *Social Forces, 82,* 445–480.

Sackler, M. (Director) (2010). *The lottery* [Motion Picture]. U.S.A.

San Francisco Bayview. (2011). What happened to Black Wall Street on June 1, 1921? *San Francisco Bayview National Black Newspaper, February 9.* Retrieved on February 25, 2012 from http://sfbayview.com/2011/what-happened-to-black-wall-street-on-june-1-1921/

Sanders, E.T.W. (2009, February). *Cleveland Metropolitan School District state of the schools address.* Speech given at CMSD State of the Schools Address at John Hay Campus.

Sankofa, B.M., Hurley, E.A., Allen, B.A. Boykin, A.W. (2005). Cultural expression and Black students' attitudes toward high achievers. *The Journal of Psychology, 139,* 247–259.

Scruggs, T.E., & Mastropieri, M.A. (Eds.) (2005). *Advances in learning and behavioral disabilities volume 18: Cognition and learning in diverse settings.* CA: Elsevier Inc.

Sellers, R.M., Caldwell, C.H., Schmeelk-Cone, K.H., & Zimmerman, M.A. (2003). Racial identity, racial discrimination, perceived stress, and psychological distress among African American young adults. *Health and Social Behavior, 44,* 302–317.

Sellers, R. M., Rowley, S.A., Chavous, T.M., Shelton, J.N., Smith, M.A. (1997). Multidimensional inventory of Black identity: A preliminary investigation of reliability and construct validity. *Journal of Personality and Social Psychology, 73,* 805–815.

Sesanti, S. (June 13, 2012) Personal communication.

The Seven Natural Wonders. (2008). Inspiring people to discover, explore & engage the natural wonders of the world: Africa. *7 Natural Wonders.* Retrieved on August 2, 2012 from http://sevennaturalwonders.org/category/africa/ .

Shabazz, A. (1999). Foreword. In A. Haley's *The autobiography of Malcolm X* (p. xiii). New York: Ballantine Books.

Sharkey, H.J. (2004). Sudan's blood memory: The legacy of war, ethnicity, and slavery in *Early* South Sudan (book). *International Journal of African Historical Studies, 37,* 359–361.

Shealey, M.W., & Lue, M.S. (2006). Why are all the Black kids still in special education? Revisiting the issue of disproportionate representation. *Multicultural Perspectives, 8,* 3–9.

Sheldon, K.M., & King, L. (2001). Why positive psychology is necessary. *American Psychologist, 56,* 216–217.

Shorey, H.S., Snyder, C.R., Rand, K.L., Hockemeyer, J.R., & Feldman, D.B. (2002). Somewhere over the rainbow: Hope theory weathers its first decade. *Psychological Inquiry, 13,* 322–331.

Skiba, R.J., Simmons, A.B., Ritter, S., Gibb, A.C., Rausch, M.K., Cuadrado, J. et al. (2008). Achieving equity in special education: history, status, and current challenges. *Exceptional Children, 74,* 264–288.

Smithsonian (2007). National museum of African American history and culture. Retrieved on February 15, 2008 from http://nmaahc.si.edu/section/education/view/85 .

Snyder, C.R. (1995). Conceptualizing, measuring, and nurturing hope. *Journal of Counseling & Development, 73,* 355–360.

Snyder, C.R. (2002). Hope theory: Rainbows in the mind. *Psychological Inquiry, 13,* 249–275.

Snyder, C.R., Harris, C., Anderson, J.R., Holleran, S.A., Irving, L.M., Sigmon, S.T. et al. (1991). The will and the ways: Development and validation of an individual-differences measure of hope. *Journal of Personality and Social Psychology, 60,* 570–585.

Snyder, C.R., Hoza, B., Pelham, W.E., Rapoff, M., Ware, L.,Danovsky, M., et al. (1997). The development and validation of the Children's Hope Scale. *Journal of Pediatric Psychology, 22,* 399–421.

Snyder, C.R., Lehman, K.A., Kluck, B., & Monsson, Y. (2006). Hope for rehabilitation and vice versa. *Rehabilitation Psychology, 51,* 89–112.

Snyder, C.R., Lopez, S.J., Shorey, H.S., Rand, K.L., & Feldman, D.B. (2003). Hope theory, measurements, and applications to school psychology. *School Psychology Quarterly, 18,* 122–139.

Snyder, C.R., Shorey, H.S., Cheavens, J., Pulvers, K.M., Adams, V.H., & Wiklund, C. (2002). Hope and academic success in college. *Journal of Educational Psychology, 94,* 820–826.

References

Stinson, D.W. (2011). When the "burden of acting White" is not a burden: School success and African American male students. *Urban Review, 43,* 43–65.

Suzuki, L.A., Ahluwalia, M.K., Mattis, J.S., & Quizon, C.A. (2005). Ethnography in counseling psychology research: Possibilities for application. *Journal of Counseling Psychology, 52,* 206–214.

Swan, Q. (2009). *Black power in Bermuda: The struggle for decolonization.* NY: Palgrave Macmillan.

Tatum, B.D. (1997). *"Why are all the Black kids sitting together in the cafeteria?" And other conversations about race.* NY: Basic Books.

Tatum, B.D. (1999). *Assimilation blues: Black families in White communities: Who succeeds and why?* NY: Greenwood Press.

Templeton, J.W. (1996). *Our Roots Run Deep: The Black Experience in California, 1950-2000.* eAccess Corporation.

Templeton, J.W. (2010). *Cakewalk: A Novel about the Untold Creators of Jazz Music.* eAccess Corporation.

Terrell, F., & Terrell, S.L. (1981). An inventory to measure cultural mistrust among Blacks. *Western Journal of Black Studies, 3,* 180–185.

Thompson, R.F. (1974). *African art in motion: Icon and act in the collection of Katherine Coryton White.* CA: University of California Press.

Thompson, V.L.S., & Akbar, M. (2003). The understanding of race and the construction of African American identity. *The Western Journal of Black Studies, 27,* 80–88.

Tully, S. (1994). Teens: The most global market of all. *Fortune, 129,* 90–96.

Ture, K., & Thelwell, E.M. (2003). *Ready for revolution: The life and struggles of Stokely Carmichael (Kwame Ture).* NY: Scribner.

Twain, M. (1999). *The adventures of Huckleberry Finn.* NY: Barron's Educational Series.

U.S. Army. (2010). *Black in the U.S. Army: Then and now.* A report by the Department of the Army, Office of Army Demographics.

U.S. Census Bureau. (2009). State & county quick facts: Cleveland (city), Ohio. Retrieved on March 15, 2009 from http://quickfacts.census.gov/qfd/states/39/3916000.html .

Valle, M.F., Huebner, E.S., & Suldo, S.M. (2004). Further evaluation of the children's hope scale. *Journal of Psychoeducational Assessment, 22,* 320–337.

Van Sertima, I. (2003). *They came before Columbus: The African presence in ancient America.*
NY: Random House Trade Paperbacks. (Original work published 1976).

Vandiver, B.J., Cross, Jr., W.E., Worrell, F.C., & Fhagen-Smith, P.E. (2002). Validating the Cross Racial Identity Scale. *Journal of Counseling Psychology, 49,* 71–85.

Vandiver, B.J., Fhagen-Smith, P.E., Cokley, K.O., Cross, W.E., & Worrell, F.C. (2001). Cross's nigrescence model: From theory to scale to theory. *Journal of Multicultural Counseling and Development, 29,* 174–200.

Vasquez, M.J.T., & Jones, J.M. (2006). Increasing the number of psychologists of color: Public policy issues for affirmative diversity. *American Psychologist, 61,* 132–142.

Ventura, M. (1985). *Shadow dancing in the U.S.A.* CA: Tarcher.

Walker, J.E.K. (2004). War, women, song: The tectonics of Black business and entrepreneurship, 1939-2001. *The Review of Black Political Economy, Winter, 65–*116.

Walker, S.S. (Ed.) (2001). *African roots/American cultures: Africa in the creation of the Americas.* Lanham, MD: Rowman & Littlefield Publishers, Inc.

Weiner, M.F. (2009). Elite versus grassroots: Disjunctures between parents' and civil rights organizations' demands for New York City's public schools. *Sociological Quarterly, 50,* 89–119.

West, C. (2001). *Race matters.* Boston, MA: Beacon Press.

WKYC (2009, March). Cleveland schools CEO travels to Washington to meet new education *secretary.* Retrieved on March 20, 2009 from http://www.wkyc.com/news/news_article.aspx?storyid= 109382 .

Williams, J., & Baron, K. (2007, October). Military sees big decline in black enlistees: Iraq war cited in 58% drop since 2000. *The Boston Globe.*

Woodson, C.G. (1968). *The African background outlined.* NY: Negro Universities Press. (Original work published 1936).

Woodson, C.G. (2000). *This mis-education of the Negro.* IL: African American Images. (Original work published 1933).

Worrell, F.C., Cross, Jr., W.E., & Vandiver, B.J. (2001). Nigrescence theory: Current status and challenges for the future. *Journal of Multicultural Counseling and Development, 29,* 201–213.

Wright, J.W. (2009). *The New York Times almanac: The almanac of record.* NY: Penguin Group.

Wu Tang. (1994). C.R.E.A.M. On *Enter the Wu-Tang: 36 Chambers.* Staten Island, NY: RCA.

Zirin, D. (2012, March 23). Jackie Robinson, Trayvon Martin, and the sad history of Sanford,

FL. *The Nation.* Retrieved on March 28, 2012 from http:// www.thenation.com/blog/166992/jackie-robinson-trayvon-martin-and-sad-history-sanford-florida .

Index

A

Academy, 155; Academic(s)(ians), 15, 24, 34-36, 47, 57, 75, 98, 104, 110, 123, 130, 145, 153, 155, 156, 158, 161; Academic achievement, 10, 11, 100, 119, 127; effort(s), 59, 81; excellence, 63, 130, 143; experiences, 23; motivation, 85; performance, 72; planning, 99; progress, 34, 47, 67, 82; outcomes, 19; resilience, 99, 108, 132, 134; resolve, 49, 74; self-concept, 11; success, 11, 108; Academically, 2, 80, 90, 118, 132

Achiever(s), xvii, xxvii, 13, 22, 25, 28, 29, 32, 34, 35, 38-40, 76, 78, 84-86, 92, 98, 99, 103, 107, 108, 110, 116, 117, 120, 143, 150, 153, 160; and behavior, 131; collectivism, 122; confidence, 131; family, 140, 141; hobbies and interests, 118; identity, 136, 139; njia, 123, 124; peers, 119; philosophy, 127, 129; quality of life, 133; values, 134-136

Achievement(s), vi, viii, xv, xviii, xxix; African American, xi, xvi, xvii, xxi, 17, 18, 20-22, 35, 47, 62, 63, 88, 89, 94, 100, 110, 120, 123, 124, 127; CHS predicted, 10; experience(s), x, 6, 9; of goal, 7, 63, 73, 80; identity, 11, 137-140; life, 43, 54, 86, 112, 116; race, 103; school, xxv, xxiv, xxvi, xxvii, 8, 27, 30, 45, 46, 48, 49, 56, 58, 63, 70, 75, 77, 93, 127, 128, 129, 139, 144, 145, 150, 159, 160; Underachievement, xvi, 26, 160

Adolsecent(s), xvi, xxvii, xxviii, 10, 29, 53, 135, 141, 157; Adolescence, 5, 28, 89

Afraid, vii, 61

Africa, ix, x, xii, xvi, xix, xxi, xxiii-xxv, xxix, 7-9, 13-15, 17, 20, 30, 37, 124, 127, 136, 139, 143, 148; and African Americans, 150, 155, 161, 162; according to Aisha, 114, 115; Assata, 85, 87-91; Kenya, 102, 103, 105; Kwame, 67, 70-72; Talibi, 64, 65; Ture, 51, 52-53; divide-and-conquer, 122; pre-colonial, 123, 135

African Diaspora, xi, xix, 22, 88, 100, 123, 143, 148, 156, 161; African Diaporic/an, xii, xvii, xx, 12, 15, 52, 53, 128, 135, 150, 152, 156

Africanity, xix-xxi

Afrocentric, ix, xi, xii, xx, xxviii, 48, 85, 88, 100, 108, 156, 160, review Chapters 2 and 3

Afrocentricity, v, xii, xix-xxi, 7-9, 12, 23, 30, 159

Afrocentrism, xxi

Agency, v, vii, viii, xx, xxvii, 2, 4, 11, 12, 18, 21, 22, 32, 35, 48, 68, 81, 99, 112, 117, 132, 139, 156
Akbar, N., vii, xi, xxi, 30, 136, 143
Amen, R.U.N., 16
Amentutankh/Tutankhamen, 149
Ancestry, xi, 65, 122, 130; African descent/descended, xi, xii, xvi, xvii, xix, xx, 6, 16, 22, 24, 56, 70, 112, 146, 148
Andre 3000, 16
Ani, M., viii, 129
Ankh, v, 15, 16, 149, 150
Anti-African, 21, 101, 149
Asante, M.K., v, ix, xi, xii, xviii, xxi, xxviii, 8-10, 30, 33, 136, 137
Asante, Jr., M.K., xxv, 133
Assimilate, 35; Assimilation, xvi, xxviii, 143; Assimilationist, 20
Ausar, vi, 79
Axum, 13, 14, 15; Axumite(s), 13
America, see also United States, v, ix, x, xii, xiii, xvii, xx, xxv, xxviii, 7-9, 11, 13, 18-20, 23, 25, 45, 56, 62, 65, 70, 89, 96, 103, 123, 136, 137, 139, 141, 155, 158, 161

B
Badu, E., xxiv, 16
Balance, 17, 34, 43, 75, 103, 127, 132, 162; Unbalanced, 63
Ballenger, C., 144
Billson, J.M., xxiv, xxvi
Black Star, 133
Brazil, xvi; Brazilian, 152, 162
Bridge, 48, 62, 82, 131, 137-139, 145
Brophy, T., xviii
Browder, A., 15, 162
Brown, L., 16

C
Career, xi, 45, 48, 56, 68, 73, 77, 80, 84, 98, 99, 109, 110, 123, 131-135, 141, 146, 148, 151, 153, 154, 156; satisfaction, 78
Caribbean, xvi, xxiii, 13, 20, 127
Centered, viii, x, xx, xxix, 8, 9, 17, 25, 31, 90, 118, 128, 133, 149, 155; Centeredness, 23, 32, 34, 63, 120

Index

Chandler, D.R., vii

Child development, see also Development, xxvii, xxviii

Chisholm, S., 149

CHS, 6, 10

Clarke, J.H., xxi, 16

Cleaver, E., 160

Cleveland (,OH), vii, xvii, xxix, 17, 25-27, 47, 56, 57, 89, 109, 110, 115, 119, 121, 138, 155

Cognition(s), 4, 29; Cognitive, x, xxiii, xxvii, xxviii, 1, 3, 4, 12, 23, 35, 45, 130, 161

College(s), v, vii, x, xi, 2, 4, 8, 11, 19, 26, 27, 35, 123, 130, 134, 135, 138, 146, 150, 154, 156, 157, 161; according to Aisha, 107, 108, 110, 111; Assata, 86, 93; Kenya, 98, 100, 101, 103; Kwame, 68, 78; Talib, 57-63, 66; Ture 44-47, 50

Collectivism, xxviii, 19, 20, 22, 34, 36, 53, 72, 110, 135, 136, 140; Collectivist, 5, 20, 35, 45, 89, 120, 129, 135, 136

Communal, 20-23, 34, 44, 63, 128, 133

Confidence, see also Self-confident/confidence, viii, xxix, 4, 25, 38, 117, 128, 131, 132, 140, 154; Confident(ly), xi, 36, 38, 131, 141; according to Aisha, 111, 112; Assata, 80, 86, 88; Kenya, 109; Kwame, 68; Talib, 60, 61; Ture, 45, 46, 53, 55

Confused, xii, xxviii, 29, 34, 71, 86, 139; Confusion, xviii, xxiv, xxviii, 13, 22, 38, 66, 89, 101, 122, 160

Conscientious(ness), xv, 25, 52, 53, 72, 78, 85, 128, 148, 152

Conscious(ly), xii, xv, xx, xxiv, 23, 45, 48, 53, 55, 60, 69, 72, 74, 80, 81, 86, 95, 103, 114, 135, 139, 149, 160; Consciousness(es), vii, x, xii, xviii, xix, 9, 22, 34, 48, 53, 63, 66, 85, 91, 108, 111, 115, 118, 120, 122, 124, 128, 136, 148, 152, 158

Continent, xix, xxi, 52, 70, 90, 91, 115, 148-150, 162; Continental, xx, xxiii, 13, 15, 53, 128, 139, 140, 147

Cool, xxiv-xxvi, xxviii, 16, 33, 54, 61, 116, 119, 120, 121, 142

Create(s)/(ing), viii, xviii, xxi, xxvii, 5, 12, 16, 18, 24, 39, 63, 65, 97, 103, 118, 119, 131, 133, 136, 137, 143-145; Creative, xxv, 34, 73, 116, 118, 149, 152; Creativity, xxiv, xxv, 20, 24, 32, 129

Cross, W., xix, 12, 19, 20, 156, 157

Cultural-esteem, xi, 141, 143

185

D

David, K., 16

Dead Prez, 133

Desegregation, xxiii, 17, 18, 122, 123, 137

Determined, see also Self-determined, ix, 11, 63, 69, 78, 80, 90, 116, 130, 132; Determination, see also Self-determination, xxvi, xxix, 4, 12, 21, 46, 48, 50, 51, 53, 56, 58, 60, 63, 66, 70, 72, 75, 80, 88, 91, 95-97, 99, 106, 108, 110, 113, 114, 123, 132-134, 138, 143, 157, 158

Develop(ed)/(ing), 3-6, 8, 9, 12, 16-18, 24, 62, 63, 81, 86, 101-103, 115, 119, 124, 137, 138, 146, 152, 158; Development(s), 1, 2, 3, 5, 6, 9, 13, 17, 24, 25, 27-30, 32, 34, 52, 86, 99, 104, 111, 112, 127, 135, 138, 140, 143, 152, 156, 162; Developmental, 2, 6, 18, 85, 96

Different(ly), xii, xiii, 3, 5, 28, 37, 39, 48, 51, 53, 58, 60, 64, 67, 68, 73, 74, 84, 95, 101, 112, 121, 144, 147-149, 159

Diop, C., v, 9, 143

Dirty, 89, 90, 139, 140

Discrimination, xxiv, 2, 12, 19, 20, 22, 50, 70, 74, 122, 128, 137, 150, 155

Dissonance, xxiv, 12, 104, 148, 154

Diverge, 48; Divergent, 62, 93, 131, 137-139, 143, 148

Dream(s)/(ing), xv, xvi, xxvii, 1, 21, 90, 97, 99, 139, 140, 149; Dreamers, 143

Du Bois, W.E.B., v, xi, 8, 11, 28, 48, 56, 159-161

E

Educate(d), ix, xvi, xvii, xxiii, xxix, 22, 66, 103, 119, 145, 158; Educator(s), vii, ix, xvi, xxii, xxv, xxvi, 6, 12, 16, 18, 34, 35, 118, 130, 131, 143, 145, ; Educating, xvii, xxii, xxv, 6, 71, 89, 144

Egypt, x, 13-15, 44, 147; Egyptian, 14, 151, 152

Elder(s), v, viii, xxiii, 30, 55, 77, 81, 85, 89, 100, 110, 121, 124, 131

Encourage(s)/(ed)/(ing), vi, vii, xi, xxi, 5, 12, 20, 85, 109, 110, 136, 138, 143, 144, 156, 158; Encouragement, 38, 47, 60, 100, 110, 141, 142

Enlighten(ed)/(ing), vii, x, xvi, xix, 153; Enlightenment, v

Ethnic, x-xii, xv, xviii, xix, xx, xxiv-xxviii, 6, 8, 9, 11, 12, 25, 56, 63, 65, 71, 117, 146, 148; and community, 85, 89, 133, 136, 139, 143, 147; pride, 50, 102, 128; Ethnicity, xi, xviii, xix, xxviii, 3, 11, 19, 50, 70, 102, 112

Ethnocentric, xxi, xxvi; Ethnocentrism, xxiii

Eurocentric(ally), ix, xxvi, 5, 35, 48, 65, 86, 95, 122, 138, 144, 149, 151, 160-162

Eurocentrism, xxi, xxii, 3, 51, 86, 95, 97, 128, 145, 160, 161

European(s), v, xv, xvi, xviii, xix-xxii, xxvi, xxix, 3, 6, 8-10, 12, 14, 15, 20, 22, 25, 52, 65, 123, 143, 144, 150, 158, 160-162; and history, 139, 145; privilege, 48; pro-European, 122; non-Europeans, 1, 8

European Slave Trade, or system, 71, 90

Excel(ed)/(ing), xvi, 17, 70, 99, 113, 117, 120, 130, 131; Excellence, ix, xxv, 17, 47, 57, 63, 108, 128, 130, 134, 138, 140, 143, 144, 148; Excellent, 43, 62, 131

Expect(ed)/(ing), xv, xxviii, 5, 18, 20, 47, 56, 61, 72, 81, 104, 106, 111, 116, 130, 132, 138, 140, 146, 151, 154; Expectation(s), xxiii, 3, 5, 17, 29, 34, 45, 47, 57, 77, 78, 98, 116, 124, 127-131, 134, 138, 140, 141, 143, 144, 146, 151, 158

F

Family, v-vii, xi, xvi, xvii, xxvii, 6, 7, 19, 21, 28, 44, 64, 65, 68, 74, 77, 83, 90, 118, 150, 154; and connectedness, 39, 49, 50, 53, 69, 72, 79-81, 85, 91, 99, 109, 124, 127, 133, 134, 136, 140, 159; dynamic, 5; extended network, 56, 83, 97, 99, 100, 107, 127; help, 71, 72, 84, 108, 115; pride, 78, 79, 128-131; school, 36, 48, 62, 82, 101, 115; support, 3, 47, 49, 57-60, 62, 93, 95, 96, 110, 111; values, 45, 46, 63, 66, 75, 83, 98, 109, 117, 120, 124, 137, 139, 143, 148, 151, 160

Fear, see also Afraid, 53, 89, 109, 133, 139

Fiasco, L., xxv, 118

Focus(ed)/(ing), 2, 4, 8, 10, 16, 23, 24, 28, 46, 54, 57, 61-63, 66, 68, 74, 78, 80, 85, 91, 94, 97, 98, 100, 105, 107, 108, 112, 116, 117, 123, 124, 127, 132-134, 140, 143, 144, 148, 150-152, 156, 161, 162

Friends(hips), vi, xvi, 29, 59-61, 66, 81, 85, 99, 100, 109, 118, 120, 124, 130, 137, 141, 142, 154

Fuller, C., xxiii

Future(s), 2, 10, 20, 29, 37, 38, 45, 47, 51, 55, 58-60, 62, 63, 65, 68, 69, 74, 84, 86, 90, 95, 106, 112, 116, 117, 122, 130, 134, 135, 137, 146, 151, 155, 158, 162

G

Goal-driven, xv, 25, 128; Goal-pursuit, xvi, 4, 12, 36, 49, 82, 93, 106; Goal-setting, 5, 32, 35, 36, 45, 69, 81, 84, 88, 103, 123, 158

God, xiii, 13, 14, 68, 79, 106, 117, 133, 136

Gould, S.J., xviii

H

Harmony, x, 30-33, 35, 78, 128, 134, 135, 153, 162; Harmonious(ly), xvi, xxviii, 15, 19, 108; Harmonizing, 135

Haitian, 89, 152

Heart(s)/(y)/(ed), viii, ix, x, xxi, xxii, 6, 22, 28, 51, 79, 122, 144

Helms, J., 154, 158

Herodotus, 14

Heroes/heroines, 102, 103, 105, 113, 130, 133, 136, 140, 160

Hill, L., 152

Hilliard, A., vii, xxi, 158

Hip hop, xv, xxiv, xxv, 32, 117-119, 133, 161

Historical(ly), v, vi, viii, xii, xx, 18, 20, 25, 33, 63, 150; Historians, 18, 146; History, 7-9, 11-13, 15-18, 25, 27, 30, 37, 49-53, 55, 56, 63, 64, 65, 70-72, 85-89, 91, 101, 102, 103, 112-117, 124, 127, 128-131, 133-135, 137, 139, 140, 141, 143-146, 149-152, 157, 159-162

Homer, 13

Hood, 47, 101, 110

I

Identity, vii, viii, xix, xx, xxiv, xxvi, xxvii, 7, 9, 11, 12, 19, 29, 35, 46, 50, 63, 64, 70, 76, 79, 85, 86, 88, 89, 101-103, 112, 114, 118, 120, 124, 127, 128, 130, 134, 136-139, 141, 152, 156, 159, 160; Identities, xxiv, xxvi, 11, 12, 20, 85, 102, 120, 129, 135, 137, 149

I-em-hotep, xiii; Imhotep, 149

Impoverished, xvii, 57, 100, 109, 115

Inequality(ies); 5, 56, 65, 70, 100, 103, 113, 135

Instruction, x, xxi, 6, 20, 40, 43, 68, 69, 103, 107, 143, 146, 157; Instructors, xi

Intelligent(ly), xv, xxii, 75, 124, 149; Intelligence, xv, xvi, xviii, 12, 13, 15, 17, 43, 61, 91, 147, 158, 161; Intellectual(s)/(ly), vii, viii, ix, xi, xii, xvii-xxi, xxv, 9, 13, 16, 17, 73, 89, 108, 113, 153, 161

Intercultural(ly), xv, 6, 54, 70, 139, 145

Intervention(s), xi, xxi, 6, 10, 20, 23, 35, 145, 153

Intracultural(ly), xxix, 7, 12, 21, 72, 102, 129, 139

Isshangi, B., 16

J
Jackson, M., 9
Jamaica, 147; Jamaican(s), 152, 162
Jochannan, Y.B., xxi, 16
John, A.N., 16
Justice, vi, 11, 22, 30, 89, 134-136, 162; injustice, 95, 124, 135
Justice Academy, 28-30, 90, 118, 146

K
Karenga, M., viii, ix, 16, 21, 120, 134, 162
Karenga, T., 16
Kemet, xix, xxviii, 13-16, 19, 23, 30, 44, 55, 79, 113, 134, 147, 150,
      152, 160; Kemite, 14; Kemetic(ally), xix, 15, 19, 44, 79, 152
King, J., viii, ix
King, Jr., Martin L., 21, 64, 65, 71, 74, 87, 91, 102, 123, 130, 137, 149
Kozol, J., xvii
Kunjufu, J., xvi, vii, 2, 17, 18, 23, 34, 160
Kush, 14, 23, 113

L
Ladson-Billings, G., xxviii, 20, 73, 137, 146, 148, 159
Legacy, xx, xxix, v, vi, 15, 16, 44, 48, 53, 72, 77, 94, 110, 116, 122, 123,
      160
Light, vi, xxii, 19, 21, 24, 67, 155, 160, 162; dim, 29; highlight(ed), 44,
      160
Live(d)/(s)/(n), xxii, 7-9, 16, 18, 20, 24, 28, 29, 36, 44, 45, 50, 51, 56,
      59, 75, 78, 79, 83, 85, 86, 97, 102, 107-109, 111, 119, 133, 135,
      136, 141, 143, 146, 149, 151-153, 161; Livelihood, 60; Alive, 16,
      44, 159
Love(s)/(ed), v-vii, ix, 58, 109, 124, 128; Lovers, 84
Lugard, L., 13, 16

M
Maafa, 55
Maat, v, x, 79, 134, 150
Majors, R., xxiv
Mandela, N., xxiii, 21, 22, 137
Marshall, T., 87, 89

Mcdougal, S., 9
Million Man March, xxiii
Miseducation, xvii, 8, 29, 53, 89, 100
Morrison, T., xxiii
Music(al), xxiv, xxv, 16-18, 23, 32-34, 38, 39, 64, 117-119, 124, 129,
      132, 136, 149, 150, 152

N
Negro, 13, 17, 18, 100, 156,
Nehanda, M., 149
Nightmare, 52
Nile, 14, 15
Njia, xxii, 123, 124, 132
Nobles, W., vii, ix, xxi, 7, 30, 136, 15

O
Obama, B., 20-22, 27, 29, 117, 120, 121, 155, 160
Object(s), xx; objectification, xx; Objective(s), 4, 8, 40, 69
Ogbu, J., xxiv, xxvi, 18, 120, 127, 128,
Oppose(ed)/(ing), 21, 35, 37, 69, 71, 149; Opposite, 131; Opposition(s),
      20, 21, 72, 120; Oppositional, xxiv-xxvi, 18, 94, 95, 97, 105, 157;
      Oppositionality, xxiv, 105
Osiris, see instead Asuar
Owens, J., 87, 89

P
Parent(al)/(ing)/(s), vi, xi, xv, xvii-xix, xxiii, xxv, xxvii, 5, 6, 18, 22, 24,
      34, 47, 48, 53, 57, 60, 61, 63, 66, 76, 77, 79, 81, 84, 97, 98, 101,
      111, 120, 124, 130, 131, 138, 141-145, 149-154, 161; -child, 82,
      118; -teacher/school, 62, 82; single-, 2, 29, 107, 109; two-, 29, 43,
      85
Parks, R., 71, 102, 130
Peace, vi, xiii, 44, 46, 50, 77, 78, 86, 93, 103, 108, 109, 112, 134, 135,
      137, 144
Phelps, R.E., 9, 154
Pitcher, G., 13-15, 150
Pointe du Sable, J., 89

Politics, 17; Political(ly), ix, xvii, xix-xxi, xxiii-xxvi, 8, 9, 17-19, 21, 25, 55, 70, 111, 152, 155; Sociopolitical, 6, 8, 18, 20, 50

Poor(ly), vii, xviii, 2, 10, 11, 20, 26, 51, 55, 63, 70, 71, 97, 101-103, 109, 114, 115, 120, 121, 139, 140; grades, 77, 138; parents, 141; teacher(s), 96

Poverty, see also Impoversihed, xxvii, 2, 26, 49, 51, 52, 70, 79, 101, 115, 117, 127

Power(ful)/(s), vi, viii, xix, 1, 5, 15-18, 21, 30, 35, 55, 63, 111, 133, 134, 141, 151, 154, 157, 159; Higher, 70; predictive, 10; will-, 4; Powerlessness, xvi

Prepare(ed)/(s), viii, 2, 59, 107, 108, 131, 135, 154; Preparedness, 65, 107, 108; unprepared, 98; Preparation, vii; Preparatory, 26

Pride, vi, xix, 12, 23, 50, 51, 63, 72, 78, 89, 90, 98, 102, 108-110, 113, 128-130, 136, 137, 140, 141, 143, 144; Proud(ly), v, xxvi, 44, 46, 50, 53, 54, 79-90, 98, 103, 106, 113, 131, 137, 139, 160

Prison, xxiii, xxvi, 152; Prisoner, 21; Imprisonment, 19, 127; -school model, 26

Proverb(ial)/(s), xxii, 28, 32

Ptah, v; Ptah-hotep, 15

Q

Qualitative(ly), xxix, 25, 38, 40, 68, 78, 148, 154, 157

Quality, 17, 26, 27, 45, 46, 73, 96, 109, 119, 133, 134, 149, 151, 155, 156

Quintana, S.M., xix, xxiv, 22, 147

R

Ra, S., 16

Race-ethnicity, 55, 69-71, 111, 113

Racial-ethnic(ically), 6, 8, 14, 25, 53, 69, 90, 113, 118, 128, 157, 161; identity, xix, xxvii, 11, 12, 19, 50, 63, 64, 70, 79, 86, 89, 101-103, 112, 114, 120, 124, 127, 129, 135-141, 156, 159

Racism, xxii, xxiv, xxvi, xxvii, xxviii, xxix, 2, 9, 11, 12, 17, 19-22, 34, 37, 51-55, 65, 66, 70, 74, 75, 82, 89, 91, 93-96, 101, 106, 112, 114, 116, 117, 121, 122, 133, 135, 137, 141, 149, 161, 162; Racist(s), xxii, 3, 13, 21, 22, 49-51, 56, 65, 74, 95, 132, 145, 149; Anti-racist, 86, 89

Ramses II, v, 149

Reciprocity, v, x, 11, 19, 79, 132, 135, 139, 162

Religion(s), ix, xx, xxiv, 16, 17, 32, 129, 136; Religious, xxiii, 15, 16, 20, 45, 136
Research, vii, viii, xx, xxiv, xxvii, xxviii, xxix, 1-3, 5, 6, 9, 10, 13, 18, 25, 30, 38, 65, 69, 103, 123, 146, 158, 160; questions, 34-36, 39; -to-practice, 153; Researcher(s), xxix, 1, 3, 8, 10, 24, 25, 30, 32, 131, 154-156
Resilience(y), viii, xxix, 1-3, 21, 39, 53, 55, 58, 63, 68, 72, 81, 97, 99, 108, 111, 132, 150; Resilient, 1, 96, 97, 107, 132, 134
Revolution, xv
Rich, xviii, 44-47, 49, 56, 58, 68, 69, 77-79, 83, 133, 134; history, 25, 103, 150, 162; Riches(t), 13, 134; Richness, 123; Enrich(ed)/(ment), 104, 134, 143
Righteous, xv
Robinson, J., 87, 89
Role model(ing)/(s), xxvi, 3, 5, 19, 36, 47, 49, 56, 62, 69, 80, 81, 96, 101, 103, 111, 122, 123, 131, 132, 141
The Roots, xxv, 18

S
Sankofa, xxii
Sankofa, B.M., xxvi, 9
Schooled, xvii; Schooling, xvii, xxii, xxvi, 34, 47, 48, 73, 75, 92, 145, 147, 149, 151, 157
Se Ptah, H.A.R.S., v, 15, 149
Segregation, 71, 122, 139; Segregated, xii
Self-confidence, 4, 5, 86, 92, 99, 110, 131; Self-confident, 63, 112
Self-determined, xvii, xxvii; Self-determination, 9, 66, 120, 132
Self-esteem, xi, 141, 143
Self-hatred, xxviii, 13; Self-hating, 34, 90
Self-knowledge, viii, 22, 32, 72, 89, 102, 116, 130, 140, 143, 149
Sellers, R.M., 19, 34, 156
Shabazz, A., 46
SigHT, x, xv, xxvi, 1, 7, 24, 25, 28, 34, 38, 48, 109, 120, 127, 128, 132, 133, 135, 143, 151, 155, 157, 160, 162
Slave(s), 56, 71, 74, 90, 114; -era, 12; Slavery, xx, 7, 10, 51, 52, 65, 70, 72, 90, 122, 139, 150
Snyder, C., 1-6, 10-12, 19, 20, 23, 24, 49, 123, 155

Soul(s), 44, 13, 160; food, 161

Spirit(s), v, vi, x, xv-xvii, 5, 8, 12, 16, 30, 49, 89, 107, 108, 119, 133, 135-138, 150, 158; Anti-spirit, 133; Spiritedness, 162; Spiritual(ly), v, vi, 8, 9, 16, 21, 68, 90, 99, 106, 108, 123, 128, 129, 136; Spirituality, vii, xi, xvii, 23, 32, 68, 85, 128, 133

Statistic(s), xvi; Statistical, 38, 132

Stokes, C., xxiii

Struggle(ing)/(s), vi, viii, xii, xxi, xxii, xxviii, 34, 39, 78, 79, 86, 111, 116, 124, 140

Subject(s), xx, 12, 31, 33, 112, 115, 132; Subjected, 51, 101; Subjectivity, 30

Succeed(ing), vii, xv, xvi, xxi, 2, 3, 25, 35, 48, 53, 58, 60, 88-91, 93, 95, 100, 105, 111, 116, 121, 130, 131, 134, 137, 138, 146, 148, 152, 158, 162

Sun, vi, xxvii, 24

Survive(d)/(ing), xxiii, 55, 106, 108, 114, 115; Survivor, 115; Survival, xv, 8

Swan, Q., xxiii

T

Tatum, B., vii, 20, 141, 151

Taylor, S., 16

Teacher(s), vi, xi, xv-xix, xxii, xxiii, xxv-xxvii, 5, 6, 16, 24, 25, 27, 29, 30, 39, 43, 46, 48, 53, 54, 57, 60-62, 66-68, 72, 73, 75-77, 81, 82, 87, 90-98, 104-107, 110, 115-117, 119, 120, 131, 132, 134, 135, 138, 140, 142-148, 150, 151, 153, 158, 161

Television, 20, 51, 80, 118, 124, 153

Templeton, J., 18

Terrell, F., 153, 155

Terrell, S.L., 153

Time(s), v, vii, x, xi, xiii, xviii, xix, xxi, xxix, 2, 4, 8, 10, 16, 17, 22, 24, 27-29, 35, 43, 56, 89, 103, 107, 113, 116, 123,131, 138, 147, 148, 160; find, 149; Timelessness, 128

Trans Atlantic Slave Trade, see instead European Slave Trade

Truth(s), viii, xv, xxi-xxiii, xxix, 7, 8, 17, 23, 32, 33, 75, 80, 89, 90, 106, 119, 133, 149, 151, 156, 157, 160, 162

Ture, K., xxiii

U
Unconscious, 144, 159
Unconventional, xxi
Unity, xix, 34, 39, 120, 122, 123; Reunited, 158; Unified, 39, 122
United States/U.S., xvi, 2, 8, 9, 13, 17, 18, 21, 23-27, 30, 34, 115, 117, 121, 127, 137, 147, 149-151, 153, 157, 161
Universe, xxiv, 1; Universal, xiii, xviii, 21, 30, 32, 44, 128
University(ies), v, x, xxix, 138, 150; University training, xi, 145

V
Van Sertima, I., xxi, 13
Vereen, B., 16
Victim, 53, 106; Victimized, 139; Victimization, 71, 90
Victory(ies), vi, ix, 2, 9, 21, 22, 30, 69, 74, 90, 108, 115, 117, 120, 135; Victorious, vii, 22, 56, 139
Vision, x, 28, 46, 48, 62, 68, 84, 86, 115, 124, 128, 141, 143; Divison, 120; Envisioned, 59, 84, 98, 108, 128, 158
Visit, 75, 82, 83, 103, 115, 118, 140, 152

W
Welsh, K., 33, 73
Wisdom, viii, xvii, xxii, 14, 15, 56, 78, 99, 124, 160; Wise, 17, 51, 74, 119, 139
Wishful thinking, xv; thinkers, 143
Woodson, C., ix, xi, 12-17, 100, 159
Wright, B., 16
Wu Tang, 133

X
X, Malcolm, 21, 46, 102, 130, 149